1 Hour Web Site: 120 Professional Web Templates and Skins

Michael Utvich, Ken Milhous, and Yana Beylinson

Wiley Publishing, Inc.

1 Hour Web Site: 120 Professional Web Templates and Skins

Published by
Wiley Publishing, Inc.
111 River Street
Hoboken, N.J. 07030-5774
www.wiley.com

Copyright © 2007 by Wiley Publishing, Inc., Indianapolis, Indiana

Published simultaneously in Canada

Library of Congress Control Number: 2006927783

ISBN-13: 978-0-471-93338-0
ISBN-10: 0-471-93338-4

Manufactured in the United States of America

10 9 8 7 6 5 4 3 2 1

1B/RT/RQ/QW/IN

About the Authors

Michael Utvich is an award-winning author and consultant. Michael has focused his consulting practice on projects that draw upon technology and interactive content to create highly effective learning, marketing and internal communication programs for clients in the corporate and high technology arena. Michael has developed both the content for the programs and the supporting methods to gather metrics, performance measurement and evaluation. His consulting client list includes such corporate clients as: Oracle, Microsoft, IBM, NCR, Deloitte & Touche, AOL Time Warner, Lexus, Nissan, Random House, Toyota, and Xerox, as well as innovative Digital Economy companies such as Inlumen, Primavera, Apogee Networks, MedWell, Intellispace, and EnCompass Knowledge.

Michael has authored eight books on electronic publishing, computer technology, and business for Random House and Bantam Doubleday Dell. Most recently, Michael was a contributing author to *Interactive Dramaturgies: New Approaches in Multimedia Content and Design,* from Springer Publishing in Frankfurt. This book was book written by an international author team around cutting edge content development concepts in gaming, interactive film and television, and interactive content design.

Ken Milhous is an Internet specialist focusing on the combination of professional graphic design with advanced logic to create complete business solutions for e-commerce, multimedia, marketing, and communication. Ken has developed hundreds of Web pages, interactive CD-ROMs, user interfaces, and print collateral pieces for a wide range of clients selling products and services.

After graduating from Purdue University with a degree in Computer Graphics, Ken developed various projects at different companies where he gained invaluable knowledge collaborating with clients and vendors to create the most appropriate solution based on requirements, budget, and available resources. Clients include Nestlé, JBL, Price Pfister, Insight, Gateway, M.H. Ross Travel Insurance Services, and Infiniti Car Club of America.

Yana Beylinson is a graphic and Web designer with an unparalleled knowledge of Web practices and Internet marketing. She is the principal of Liquid Pixel Studio, an innovative Web and graphic design company. Her extensive Web development experience is coupled with rigorous training in graphic design and a fine art foundation, making her work a perfect fusion of form and function. The result is well-built sites with a distinct fresh look, attention-grabbing e-flyers and logos. Over the years Yana is proud to have worked with such clients as Archdiocese of New York, Waterford/Wedgwood, and many others. She currently lives and works in New York.

Credits

Acquisitions Editor
Michael Roney

Project Editor
Cricket Krengel

Technical Editor
Jon McFarland

Copy Editor
Lauren Kennedy

Editorial Manager
Robyn B. Siesky

Business Manager
Amy Knies

Vice President & Group Executive Publisher
Richard Swadley

Vice President & Publisher
Barry Pruett

Project Coordinator
Adrienne Martinez

Graphics and Production Specialists
Sean Decker
Jennifer Mayberry
Joyce Haughey
Barbara Moore

Proofreading
Sossity R. Smith

Indexing
Lynnzee Elze

Quality Control Technician
Brian H. Walls

Permissions Editor
Laura Moss

Media Development Specialist
Steven Kudirka

Special Help
Courtney Allen
Laura Sinise

To our wives, Sharon and Judy

Thank you for your support, encouragement, and above all, your patience.

~Michael and Ken

Preface

The World Wide Web is the least expensive and most efficient way to communicate content anywhere — from around the world, to across the street. Sure, there are other media you could use but they all have very distinct limitations when it comes to communication power, cost, and access. A book has to be printed and distributed, a television show has to be broadcast (or cabled), a DVD has to be packaged, e-mail needs an address list of the audience you want to reach, and sending information through the mail requires printing, packaging, as well as postage.

The Web uses computer technology and a vast worldwide network to overcome many of the limitations and costs associated with other communications media. Electronic transfer of words, pictures, music, and moving images enables you to bypass the physical media (such as paper and discs) that make other media so costly, while allowing you the ability to reach out and find an audience just like broadcast media networks do.

At the outset, the Web was a plaything for technical experts and an area of experimentation for forward-looking businesses. Today the Web is a fully mature medium — global and universally used in the worlds of business, culture, news, and information. Unlike other media, such as broadcast television, the price of access and use for the Web is low and easily affordable by individuals and small businesses.

The singular power of the Web is that it enables other people find you. Putting up a site allows you to tap into the network and create a Web presence. At the most basic and simple level, you can create a Web presence by having a URL — for example, `www.mywebsite.com` — that opens a home page with whatever information or message you want to include. Once people have connected with your Web presence, they can interact with you and share your Web presence with others in their own network.

The key to building and maintaining a useful Web presence is capturing and holding the attention of your readers or target audience. In the dozen years since the Web made its debut, accessible Web pages have proliferated into the billions, with no end in sight. In other words, there is considerable competition for audience attention.

High quality Web design is the key to holding and maintaining attention. A successful Web presence creates a unity of impression between the design of the screen, the name and key message you have chosen, and the key ideas or actions that you have selected to draw your audience to click through and participate in your content.

With high quality Web design and the low costs of access, the Web can be your face to the world for whatever purpose you have in mind. Use the Web to create a presence for your existing business or startup venture. Publish your resume or build a creative personal profile site to help network yourself professionally. Create a site on your personal interests or build a community of interest around ideas or activities you find interesting. Set up an interactive photo gallery to share family pictures across the country or around the world. Whatever the reason, your Web presence gives you the ability to reach out, generate impact, and build an ongoing dialog with other people.

This book and the accompanying system of designer templates is about helping you to easily make use of high-quality design to build an attention-getting Web presence for your business or any personal project. The templates enable you to select a style for your Web pages and use the guidelines and structure of the templates to build the content and information in your site. Following the rules and using the structures of the 1 Hour Web Site templates, you can build and publish your own Web site in no time whatsoever.

Acknowledgments

We undertook this project as a creative challenge to build a truly easy way for everybody to make use of the incredible power of the World Wide Web. Writing any book is not for the faint of heart, and this project contained many special challenges in building an array of exciting and useful designs and supporting them with procedures and operations that make them truly easy for anyone with fundamental computer skills to use.

In undertaking this project we knew we could not walk alone and we are indebted to the contributions and support of friends and colleagues for their suggestions, input, and all around patience.

Ken would like to thank Logoworks for providing samples of their excellent logo designs used in the examples of many of our template designs. One of the fundamental sources for inspiration for this book was CSS Zen Garden, a site that has led in advancing the use of CSS technology as a powerful design and web development solution. John Utter has been invaluable for his assistance to Ken in supporting, reviewing, and testing the templates. Mike Davidson with SIFR has provided valuable input on our customized font solution using Flash technology.

Michael would like to thank our editors, Mike Roney and Cricket Krengel for their support and invaluable counsel in moving this project forward. Even with a number of books under Michael's belt, this particular project involved logistical and creative challenges, and the editor's help and creative input was invaluable throughout.

Contents

Introduction

This book has been designed to help you overcome the obstacles and get your presence on the Web as fast as possible. 1 Hour Web site templates are a system that allows you to create a professional Web site using a simple text editor alone, with no specialized Web or graphic software required.

The design template family included in this book is your integrated tool to find the right presentation for your Web presence and help you to build and structure your content into a compelling and engaging experience for your audience.

Book features

This book is designed to be a working companion to the 1 Hour Web Site family of templates. To help you get the best results from this book and CD-ROM package, the coverage has been structured as a practical handbook of key information, procedures and strategic tips on how to plan your site development and create content to align with the templates. Note the following key points about the book coverage and the accompanying CD-ROM.

Part I: Getting Started

Part I of the book contains a description of the underlying concepts and mechanics of the 1 Hour Web Site family of templates and how they make your life easier when creating your own Web site. Chapters in this section provide references and detail on the key Web concepts you need to understand to create and publish your site and a complete run-down of the template creation operations.

Part II: Templates

Part II of the book contains detailed descriptions of the core template designs and creative variations on them. This section functions as a complete detailed catalog to the templates provided on the CD-ROM. Detail coverage for master templates includes illustrations of the template design, with additional illustration showing the key headings, body text, and other features of the design to use when creating your content. Each template has its own step-by-step instructions to populate the template with your custom information, making it easy to publish a custom site — whether it is for your business, organization, or family. Templates are presented in chapters that represent functional groups to make it easy for you to find the right design to suit your application requirements.

About the CD-ROM

The CD-ROM contains the working Web files for each of the templates. There are 120 separate templates with files for each one stored in a separate subdirectory. Files for standard templates are the same in all cases; some templates include a Flash movie component and they have a couple of additional files.

Files for standard templates

+ **Template CSS (.css).** The template design file.

+ **Content builder form (.htm, .xhtml).** The content entry form that works with the design file.

+ **Photoshop (PSD format).** This is the original artwork files used to create the Web templates. It is provided for users who want to customize the art in their site. Its use is not required for standard 1 Hour Web Site operations. Use the Photoshop Elements trial version (also on the CD-ROM) to edit type, colors, photos, etc. to customize the template art.

+ **Font swapping files (.swf).** Flash movie files are provided containing individual fonts. These fonts can be used during customization operations to change the selected Heading fonts within a given template design. Use of these files is not required for standard 1-Hour Web Site operations.

About Art and Logos

The art and logos provided in the samples are only for your reference. Logos can't be reused in any way and are not to be manipulated or altered in any way. You should replace the logo in your chosen template with your own logo or artwork.

 Tip If you or your organization needs a professional-quality image, contact Logoworks.com (www.logoworks.com).

Files for templates with Flash

Flash templates include each of the file types listed in the previous section and two additional files to present and configure the content of the Flash movie:

+ **Flash file (.fla).** Flash movies on any Web site are compiled movies. They are first created in the developers program, and then exported or compiled. The .fla files allow users to do anything they want to the original file and aren't limited only to the customization built when using an XML file.

+ **Flash configuration file (.txt).** This is the XML file that contains settings for the Flash movie. It is plain text, but has a name like "flashconfig.xml".

Software

The CD-ROM contains a 30-day trial version Photoshop Elements, which is used for customization of the Web site art and logo files. You may install this application and try out the software if you are considering acquiring them. Versions for both Windows and Mac are on the CD-ROM.

Getting Started

✦   ✦   ✦   ✦

In This Part

✦   ✦   ✦   ✦

Understanding 1 Hour Web Site Templates

The fundamental challenge in all Web site projects is to frame your content in a design that presents your story in the most compelling way possible. Web sites are information machines that connect with and engage the audiences that matter to you. When you create a Web site from a blank screen, you wear many hats: content specialist, communications expert, graphic designer, and Web technologist to name a few. 1 Hour Web Site templates enable you to draw on the specialized skills necessary to create a professional Web site.

This chapter introduces the suite of 1 Hour Web Site templates and explains how they are designed to streamline your access to and use of the Web as a communications tool. A common perception of Web templates, in general, is that they are simply formatting tools for content. 1 Hour Web Site templates, however, are designed to simplify both the tools you need and the process you use to create a finished Web site.

1 Hour Web Site templates are also designed to function as an integrated system built around a set of common tokens, or markers, that allow you to easily enter content and place links within each design. The 1 Hour Web Site family includes an easy content development process and tools to help you select a design that best reflects your message and structures your content to fit within that design.

Template Power

Web design templates are design models or formats that enable you to create a Web site that is professional and polished. Beyond that basic definition, the quality, features, and flexibility of these templates varies greatly.

Those of you who have used Microsoft PowerPoint are familiar with the template system built into the software. PowerPoint provides design templates you can load as computer files, which contain complete design layouts with color, fonts, and formatting for the title page and regular presentation slides. The PowerPoint system is an example of a fully integrated template system that offers design intelligence and gives you fast features you can use to enter and frame your content.

1 Hour Web Site templates have been designed with this ease of use and flexibility in mind. The objective is to reduce or eliminate as much technical complexity as possible and let you work creatively with designer resources.

The 1 Hour Web Site Suite of Templates

The 1 Hour Web Site templates that come with this book are organized into functional groups that reflect common business and personal applications for Web sites. Within each group, you have a range of designs with different layouts and communication approaches to choose from.

Template categories

Each design in the 1 Hour Web Site system is modeled around an example business entity, individual, or organization to showcase how the design acts as a skeleton for content. The following section provides a brief introduction to the functional groups and the design logic behind each one.

Chapters 4 through 12 of this book have been designed as a catalog of the available templates, and include details on the key communication points and recommended use for the particular template.

You can preview each template in color on the CD-ROM. A gallery of template illustrations can be found on the CD-ROM.

General business

General business templates are designed to clearly present the business name, its tagline or core message, and the principal information defining its products and services. Page links are the next layer of the story behind the business, and they motivate the user to access content presented on sub-pages.

A range of general business templates gives you a selection of styles that you can customize to fit the business type you're representing. This way, the overall character of the offering and its public face on the Web embodies its essence in style and design.

Professional service

Professionals need to communicate personal and organizational credibility to their audience. The individual or organization is the product. Whether the professional focus is medical, legal, financial, or consult services, the communication must focus on the experience, background, and service offerings in a way that builds a rapport, and a level of trust, with the audience.

Templates for professionals tend to be conservative, with designs that showcase the range of services offered and provide evidence of business credibility beginning at the home page. These sites can include testimonial quotes as well as cite professional recognition and achievements that help to differentiate the individual or organization from others in the field.

Retail business

Retail Web sites are designed to stimulate sales. While they share all of the characteristics of general business Web sites, they need to have special design features that showcase a product or service offering or present an array of product categories offered through a store or online retail outlet. A retail site must carry the brand for the business and incorporate presentations of product offerings, potentially involving specific pricing, sale, and product configuration options.

Templates for retail businesses focus on specific types of retail businesses, such as restaurants, banks, auto dealerships, grocery stores, and more. The default designs presented serve to exemplify certain retail models. Most of these designs can be easily adapted to serve any retail purpose.

Nonprofit organization

Nonprofit organizations seek to align audiences interested in topics centered on core messages and objectives. Whether the mission of the organization is social, political, educational, or religious, all organizations share the same fundamental communication challenges. The identity and intention of the organization must be clear and credible, and the site must present information about the group or ways they can become involved in its work. These sites are similar to Community templates in that they often focus on motivating the audience to join, contribute, or participate in an organization's activities.

Entertainment

Show business and entertainment Web sites are the dramatic expression of a show, performer, or cultural style. These sites tend to be pure style, and use graphics and images to convey the quality of an entertainment experience and to define the personality behind it. On a design level, these sites must convey a strong visual brand that defines the entertainment product; on a detail level, they can include summary information about the experience, quotes and comments from members of the site's audience, comments from critics, and calendar or broadcast information.

E-commerce

E-commerce Web sites are designed to generate business over the Web. They share many communication objectives with the general business and retail business sites. Their purpose is to build and retain a Web audience through business-to-customer (B2C) retail offerings, or business-to-business (B2B) offerings of products, services, and professional expertise. These sites include transactional pages that require related business services to manage online sales.

Information and e-publishing

Web information publishing draws audiences with collections of content, including articles, listings, links, and other types of information. Forms of e-publishing include everything from newsletters, electronic magazines, and collections of

articles to general grab-bag sites containing articles and links around one or more topics. Typically information sites use dense formatting on the home page to maximize the number of headlines, story leads, and links to subpages that can seize audience attention.

Community

Community Web sites are a means for individuals or groups to engage people around particular community projects and objectives. These Web sites are designed to help individuals and groups who are not organized into a formal non-profit or business entity communicate their message and encourage members of an audience to participate. Community Web sites are often built around a local calendar or roster of activities and serve to coordinate volunteer activity. They may also include public postings or blogs that enable members of the community to interact and post information of common interest.

Personal

Personal Web sites are electronic outreach for an individual or a family. They are designed for everyday people using the Web for personal and social tasks, ranging from posting a résumé online to sharing a gallery of digital family pictures with other family members and friends around the world. Templates in this group are simple and direct and enable visitors to easily view information.

Template groups

Web site designs vary in many ways, such as in their use of color, fonts, backgrounds, and graphics. These elements are integral to the design, and coverage of individual templates in later chapters helps you understand the underlying logic of a given design and how to best use it.

One of the most critical variations among designs used in the 1 Hour Web Site template family is the amount of content the home page and subpage formats feature. Content density is a key element in generating the kind of impact you want to achieve. Typically, content density is more of a factor on the home page, where the audience first interacts with your organization or message. Subpages carry more detailed content and usually feature more dense layouts to deliver your supporting information.

For example, in a situation where you want to convey a strong brand message for a company or product, you want to avoid a lot of extraneous copy that detracts from or obscures that message. In this situation, you should choose a site design that uses color and graphics to clearly communicate an emotional connection with the audience. You would want a low-density content array that puts heavy emphasis in your home page on the business or product name and features your brand message prominently.

However, if you are creating a news or information site, or posting your résumé directly on the Web, you might want a design that supports more content on the screen on the home page and in subpages as well. In this case, you would select a high-density content array that enables you to place lists, links, and paragraph copy directly on the home page to capture your audience's attention instantly. Headlines clustered on the home page would present many topics to draw the attention of the largest number of readers, and links would take them to the content, presented on subpages within the site.

Group 1: Low-density templates

Low-density templates focus on your organization name and message, and include obvious links to subpages that enable you to engage the audience (see Figure 1-1). When visitors select the subpages, they access supporting content and information on your organization. Typically these templates present photographs or design patterns prominently and use vivid color and/or background shapes to create a visual environment that is compelling and engaging.

Subpages supporting these designs carry through the visual look and feel of the home page. They use white space or blank areas of the background to set off your page headlines and subheads while clearly presenting paragraph text and lists.

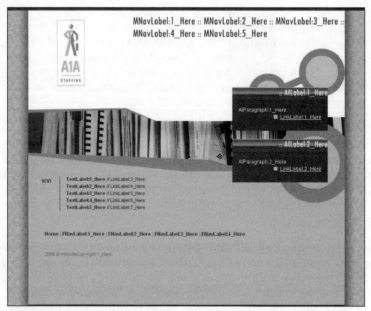

Figure 1-1: Low-density templates, such as template 440, use open space and strong headline treatment to generate impact for a company, a product, or an organizational message. Detailed content is placed on subpages.

Group 2: Medium-density templates

Medium-density templates are designed to combine a strong visual presentation with areas reserved for more detailed content directly on the home page. These designs enable you to present your site name and message accompanied by the lead-in paragraph of an article or lists of key points of information, such as product or service features, or a member calendar, on the home page to make an initial impression (see Figure 1-2).

Subpages supporting these designs offer you the option of placing more text and information within the page, using headings and subheadings to guide the users through your content.

Figure 1-2: Medium-density templates, such as template 620, integrate a strong use of open space to carry the brand message with areas for paragraph content, engaging the audience with summary content or article leads in subpages.

Group 3: High-density templates

High-density templates are designed to get as much content onto the page as possible while maintaining a strong site identity and clear headlines to carry your message and maintain content organization. Virtually every news and information site uses some variation on this type of design. You have the option to place article information directly on the home page or to include a series of article lead paragraphs that link directly to a full article presentation on a subpage.

Subpages supporting these designs support article and content presentation with more emphasis on headlines than white space or graphic visual elements to organize the information. Typically these pages employ a strong banner-style page heading that maintains your site identity throughout and offer you more room within the page to present information. These sites also offer pages where you can present standalone articles.

Group 4: Flash templates

Some templates in the 1 Hour Web Site family include Flash elements in the home and subpage layouts. Flash is a multimedia presentation technology used to place animated movies and text effects in Web sites. Some Web sites are programmed entirely in Flash; others, such as those included in the 1 Hour Web Site family, include embedded Flash elements in the design that automatically activate when the page is displayed.

Typically, Flash templates are set up to animate your company name and/or message for greater impact. Note that the Flash templates work just like standard templates do; the Flash component is simply an element in the overall design and not the entire Web site. Flash templates use animation to bring attention to your message so they are treated as a group by themselves.

Subpages supporting these designs can incorporate variations of the Flash effects featured on the home page integrated into the subpage headings, or they can pick up design elements from the Flash and incorporate them as graphic backgrounds supporting the page heading.

About Creating Your Web Site Content

For many people, the major obstacle to creating a Web site is coming to terms with what to say and how to present it. 1 Hour Web Site templates have been designed to do more than just make Web technology easy to use. They provide you with a creative resource that helps you to conceptualize, write, and edit your content.

Each template is presented using a standard Design Summary. It breaks down the key elements of the design to help you select the template that best communicates your content.

To make the best use of the provided templates, you need to understand the logic of the design and the key features that make up the layout. This helps you understand the communication power of the design and better frame and express your ideas. Each template includes a default story, example business, or other content to give you ideas as well as a clearer understanding of the best use for each design.

Your Web site audience

Perhaps the most important consideration when designing your site is to define your target site audience or audiences. Many people ignore or pay little attention to this consideration, and consider their audience is everybody. But "everybody" is not an audience; it means only that you have not taken the time or made the effort to define who you want to communicate with.

Whatever your content or message is, it will have more interest to certain groups of people than others. Understanding who those primary interest groups are enables you to more effectively target your message and site content to engage their interest.

An audience can best be understood by breaking them down into basic groups, often called demographic groups. Test your content and message against these groups and key questions:

✦ **Age.** Does your content appeal to people of a certain age group?

✦ **Gender.** Does your content appeal more to men or to women?

✦ **Profession.** Is your content of special interest to people belonging to a specific professional group?

✦ **Level of education.** Does your site content address people with a particular level of education or educational specialty?

✦ **Geographic location.** Is your content directed to people in a certain local, regional, or national area?

✦ **Creed or affiliation.** Does your content address the interests of people who share particular religious, political, or social beliefs or affiliations?

The process of narrowing down "everybody" to a defined group is called *targeting an audience*. You might find that your target is a combination of the demographic factors noted previously. For example, you might find that your real target is people 18 to 35 (age) who work in medicine (profession) in the state of California (geographic).

Note that when you target an audience, you are not necessarily trying to limit your Web site to just that group of individuals. The goal of targeting an audience is to identify those individuals most interested in your content and most likely to connect with your message.

Whoever your target audience might be, once you have identified and described them, you are in the position to pose questions about what information members are interested in and how you can best present that information to attract and hold their interest. The following are some considerations that will help you further define your audience's interests:

✦ **Key questions.** Which key questions about your topic will typical audience members want answered?

✦ **Hot topics.** Which aspects of the topic are your audience very interested in?

✦ **Updates.** How often does your audience expect content updates and fresh information?

✦ **Level of detail.** How much detail does your audience expect for the information to be considered credible?

The more you know about your audience, the more you are prepared to develop a site that draws on their interests, hot buttons, and curiosity. Failure to understand your audience often results in a site that does not attract visitors because it is simply not relevant to its intended audience.

Design Summary

Each template in the 1 Hour Web Site family has its own Design Summary, which is based on a group of standard parameters that reflect key communication and style considerations. Each Design Summary gives you concepts, commentary, and recommendations that identify the communication power of that design. When you use the Design Summary to create the content for your Web site, it is important to keep one central factor in mind: Your Web site is a communication tool that must connect with, and engage, other people. The Design Summary suggestions help you frame your message so that the content and the design you select complement each other, making your site compelling and useful.

The standard parameters of a Design Summary identify key communication issues you should consider to make the best use of a design.

Recommended Use

The first consideration in the Design Summary is Recommended Use. This parameter contains suggestions and ideas on how to use the template for different communication purposes.

For example, a site under the General Business category (see Figure 1-3) features an example company or organization with a logo to show off the design. Recommended Use comments describe how you can apply this design to showcase a company or a specific product or service and include guidelines on how to employ creative applications for the template that go beyond what you see in the example.

Recommended Use comments help you match your content and message with an appropriate design. The message is the core value that you want your customers to remember. In a Web site, the message should be reflected in home pages and subpages as often as possible. Once you grasp your audience with your message and content, you can lead them to dense and complex information deeper in the site.

Figure 1-3: Template 1010 is recommended for general information listings and information publishing, but the simple open design can be adapted for many uses.

Look and Feel

Look and Feel is the second element in the Design Summary. This parameter serves to break down the design elements so you can understand how they contribute individually to the communication power in the design. The site design creates an impression and an emotional state in your audience that strongly influences their perception of the content. For a Web site, the color and format play the same role in shaping audience emotional reactions as the music and soundtrack do in a film. Some of the key elements that contribute to Look and Feel include color, texture, fonts, and graphics (see Figure 1-4).

Figure 1-4: Template 710 uses shades of blue and gray to break up the screen space and focus attention on items of major interest. The effect is crisp and businesslike.

Color and texture

Color, pattern, texture, and images can all add emotional focus and direction to your Web content. Backgrounds serve primarily to set the emotional stage and guide your audience as they visit different areas of your site. As you develop your content, be sensitive to its emotional character, and how color can reflect and amplify your message (see Figure 1-5). For uplifting, inspirational messages, light backgrounds and bright colors are more likely to convey a positive message than morose looking grays or very dark backgrounds. There are no absolute hard and fast rules, but use your common sense when selecting templates that reflect the emotional message and underlying credibility of what you have to say.

Figure 1-5: Template 540 uses floral imagery for a powerful and colorful impression that is complex and emotionally involving.

Fonts

Fonts give character to content and are a critical element in creating the look and feel of a site. For example, heavyset fonts using thick black lines correspond to a loud voice or shouting, while ultra-thin line width suggests a quieter, more subtle voice.

You should be aware of two principal types of fonts:

✦ **Display or headline fonts.** These typefaces are ornamental graphic series that are designed to create an emotional effect and generate cultural associations. The shape of the characters could be graphic mimics of cowboy lassos; suggest exaggerated calligraphy such as bridal invitation script; or, be the curved, sculptured characters commonly used in the sixties. Display fonts are used for titles and major headings.

✦ **Text fonts:** These fonts are designed to present smaller text headings and paragraph text in readable forms. Many of them exist and the differences between them are much more subtle than those in display fonts.

Images and graphics

Enhance your site with graphics and photographs as appropriate. You can integrate them into the content and text flow or present them as part of the layout. However, it's important to monitor graphic use carefully; these elements require longer load times than text and can slow or stop a site from loading, giving the user reason to get bored or start looking for another site.

Within your site, you can identify content elements using complex graphic labeling, either graphic logos or graphic composites that visually summarize a type of information, character attributes, or other story values.

✦   ✦   ✦

Web Technology for Templates

1 Hour Web Site templates are designed to simplify the operations you perform and the related terms and concepts you need to understand. Using the templates is an opportunity for you to learn the Web from the inside out and to develop a deeper comprehension of the communication power and capabilities you can access through it. It's important to remember that much of the language only seems complicated; the ideas referenced by the terms are simple and intuitive.

This chapter gives you a quick, focused tour of the terms, concepts, and publishing operations you need to understand to design and publish your Web site using 1 Hour Web Site templates.

A Brief Tour of the World Wide Web

People sometimes confuse the World Wide Web with the Internet as a whole. The Web is a publishing system that runs over the Internet. It is one of a number of interactive applications that run over the Net, such as e-mail, chat, and newsgroups. Given the extraordinary flexibility of the electronic network, the Web can be linked to, or integrate elements with, other Internet functions.

The technologies that collectively define the Web serve to define the system and its rules of operation and identify the technology tools that you use to access it. The following brief tour should provide a level set on the basics.

It is useful to understand the Web as an electronic form of real estate. Many of the terms commonly used to define it, including *domain*, *site*, *address*, and *navigation*, refer to the physical space in which we live. As you take the tour through the fundamental Web terms and concepts, remember that when you create a Web site, you create a place in an electronic universe where people can locate, visit, and interact with you.

Internet addresses

The Internet is, fundamentally, an address book. When it was first developed, decades ago, technologists in the academic and government arena were looking for an easy way for large computer banks to exchange information. The Internet emerged as a *protocol*—a set of rules and communication conventions—that defined a specific common format that could be used to establish a unique address for each computer. These addresses were called *Internet Protocol*, or IP, addresses, and they took the form of a series of numbers: four groups of up to three numbers separated by three decimal points. So an IP address could be as simple as:

1.2.3.4

On the other hand, it might look like this:

123.456.789.012

The structure of the IP address was simple and enabled large computers to connect over telephone lines and access specific computers to exchange information. Once this connective foundation was built, it quickly became clear to users that it had many potential applications beyond simple computer file sharing (see Figure 2-1). Specialized systems emerged supporting basic e-mail and online discussions (similar to today's blogs). Tools to access these capabilities were basic and required a relatively high level of computer skill to use. But that was soon to change.

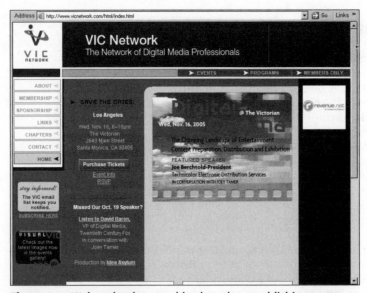

Figure 2-1: Web technology enables broadcast publishing across the Internet, with fonts, graphics, design layouts, and Flash movies embedded within the page.

The Web's make up

In the beginning, the Internet was essentially black screen, character computing that transmitted basic text. The World Wide Web emerged in the early nineties as a new Internet system that would permit the exchange of formatted documents with custom layout, specialized fonts, and computer graphics.

HTML

The magic ingredient of the Web is a specialized text markup language called HTML (Hypertext Markup Language). In essence, the way that HTML works is not dissimilar to the way your word processor uses automated style tags to set your document headings, bullets, numbered lists, and so forth. HTML defines a set of text codes that can be assigned to various elements in a page, which are read by a specialized reader called a *browser*. When an HTML document is opened in a browser, it interprets the text codes and formats the document on screen according to the settings coded in the HTML tags within the document. An example of both is shown in Figure 2-2.

HTML defined a new means to exchange formatted text and make it available in electronically readable pages through the browser. However, for the Web to be truly usable, it also needed to provide a simplified method of locating and reading pages. The basic IP address system was workable, but the clusters of numbers that made up the address were difficult to remember and didn't carry any information that easily identified and labeled the contents of the Web pages.

URL

The solution to the Web addressing problem is the Uniform Resource Locator or URL. Basically, this is a name identifier that can be used instead of the underlying numeric IP address. The URL is just another term for the common Web address; for example, `http://www.wiley.com` or `http://www.google.com`.

Users can type each of these URLs into a browser and access Web pages created in HTML. Like all URLs, they have a corresponding, numeric IP address like those shown in the previous section. The URL enables you to name and identify a type or group for a page of Web content.

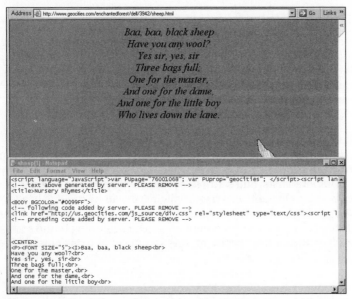

Figure 2-2: The nursery rhyme shown in the Web page at the top has been coded to appear on the Web using HTML. The source code that creates the Web display can be seen in the window in the bottom of the illustration, with the HTML code appearing in brackets (< >).

The URL is composed of three fundamental elements that enable you to use it to locate and use Web sites:

✦ **Web protocol.** In `http://www.wiley.com`, for example, the `http://` identifies the type of Web document or format that is used. HTTP (Hypertext Transfer Protocol) identifies the site as a Web page. Other protocols such as FTP (File Transfer Protocol) can be used to access information in other Internet formats.

✦ **Domain name.** In `http://www.wiley.com`, `wiley` identifies the name for the site destination. The domain name is the central identifier for the site and the home page and all subpages are identified by it.

✦ **Domain extension.** In `http://www.wiley.com`, `.com` identifies the category or group identifier for the site. There are many defined domain extensions, including `.com` (for commercial or business sites), `.gov` (identifies a government site), and `.edu` (represents an educational site). Others identify sites geographically by country, and within the United States, by state.

The URL can also carry the identity of pages within the Web site so they can be directly addressed from the browser. The syntax is identical to the structure used in many computer File Manager tools. A simple formulation that would directly access a subpage in a site might look like this:

```
http://www.cnn.com/CNN/Programs/situation.room/
```

```
http://www.wiley.com/1HourWebsite
```

This simple system makes it easier for most people to remember, use, and access the Web easily. Not incidentally, the URL enables you to brand your Web site with your name or the name of your business, organization, or product.

Domain names

The first thing you must do to put a site on the Web is rent your own domain name. There are many vendors on the Internet that sell and register domain names for fees that can vary widely. When you rent a domain name, it is assigned to you, along with a specific, related IP address (also called a Domain Name System [DNS]) that is the basic numeric Internet address format.

You can rent a domain name for a set period of time (see Figure 2-3). Web registrars often offer package deals that allow you to select the term to rent the address. Two years is typical, but you might opt for longer. Once your term has expired, you must renew the domain name and pay new fees to secure it. If your rental period expires, the name reverts to a pool of available names that can be rented by anyone else. You may elect to secure your preferred URL in more than one domain extension, for example, .com, .net, .org, .biz and more. This approach helps you to minimize confusion with potential competitors who might secure your preferred URL with a different extension.

Figure 2-3: Nexcess.net is an Internet Service Provider that offers domain registration as one of its services. The domain registration screen shows pricing for typical domain packages, which are presented as a rental agreement, with a cost for a specific term.

When you rent a domain name, the registration agency provides you with Web registration codes. This package of information includes your URL and your IP address. This information is used to make your site accessible to register and accessible from any Web browser.

When you create your Web pages, they will be assigned to your domain name so that anyone entering your URL will be brought directly to your site.

Web site content

Once you have a URL, you have an address on the Web. Now you are ready to create your Web content, and this is where 1 Hour Web Site templates come in. Using the templates, you can select a site design you feel is right for your Web communication needs and enter your content into specially prepared files that eliminate the need for you to do any coding or technical work, which is specifically addressed in Part II of the book.

Once you complete your content and apply the desired 1 Hour Web Site style sheet, your content is formatted and ready to go. At this point you prepare your Web site pages as directed in this book, and you will be ready to deliver them for publishing.

Web hosting service

Once you have rented and registered a domain name and developed your content in HTML, or one of the other Web-supported markup formats, you are ready to publish a Web site. At this point, you need to place your content where it can be linked to your domain name and identified with your site URL: for example, www.mysite.com.

Placing a site onto the Web is called *hosting*. The companies that offer this service are called *Web hosting services* (see Figure 2-4). They maintain large computer systems, called *servers*, designed to store and distribute masses of content. Their business is to sell you space on their servers to store your Web site computer files and to link your URL to their server locations. Hosting packages range from simple, basic site placement to large-scale content areas and specialized services. Be sure to ask questions before signing up so you avoid buying a service package that is more than you need.

When you sign up with a Web hosting service, you provide your Web site files, developed from one of the 1 Hour Web Site templates, along with the Web registration information you received when you rented your domain name. The Web hosting service uses this information as a key to identify and set up your URL so the user can find it on the Internet. Users accessing your URL are taken to your initial, or home, page, and can link to other pages or links within your site from there.

Figure 2-4: Web hosting services sell you electronic real estate where you place and operate your site.

Web hosting services are in the business of money and they usually package their services in an array of price packages, structured by month or by year, that include an amount of computer storage area, in megabytes (MB) or gigabytes (GB). The amount of space you need is determined by the size of your Web site files, as well as additional files you might want to store as galleries, or data that site users might upload to your site.

It is common for Web hosting services to offer packages that include domain-based e-mail with your Web publishing service, with the price that corresponds to the number of available Web mailboxes. This service enables you to extend your Web site with e-mail that is branded to your domain name, such as:

Michael@mysite.com

Sara@mysite.com

Hosting packages often include additional services, such as ones that optimize your site with various search engines, monitor your site traffic, and more. If you're just getting your feet wet, it's a good idea to go with one of the more basic and less expensive plans first. Once you gain experience with the Web and assess the amount of traffic your site receives, you can elect to upgrade your services with the Web hosting company at any time.

Browser

Once you have developed, hosted, and published your site, anyone in the world who has access to a Web browser can enter your URL in the address line and display your Web pages on her system.

Of the variety of Web browsers in use, the most common ones are Microsoft Internet Explorer and Mozilla Firefox. Whichever brand of browser you opt to use, they all do the same thing: deliver your pages through the Internet.

When developing your site using 1 Hour Web Site templates, you test your site in the browser on your system. However, once your pages are actually on the Internet, you should test them, reading them through several browsers, including Microsoft Internet Explorer and Mozilla Firefox , and others such as AOL, to make sure they display correctly. If you notice problems displaying the pages, you can contact your Web hosting service for assistance to make sure you have placed your files correctly.

You should also review your pages using different screen resolutions. The *screen resolution* determines how much information can be displayed on your computer screen. The amount of your Web page that a user can view when the page is opened depends on the screen resolution that user has selected. Screen resolution is usually controlled through the Settings or Properties options, depending on your operating system.

Standard screen resolution is 800×600 pixels; on newer monitors you may have the option to set higher screen resolutions, such as 1024×768, or 1280×1024. Settings are determined by the graphics card in your particular computer. The bottom line is that the higher the screen resolution, the more information is displayed when the page is opened, and the less information that is concealed off screen where the reader must use scroll bars to see it.

It is a good idea to benchmark your site at 800×600 pixels and be sure your initial messages show up at that resolution, so that the greatest possible number of readers can get the full impact of your site.

Search engines

The first place you go on the Web when you are looking for something is usually a search engine. The most visible search engine in today's Web universe is Google, shown in Figure 2-5, but there are many others, some of them longtime-established players such as Yahoo! and America Online to name a few.

Figure 2-5: Search engines are commercial tools that search for information links and feature advertisements in the form of sponsored links.

Your Web site is complete . . . now what?

Once you obtain your Web domain and URL and develop the pages and publish them through a hosting provider, you are in business. Your Web site is available to the world.

Unless you inform the world, however, your site has the impact of the proverbial one hand clapping effect. So before you rest on your laurels, take a moment and think out a plan to let your audience – whether they are customers, family, friends, or club members – know it is up and operational.

Given how difficult it can be for a new site to gain exposure through search engines without involved and sometimes expensive optimization, consider these three key ways you can get the world to take notice:

✦ **E-mail.** Make up a polite announcement letter—you don't want your message to look like spam after all—and send out the URL of your new site to personal friends and/or business associates you think will be interested. Be sure to request that they forward your e-mail to any of their contacts who might be interested as well.

Search Engine Optimization

Search engines work within your browser and use a variety of proprietary technologies to respond to a search request and navigate through the many millions of Web pages on the Internet to locate sites that match that request. Given the number of pages on the Web and the ten or 25 hits that typically show up in the initial page showing the results of a search (with sometimes thousands of hits on following pages), it is often difficult to have your site located and featured near the top of the list.

It is possible to add additional markup information in the form of text tags, called *metadata*, to your site that serve to connect with search engine indexes and make your site more prominent in the search engine. *Search engine optimization* refers to metadata placement strategies used to improve your visibility on the Web. The fundamental goal of search engine optimization is to move your site up in the priority rankings of the search engine so it appears closer to the top of the list. The higher your site places on the search list – such as in the top two or three results pages – the more likely you are to be found, and your site to be accessed.

Search engine optimization is beyond the reach and scope of Web templates because the metadata tags are based in your specific content and on the key words or concepts you want to associate with your site. Web hosting services often offer some form of optimization services, and many independent providers provide specialized methods and techniques for optimization as well.

A big buyer beware is called for here. Despite the many claims providers make, no magic bullet or surefire strategy exists to increase the visibility of your site on the Web. Note further that optimization techniques that are targeted to the search patterns of one engine, such as Google, might not be effective for another, say, Yahoo!. So before you consider using optimization services, be very clear about what each provider offers.

✦ **Shared links.** Ask any friends or associates who have their own pages to include links to yours, and return the favor. Having your site link placed on other people's sites is an implicit recommendation and helps drive their readers to you.

✦ **Word of mouth.** Talk up your site whenever possible. Yes, have it on your business card, but don't be afraid to mention it in casual or business conversation. Note that there is a great advantage to having a simple and memorable domain name when you want to talk up your site. The greater the length and the more convoluted your domain name is, no matter how clever it might be, the harder it is to get people to remember your address.

Once you have informed the world, your site is truly published. Just don't forget that a periodic update to the content, and even the overall look of the site, through your hosting provider once in awhile is a great idea to keep people coming back to visit.

✦   ✦   ✦

Building Your Web Site

Choose your metaphor: creating your own Web site is like building a house, cooking a gourmet meal, or even writing a book. These complex processes are all alike in that they all demand preparation, attention to detail, and making the best and most efficient use of your time and energy to complete them. Creating a Web site is a process with many variables. As with any process-based activity, you have to clearly understand the task ahead, gather the resources you will need as a foundation, and work through the process to the final outcome.

1 Hour Web Site templates have been designed to streamline the technical complexities of Web site development so you can focus your energies on what is the most challenging aspect of any Web site project: figuring out what you want to say, and how best to communicate it.

Building a Web site is a continuous interplay between writing the words and placing them into a coherent and meaningful design. The way your message looks on the Web is a big part of how effectively it communicates. The design is made up of colors, images, graphic elements, and fonts; and its impact on your readers is to grab their attention, to shape their rational and emotional reactions to your message, and ultimately, to communicate the credibility and value of what you want to say.

1 Hour Web Site templates allow you to easily edit Web code using the Find feature in a simple text editor — you can use WordPad or Notepad, for example, if you are working on a PC. Each blank template contains a set of easily locatable content tokens that take you to the precise location in the code to enter your Web site headings, announcements, and copy. Link tokens allow you to place link destinations within your site or to external Web pages by simply placing the page filename or

site URL. This token-based placement system for content and links in 1 Hour Web Site templates allows you to concentrate on building your content and building your Web site even if you have only basic word processing skills.

In this chapter, you learn how to execute the site creation process. This chapter explains how the system of content and link tokens works and provides you with a background and examples to help you make use of the individual site creation profiles presented in Chapters 4 through 12.

About the Templates

The 1 Hour Web Site family of templates is a system of designs created to afford you the maximum flexibility to create the Web site you want. To make the best use of the templates, it's important you understand the range of options you have, from basic implementation of templates to advanced enhancements.

A Web site is an integrated electronic publication that combines text and images within a visual design, and provides electronic links to navigate the content. These fundamentals are universally known by Web users. As a Web site creator, it is important to understand that Web pages are created through an electronic network that pulls together separate content elements, such as text files and images, and integrates them into the design structure, which contains page headings, navigation features, and links.

1 Hour Web Site templates are blank Web sites that contain the design format and linking and navigation features but are empty of content. Tokens, or marker text, are placed in the precise locations in the code where headings, content, and link destinations must be placed. This approach simplifies Web site development to essentially locating the desired tokens using the Find feature of any basic text editor and replacing them with your content.

1 Hour Web Site templates are written in XHTML, which is an Internet-industry standard markup language. The XHTML markup language contains defined code elements that a Web browser reads and then translates into the page you see on the screen. Some templates in the 1 Hour Web Site family make use of additional programming elements such as Flash, but the primary programming approach is built around XTML code (see Figure 3-1).

```
<div id="mainContent">
    <div id="topmenu">
        <ul>
            <li><a href="index.html"><span>Home</span></a></li>
            <li><a href="MNavURL:1_Here"><span>MNavLabel:1_Here</span></a></li>
            <li><a href="MNavURL:2_Here"><span>MNavLabel:2_Here</span></a></li>
            <li><a href="MNavURL:2_Here"><span>MNavLabel:3_Here</span></a></li>
            <li><a href="MNavURL:2_Here"><span>MNavLabel:4_Here</span></a></li>
        </ul>
    </div>

    <div id="mainImage"><img alt="" src="images/main.jpg" /></div>

    <div id="ActionItems" class="ActionItems">
        <div id="Item1">
            <h2><a href="AIURL:1_Here">AILabel:1_Here</a></h2>
            <p>
                AIParagraph:1_Here
            </p>
        </div>
        <div id="Item2">
            <h2><a href="AIURL:2_Here">AILabel:2_Here</a></h2>
            <p>
                AIParagraph:2_Here
            </p>
        </div>
    </div>

    <div id="Content">
        <h1>Heading:2_Here</h1>
        <p>
            Paragraph:2_Here
        </p>
        <p>
```

Figure 3-1: The 610 template `index.html` (home page) code as it appears in a text editor. This code is written in the Web standard language, XHTML.

Each 1 Hour Web Site template contains two foundation files written in XHTML. Note that the file extension for both is .HTML, which is a Web standard used for many different variations of Hypertext Markup Language, including XHTML.

✦ `index.html` contains the code and layout for the default home page. You use this file to create the home page content only.

✦ `subpage.html` contains the standard format for the template subpage. You use this file to create all subpages for your Web site by saving this file into separate files for each subpage; for example, `Contact.html` for the contact information page.

Within each of these files, content and link tokens mark the precise places where you must enter text for headings and body copy, and identify locations for Web links.

These files display in your browser when opened and the browser title bar reads "PageTitle_Here." This site title is controlled through page description content features, which are detailed later in this chapter.

Note

Some browsers, particularly Microsoft Internet Explorer, have built in safeguards against automatically opening files that may contain active content. When you open `index.html` or `subpage.html`, you many need to select the option to "Allow Blocked Content" so that the files can display correctly.

Figure 3-2: The 610 template `index.html` (home page) as it appears when it is displayed in a Web browser. 1 Hour Web Site tokens are displayed in the layout that serves as markers in the code that guide you where to enter your content.

1 Hour Web Site templates have been designed to provide a skeleton for your content. The arrangement of site content and images gives you a variety of options on where and how to present your material. The core assumption in the design of all these templates is that you will use them as-is, and make changes to content, links, and images only, without attempting to change the layout or design. If you have the skill and access to advanced Web development tools, you may make any changes you want to the design, but those operations are beyond the scope of this book.

The 1 Hour Web Site Design Process

1 Hour Web Site templates have been designed to be as flexible for your communication needs and content requirements as possible.

A basic approach to templates might dictate a hard-structured, locked-down approach, in which every template features a home page and a standard cluster of subpages and links. This would force you to trim your content to fit into a standard frame, without being able to control how much space you really need to tell your story.

However, the structure of the 1 Hour Web Site templates combines standard page layouts with flexible content and link tokens that gives you extraordinary flexibility in determining how many pages you want for your Web site, how those pages are named, and how information is linked throughout your content, as shown in Figure 3-3.

Figure 3-3: Template 710 is just one of the many templates that offers many choices for placing text elements and links.

The following sections provide a basic overview of how to approach the specific work you do to the template or templates you choose when going through the chapters in the next section of the book. The information in these sections applies to all the templates in the 1 Hour Web Site family.

Step 1: Choosing your template

Build your Web site by shopping for the template that best reflects the design look and feel for your content. Default templates have been organized into a variety of business, organizational, and information groups in Part II. You may want to begin by looking at the collection of templates that most closely matches your business requirements. However, you can adapt many of the templates to the specific use and purpose you have in mind.

There are 40 master, or default, template designs in the 1 Hour Web Site family. Each one has two accompanying design variations that use different background color and fonts within the same structure.

The templates are organized into a series of theme chapters. Each default template has fully documented design process instructions, with accompanying illustrations of both the design layout and special illustrations that show the placement of the content and link tokens in the home page and subpages.

Organization

Templates are organized by number based on the chapter they appear in. The numbering scheme helps you identify the default and variations on a given template. A quick breakdown of the numbering system, using template 740 as an example, is

- ✦ **7.** The number of the chapter in which the template appears.

- ✦ **4.** The sequence number of the template within that chapter; in this case, it is the fourth template in Chapter 7.

- ✦ **0.** The number 0 designates this template as the default version of this design layout.

    - • **1.** The number 1 identifies variation 1 of this design (the template number would then be 741).

    - • **2.** The number 2 identifies variation 2 (in this case, the template would be 742).

This numbering system is used throughout the 1 Hour Web Site family. As you look through the book at various template layouts, note the number of the template you are interested in and you can find color images of it on the CD-ROM.

CD-ROM Gallery

Template profiles and site design process instructions appear in Part II of this book with illustrations shown in black and white. To view template designs in full color, you can access the Gallery on the CD-ROM.

When the 1 Hour Web Site CD-ROM is placed in your computer's CD drive, it automatically boots. Once you click through the software Accept screen, the CD-ROM main menu appears. You can then click Gallery from the menu of buttons across the top of the autorun interface.

From CD-ROM to computer

Template code can be found in the Templates folder on the CD-ROM. To begin the process of building a Web site from a template you select, you must first copy or drag the code folder from the CD-ROM to a chosen location on your computer.

Move the complete template folder including the `images` and `includes` subdirectories to your hard drive or other editable media either by clicking and dragging or by copying and pasting. You can retain template number as the name of the folder or can rename it to the name of your URL, such as `mywebsite`.

 Note   Given the wide variety of flexible media available, you can place these files on any media you choose including a removable disk or memory stick. It doesn't have to be stored on your primary hard drive.

All the files you need to edit the template are contained in the folder that you dragged over. For example, if you dragged the 610 folder to your hard drive, you will find two subfolders: images and includes.

Step 2: Building your content plan

The second step in the 1 Hour Web Site design process is to complete a content plan for your site. There is a specific, recommended content plan included for every default template that contains details on the site features and how you should plan your site and identify your subpages using that particular design.

Each template in the 1 Hour Web Site family offers different arrays of content presentation features and link options. The purpose of the content plan is for you to review the information you need to communicate and assign it to either the home page or subpages. During this process, you make a list of all the subpages you need to create your site and assign names to them that are used to create screen labels and links.

The content plan is a key to the most efficient method to build a site using 1 Hour Web Site templates. If you set up the subpages that contain your content first, you can eliminate a great deal of editing and link placement during site building operations. It is useful to think of the subpages you create in two groups. The principal subpages that appear in the navigation bar at the top and bottom of your site, and additional subpages you create to hold articles or other site content.

Navigation bars: Principal subpages

The most prominently featured links in many Web sites are those that appear in the navigation bar placed either at the very top or left edge of a site design, and the footer navigation bar placed at the bottom. These navigation bars are usually programmed to appear on the home page and all subpages and provide a uniform access tool to the main areas of information within the Web site. In most cases, the navigation bar presented at the top or left of the design is the most visible and contains a full set of links. The bottom bar can contain the same links as the top bar or a subset (see Figure 3-4).

Figure 3-4: Template 620 illustrates the placement of top and bottom navigation bars. When user content replaces the tokens with short single-word text labels both the main and footer navigation bars appear as a single line across the screen.

The navigation bar typically contains links to pages that collectively define the site and provide the reader with instant access to information that defines the business, organization, or project the Web site is designed to present. Pages that are typically presented through the navigation bar include

✦ **Home.** Direct link to the home page from subpages.

✦ **Product.** Description or listing of products offered.

✦ **Services.** Description or listing of services offered.

✦ **About Us.** Description of the company, its background, and mission.

✦ **Contact Us.** Contains contact information, such as mailing address, telephone numbers, and e-mail addresses.

✦ **Customer Service.** Contains information about customer service programs and supporting products and services.

✦ **Press.** Contains links to press notices about the company or its products.

✦ **News.** Contains the company newsletter or news stories about products and services.

Links to subpages presented on the navigation bar vary by the needs of the business. When selecting these pages, make sure that they are relevant to the reader. They should provide links to important information that many readers are likely to be interested in. For example, a restaurant would likely place links to a Menu page and an About Us page in the navigation bar.

Article subpages

The body of your Web site content can be presented in the form of articles or information listings that appear on the home page or subpages. 1 Hour Web Site templates have a number of presentation features that support the placement of content articles. These include

✦ Main page headings and paragraph text with a continuing link

✦ Sidebar heading and paragraph text with a continuing link

✦ Action item headings, paragraph text, and links

Depending on the template you select, you may have features to create a number of home page links, including link labels and action items that can link to a subpage containing an article on a particular topic. Some templates provide these links on subpages as well. Whatever the structure of the template you are using might be, you need to identify the specific articles you want to publish as well as the subpages you need to contain this content.

Many templates support article content presented using continuing links. In this format, one or more groups containing headings and related paragraph text are presented, with a link label following the paragraph text token. This allows you to place a paragraph or two of an article on the home page, and then use the link label to place a "Read More" or "Additional Information" type of link to a subpage where the article is completed. This type of design allows you to begin several articles on the home page and continue them on a subpage.

Subpage list

To complete your content plan you should make a list of all the subpages you need to create before moving on. For each subpage, you should identify the label, the text that you want to appear as the link on screen, and the subpage filename that you use to place the destination of the link using the link tokens.

Table 3-1 is a sample of a simple content plan that shows the type of information you need to assemble. It's very important to write down and make lists of your subpage names and filenames so you can accurately and consistently enter them into the template code.

Table 3-1 Sample Content Plan		
Token Type / Group	**Label Name**	**Filename**
Main Navigation — Top		
MNav1	Product	Product.html
MNav2	Service	Service.html
MNav3	About Us	About.html
MNav4	Contact Us	Contact.html
Mnav5	News	News.html
Footer Navigation — Bottom		
FNav1	About Us	About.html
FNav2	Contact Us	Contact.html
FNav3	News	News.html
Articles		
Heading 1 Group (Home)	Article 1	Article1.html
Heading 2 Group (Home)	Article 2	Article2.html
Heading 3 Group (Home)	Article 3	Article3.html

Step 3: Building the site skeleton

Certain features of your Web site, particularly elements such as navigation links and the Web site copyright, are common features that appear on all pages. Most sites include at least five main navigation items at the top and the same number at the bottom. If you were to edit these navigation features on each individual sub-page, it could be a very long and time consuming process.

To save you time and effort, the 1 Hour Web Site design process guides you to build a complete site skeleton before you enter your article content on individual pages. To build the site skeleton, you first enter all common page elements into `index.html`, which contains the home page layout and `subpage.html`, which contains the subpage design. The common page elements include the main and footer navigation bars, the Web site copyright, and any other features that appear globally within the particular design.

Once the common page elements are placed in the two template files, the work of setting up navigation links is complete. `subpage.html` is the master template for all the subpages in your site, and all you have to do is save it under the names you selected for your subpages in the content plan (see the example in Table 3-1). When you save `subpage.html`, you have already placed all the navigation features and the site skeleton is complete (see Figure 3-5). The only work you have left to do is to enter the specific content for that page and your work is complete.

Instructions provided in Part 2 of the book for each default template contain detailed steps on how to set up the common page features, save the subpages, and build the site skeleton for that particular template.

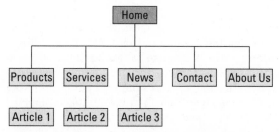

Figure 3-5: The site skeleton is a fully linked Web site with all of your subpages created and all major navigation links in place, which saves you the effort of entering main and footer navigation and other global features individually into each subpage.

Step 4: Entering content

When the site skeleton is complete, you have created a full Web site with all principal navigation features in place and all home page and subpage files ready to receive content. You can now open the home page and individual subpages and use the tokens provided to enter your content into the template design.

Placing content elements

Instructions provided for each default template contain detailed steps on using the content and link tokens available for that particular design for the home page and subpages. These process steps include coverage to place content elements including

+ Headings and subheadings

+ Paragraph content

+ Action items

+ Text labels

+ Web site special features

+ Sidebar areas with headings and paragraph text

Content editing techniques

As you build your Web site, at any time you want to see the site displayed so you can check on your progress, open `index.html` from the template folder and your site displays in your browser. Usually the easiest way to do this is to double-click on the filename in your file explorer or file list, and your default browser opens automatically to display the site.

When placing your content, you may need to experiment with the amount of content that fits within each token. The amount of content that label and heading tokens support is relatively standard, and you can use Tables 3-2, 3-3, and 3-4 for guidelines. The amount of content that paragraph tokens accept may vary depending on the placement of that token in the design. For example, a paragraph token placed in a sidebar layout may accept less text than a paragraph token placed under a Heading 1 or Heading 2 in the main page area.

During content placement and editing operations, you may find it useful to enter your content and retain the tokens in place. Once you have deleted a token from the code, that token won't be available for you to locate the related content for editing. Retaining the token during editing allows you to easily go back and find a specific token in the layout and make progressive edits to it until you are satisfied with the content.

However, make sure that once you have completed editing operations, you delete the token, so the final code looks like this:

```
<h1>New Product Announcement</h1>
```

The text of the heading is now the only thing that appears within the code blocks for Heading 1 and appears in your Web page correctly. If you don't remove the token text and view this in your Web browser, you'll see a heading that reads "Heading:1_HereNew Product Announcement."

Note that all tokens end with the common expression "_Here". So when you complete editing, if you are concerned that you may have left a token somewhere, just search for that expression to find all remaining tokens in the code to delete them.

Logo and image editing

Before completing your Web site design, you should replace the default logo provided in the template with your own logo or with another art element. Instructions on image editing are provided later in this chapter.

You can also elect to make changes to the main illustration or accent illustrations provided in the template you have chosen, and these instructions on editing site pictures are also provided later in this chapter.

Step 5: Publishing your site

Once you have completed content placement for your site, and viewed the site on the Web, you are ready to deliver the Web site files to your hosting provider. Your hosting provider will provide instructions on where to send your Web site files and how to upload them.

When delivering files to your hosting provider, you should deliver your main template folder (which is best named with your Web domain name, such as www.mysite.com) and all files it contains. You should include the entire template folder, with both subfolders in place:

```
620
   images
   includes
```

This includes all of your home and subpage files, artwork, and other files necessary to present your Web site online. Once your site has been copied up to the host's server, your hosting partner takes care of placing the site on the Internet.

It is advised that you retain a complete copy of the full site on your hard drive, so you can make necessary and desired changes and edits to the site from there. Depending on the arrangement with your Web site hosting provider, you usually can provide updates and replace the published version of your site with the updated version as needed.

Using Tokens

1 Hour Web Site templates use a system of text tokens, written into the XHTML code, that enable you to pinpoint the precise places to enter your content and links correctly. The tokens are a system of markers with simple and easy to understand names and structure. This section provides a complete explanation of how the tokens work, the token naming conventions, and the how to place tokens correctly into the code for any of the templates.

Note The detailed instructions that accompany each of the templates in Part 2 of this book provide directions on how to enter content for the tokens used in that particular template.

Content tokens

Content tokens are markers placed within the XHTML code at the precise location where you must place content for your site (which you can easily do if your text editor has a Find feature). This means every type of text element, from headings to paragraph copy, and the labels for page links within the site.

Content token syntax

Tokens have been designed to a standard syntax or text structure so you can easily locate them as well as differentiate them from surrounding code elements to reduce the possibility of error. To make things even easier, tokens within a given home page (`index.html`) or subpage (`subpage.html`) file are unique: there is only one occurrence of a given token in that file, so you don't have to worry that you are placing your content in the wrong place (see Figure 3-6).

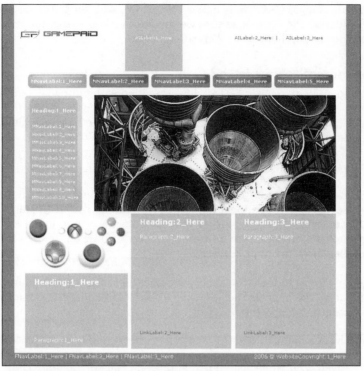

Figure 3-6: Shown here in template 930, you can see the token reference image of the home page.

Each token contains a cluster of information, uniformly structured, to make it easily recognizable. For example, Heading 1 is the standard element that identifies the principal heading on a home page or subpage. The token universally used in 1 Hour Web Site templates to express Heading 1 is Heading:1_Here. The key information elements in this token are

- ✦ **Element type:** Heading. This is the name that defines the type of content element you enter.

- ✦ **Element number:** :1. The number of the element is set off by a colon to keep the syntax clear, consistent, and easy to read.

- ✦ **Token identifier:** _Here. All tokens end with this universal identifier — the word "Here" set off by an underline. You can search for this string during your content editing to locate all tokens that have not been used or replaced in the file.

This same structure is used universally in the 1 Hour Web Site templates for content tokens. It is intended to make it as easy as possible for you to identify the tokens with confidence and build your Web site quickly.

Placement of content tokens in code

When you edit one of the two basic XHTML files provided with your selected template, what you see in your text editor is the actual XTHML code itself with the tokens embedded. Note that in the following example, the token has been highlighted with boldface for emphasis.

```
<h1>Heading:1_Here</h1>
```

This example shows how a Heading 1 token might appear within the code. Note that there are code markers that appear immediately before and after the highlighted token. It is essential that you replace only the token text and do not disturb any of the surrounding code, not even a single character or bracket item, or the heading will not display in the page correctly!

To use the token to place content, you simply replace the token with the content you want to appear on the page. In the following example, Heading 1 carries the text: Company Background, and the resulting code looks like this:

```
<h1>Company Background</h1>
```

By replacing the token with your desired text and leaving all surrounding code information undisturbed, you can enter your text simply, easily, and quickly.

Link tokens

Link tokens are markers placed within the XHTML code at the precise location where you want to place a clickable electronic link to other pages in your site or to external Web pages. Link tokens are used to create the navigation bar features that connect the user to subpages and are usually featured at the top and bottom of the home page and subpages. You can also use them as connecting links to "Read More" or "More Information" type material.

There are two tokens you use to create a Web link, as shown in Figure 3-7. The label token places the text of the link in the Web page. The destination token contains the name of the page that is displayed when the link is clicked. Figure 3-7 presents an example in which the Main Navigation item "Contact Us" is placed on the home page, using the label token MNavLabel:1_Here. The destination token, MNavURL:1_Here contains the filename for the Contact Us page, contact.html. When the Main Navigation label "Contact Us" is clicked, the Contact Us subpage is opened and displayed.

Home page (index.html)

Subpage (subpage.html)
Becomes Contact Us (contact.html)

Label token: MNavLabel:1_Here
Display text: Contact Us

Destination token: MNavURL:1_Here
Contains destination filename: contact.html

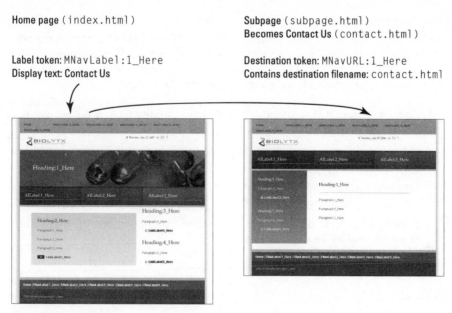

Figure 3-7: Two tokens used to create a Web link.

Several key token groups are designed to place and direct links within your Web site. These include

✦ **Main navigation (**MNav **tokens).** These present the options in the main navigation bar, which is usually placed at the top of the page.

✦ **Footer navigation (**FNav **tokens).** These present the options in the navigation bar at the bottom of the page.

✦ **Action items (**AI **tokens).** These present announcements or featured items of interest that are linked directly to a subpage.

✦ **Link Labels.** These links are used to continue articles from the home page to a subpage. These may be used to continue an article from one page to a subpage (with labels such as "Read More") and are used for a variety of similar continuation linking functions in different templates within the 1 Hour Web Site family.

Link tokens are structured similarly to content tokens, with a couple of distinct differences. As mentioned, link tokens always come in pairs — there is a token used to create the label for the link, which is the clickable text element that appears in the page, and the Link URL, which identifies the link destination. For each link, there are two tokens to edit.

Label token syntax

The label tokens (for example, Main Navigation Label 1) present the text of the clickable link in the Web page on the screen. The token universally used to express this label is MNavLabel:1_Here. Figure 3-8 shows a blank template page featuring this token. The key information elements in this token are

✦ **Element name:** MNav. This is the text that identifies this as a main navigation element.

✦ **Label identifier:** Label. This identifier specifies that this token is used to place the screen label for a link. This term is used only in link tokens.

✦ **Element number:** :1. The number of the element is set off by a colon to keep the syntax clear, consistent, and easy to read.

✦ **Token identifier:** _Here. All tokens end with this universal identifier, the word "Here" set off by an underscore.

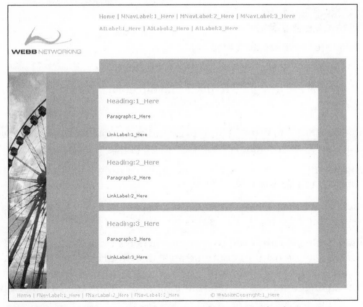

Figure 3-8: In this example from template 1010, the home page presents Main Navigation links at the top to link to principal subpages. Each Main Navigation item in the design has a label token to enter the title and a destination token to place the filename of the page to be displayed when the link is activated.

Destination token syntax

Destination tokens (for example, MNavURL 1) contain the filename of the page you want to link to, or the Web site URL of an external site. The token used to express this destination is MNavURL:1_Here. The key information elements in this token are

✦ **Element name:** MNav. This is the text that identifies this as a main navigation element.

✦ **URL identifier:** URL. This identifier is used for every destination token and signifies that you must replace this token with a subpage filename (for example, Contact.html) or other Web site URL that is the destination of the link.

✦ **Element number:** :1. The number of the element is set off by a colon to keep the syntax clear, consistent, and easy to read.

✦ **Token identifier:** _Here. All tokens end with this universal identifier, the word "Here" set off by an underscore.

This same structure is used universally in the 1 Hour Web Site templates for content tokens. It is intended to make it as easy as possible for you to identify the tokens with confidence and build your Web site quickly.

Placement of link tokens in code

Tokens for links are placed in the Web site code in the home page and subpage files just like content tokens. They are always placed in pairs of one label token and one destination token, but not necessarily in that specific order. Note that in the following example, the tokens have been highlighted with boldface for emphasis.

```
href="MNavURL:1_Here"><span>MNavLabel:1_Here</span></a></li>
```

This example shows that a pair of link tokens can be presented in a single line of code. To see how this works, assume there is a subpage in your site called "Contact Information" that has been saved in a subpage file called contact.html. To create a link, you need to replace the MNavLabel token with the text of the label to appear on the screen. Note that you must place the text between the surrounding brackets > <.

```
href="MNavURL:1_Here"><span>Contact Information</span></a></li>
```

Having defined the label for the link, you must now set the page or Web site address that the link will open when the user clicks on the label. To do this you replace the MNavURL token with the filename of the Contact Information subpage, Contact.html. Note that you must place the filename between the quotation marks in the code:

```
href="Contact.html"><span>Contact Information</span></a></li>
```

A Note about Navigation Link Token Alignment

Typically navigation links that commonly appear in a bar at the top and bottom of the page are one or two words maximum. The length of the token code, for example, MNavLabel:1_Here, is a very long word. In some designs, you may notice that the tokens in the Main Navigation bar, Footer Navigation bar or both will wrap around to a second line, due to the length of the token strings.

When the tokens are replaced with a shorter single word label item, such as "Contact" or "About", the navigation items will align correctly on a single bar and display correctly.

With both the label and destination tokens edited, this link operates correctly when "Contact Information" is clicked in the home page, taking the reader to the subpage containing the contact information.

Page definition tokens

There is a special group of tokens that define the content of your page so you can be more easily found by search engines. These tokens are present in all templates in this book. The three tags in this family are

✦ **Page title.** The `PageTitle:1_Here` token contains a short description of a Web page that appears in the browser title bar at the very top of the browser window when the page is displayed. Content for these tokens should be roughly 6 to12 words in length. For example, ACME Painting provides professional residential and commercial painting services

✦ **Page description.** The `PageDescription:1_Here` token is used for search engine optimization. The text associated with this token does not appear anywhere in the your Web page or in the browser window. The length of content associated with this token should be twice as long as the page title, or up to 24 words. For example, ACME painting is a professional residential and commercial painting company in Los Angeles specializing in decorative painting and faux finishes.

✦ **Page keywords.** The `PageKeywords:1_Here` token contains a list of key words and terms you want to associate with your site for search engine optimization. The length of content associated with this token is typically twice as long as the description. For example, los angeles commercial painter, los angeles residential painter, los angeles painter, acme painting company, home interior painting, professional painter, licensed painter, paint company, decorative painting, faux finishes, latex paint, enamel paint, wood stain.

Using page definition tokens

Page definition tokens identify individual pages within your site. The tokens are present in both `index.html` and `subpage.html`. The best time to place these tokens is when you have completed work on all pages of your site and you are ready to publish. At that point, you should open up all the individual files that make up your site and place page definition information.

Note that there are no specific instructions for replacing these tokens in the instruction set for individual templates.

There are several important principles to keep in mind when entering information for these tags.

✦ **Page differentiation.** Enter content for these tokens to each individual page in your Web site. Content for these tokens should be different on each page for the greatest possible effectiveness in search engine optimization. These tokens allow you to identify each individual page in your site so that your content can be found more readily. For example, you could define different page title content for your home page and specific subpages:

- **Home page.** ACME Painting provides professional residential and commercial painting services

- **Product page.** ACME Painting features award-winning ACME Spread paint.

- **Services page.** ACME Painting provides professional decorative design consultants.

- **Featured article.** ACME Painting develops innovative commercial painting system.

Note that each segment of page title content here includes the name ACME Painting, and each one offers a different perspective on the quality the company offers. This creates greater reach and potential for hits by search engines.

✦ **Content alignment.** Page definition tokens you create for an individual page in your Web site should maintain clear content alignment. Every word in the page title should appear in the page description and every word in the page description should appear in the page keywords. So in this sense, the content for each token builds on the one before it. Content alignment helps to focus the key points of definition for each individual page. Note that you may have different points of emphasis for the content you enter in page definition tokens in different subpages.

✦ **Placing keywords.** Keywords are the hooks that search engines are programmed to search for when locating sites in response to user requests. A keyword may be a single word, two words, or a longer phrase. It is best to keep phrases as short as possible.

Keywords token can also contain common misspelling of important keywords. If customers are likely to use a colloquial or misspelled term in a search engine when searching for your specialty then you should include those common errors as key words.

Avoid repeating the same word more than a few times. It is best to have a range of keywords that define the business to have a greater reach and impact on search engines. Words in the keywords section can be phrases and should start with larger phrases at the beginning — three-word phrases, then two-word phrases, and then one-word phrases.

Placing page definition tokens

Developing keywords and definitional material is best done after the site has been fully written and created. When placing page definition tokens, you should follow a few simple guidelines, preferably in this order:

✦ **Develop a page definition plan.** Make a list of the home and all subpages in your Web site by file name. For each file name, write the content for each of the three page definition tokens. You can use the examples presented earlier as a model.

✦ **Create page titles.** The page title token is the most visible of the three, because the content associated with it appears in the title bar of the browser window when the page is displayed. It is important to place content for this token, even if it is simply your company or organization name.

✦ **Create description.** Use the text from your page title as the starting point for the content you place for the page description token. Expand the content of the page title to create a more detailed description. Remember you have twice the length of the page title, or up to 24 words, for this element.

✦ **Create keywords.** Use the text from your page description as the starting point for the content you place in the page keywords. In this token you have twice the amount of content as for the page description, or up to 48 words. You may enter keywords ranging from single words to phrases, set off by commas.

Tip   Consult with your hosting provider to see if they recommend other search optimization strategies or resources to get the maximum benefit from your use of page definition tokens.

Token list

The system of tokens used in 1 Hour Web Site templates are your Web site creation tools. They give you easy access to the code and eliminate any need for you to learn to read code or master tricky technical editing operations. The following Tables (3-2, 3-3, 3-4, 3-5, and 3-6) list all of the principal content and link tokens in the templates.

Note that the tables use the default number 1 (such as `Heading:1_Here`), but all of these tokens can be presented in number series up to 9 (such as `Heading:2_Here`, `Heading:3_Here`, and so forth.)

Table 3-2
Home Page Content and Link Tokens

Token Name	Use	Space Limitations
Home Page Tagline		
`Tagline:1_Here`	Only in the Flash configuration file used for displaying larger headline text for a logo or promotion, such as "Quality service since 1990." (In most cases.)	Five to eight words usually.
Action Items – Principal Headlines (with Associated Articles)		
`AILabel:1_Here`	Larger title text in each action item. In some templates, this links to a page and in others, these are just headlines.	Two to four words usually.
`AILink:1_Here`	URL for each action item (if a link exists). Each action item can go to a separate page or to the same page, but use anchors to direct the users to a specific part of the page. For example "news.html."	Link token: Space constraints are not applicable.
Article Headings and Text (Used on Home Page and Interior Pages)		
`Heading:1_Here`	Larger text usually found above paragraphs of text. It should describe the content found on the page. Make sure keywords are in headings because search engines give special weight to headings.	Four to six words usually.
`Paragraph:1_Here`	Body of text usually more than a couple sentences long. Typically is found right beneath headings. It should be written well, with keywords at the beginning of the paragraph and sentences for search engine optimization.	Three to seven sentences usually look best, but there is typically no limit to the size of paragraphs.

Continued

Table 3-2 *(continued)*

Token Name	Use	Space Limitations
Connecting Links (Such As "Read More")		
LinkLabel:1_Here	Text the user reads and clicks for any generic links in the template. Usually each template has one to four generic links scattered around the page.	Usually one to four words.
LinkURL:1_Here	Destination token for a link label that sets the URL for a link in the main navigation. Should be either a filename for one of the subpages in your site, such as Product.html. Also used to set a link to an external Web site, such as www.wiley.com. Can be used as a standalone to set the link destination for graphic icons that appear in the top of page navigation bar in some designs.	Link token; space constraints are not applicable.
Text Special Features (Announcements with/without Related Links)		
TextLabel:1_Here	Line or two of generic text in the template. Can be a description of services or just a phone number. Primarily serves as filler. Examples are "Call us at 888-555-1212!" or "Web specials below."	Usually four to eight words, but it can vary.

Table 3-3
Subpage Content and Link Tokens

Token Name	Use	Space Limitations
Top of Page Links to Subpages		
MNavLabel:1_Here	Text the user reads and clicks in the main navigation for each link. Should be something like "About Us" or "Contact Us."	Usually one to two words.
MNavURL:1_Here	Destination token for the main navigation link. Should be a filename for one of the subpages in your site, such as, aboutus.html or news.html.	Link token; space constraints are not applicable.
Bottom of Page/Navigation Bar Links to Subpages (Redundant with MNav)		
FNavLabel:1_Here	Text the user reads and clicks in the bottom of page navigation bar. Should be something like "About Us" or "Contact Us."	Usually one to two words.
FNavURL:1_Here	Destination token for the bottom of page navigation link. Should be a filename for one of the subpages in your site, such as, aboutus.html or news.html.	Link token; space constraints are not applicable.
Subnavigation Tokens (Links to Subpages from Interior Pages)		
SNavLabel:1_Here	Second level of links beneath main navigation. Usually presented on a subpage sidebar to link a series of articles or other information to that subpage. Structured the same as MNav and FNav labels.	Usually one to two words.
SNavURL:1_Here	Destination token for subnavigation link. Should be a filename for one of the subpages in your site, such as, article1.html.	Link token; space constraints are not

Table 3-4
Image Tokens

Token Name	Use	Space Limitations
ImageLabel:1_Here	Text a user sees if he hovers his mouse over an image. An image label should describe what the image is. An example is "White cotton men's shirt." It is used in a small number of designs.	Typically no more than about seven to eight words. Ideally, text should not exceed what you would type into the image area using a normal size font. A small image shouldn't be more than a few words, but a large banner can be up to ten words. These suggestions are only for search engine optimization.

Table 3-5
Web Site Copyright Token

Token Name	Use	Space Limitations
WebsiteCopyright:1_Here	Line of text users can use to display a copyright line or possibly links to a Web site disclaimer and privacy policy. There are no links in this section, so you have to create them if you want to have links to a disclaimer or privacy policy.	Usually four to 15 words.

Table 3-6
Web Site Page Definition Tokens

Token Name	Use	Space Limitations
PageTitle:1_Here	Present brief summary of site — text appears in the browser Title Bar.	Usually 6 to 12 words.
PageDescription:1_Here	Present expanded summary of the site, used by search engines. Text does not appear on screen.	Usually twice as long as the title.
PageKeywords:1_Here	Present detailed list of search key words used by search engines. Text does not appear on screen.	Usually twice as long as the description.

Flash headings and taglines

A number of templates within the 1 Hour Web Site family make use of design elements created with Macromedia Flash technology. Flash is commonly used in Web designs to create design elements that incorporate movement and animation, as well as present full Web movies. Flash is used in these templates to present animated headings and taglines with accompanying graphic layouts on the home page primarily. Figure 3-9 shows a template design that includes animated taglines that fly in over the anchor image at the top of the page.

The templates in the 1 Hour Web Site family with Flash design elements include a third editable file, flashconfig.xml, in addition to the two XHTML files containing the layout for the home page and subpage. This file is a simple tool that allows you to place the text for the animated headings or taglines that display in the Flash movie. Listing 3-1 shows the entire flashconfig.xml file for template 410. Note that the content tokens appear in bold for emphasis.

Figure 3-9: Template 410 is one example of a template that contains an animated flash heading. The two taglines move when the home page is displayed. You can place the tagline text using a simple text file called flashconfig.xml.

Listing 3-1: **Flashconfig.xml for Template 410**

```
<?xml version="1.0" encoding="UTF-8" ?>
- <settings>
- <tagline>
<line>Tagline:1_Here</line>
<line>Tagline:2_Here</line>
</tagline>
</settings>
```

To edit this file, you simply open flashconfig.xml in your text editor, just as you would to edit the home page or subpage files, and replace the appropriate tokens with your desired heading or tagline text, depending on which tokens are included.

Web Site Images

Each template in the 1 Hour Web Site family is contained within a unique blank Web site folder that contains all the design files you need to create a Web site based on that template. Every template includes a subfolder called Images. Using template 910 as an example, the structure of the template folder looks like this:

```
910
   images
   includes
```

This subfolder contains all of the images, including the site logo, illustrative photographs, and other artwork that makes up the design. The images stored in this folder are visual elements assembled through the home page (`index.html`) and the subpage (`subpage.html`) code. Step-by-step operations appear later in this chapter to show you to how to replace the default logos and default illustrations in the Web site designs with your own.

Image files

1 Hour Web Site templates include several types of image files that you can edit in the course of developing your Web site. All picture files for each template are stored in the \images subfolder for that template. Figure 3-10 shows template 1140 which incorporates a logo and multiple images in the design.

✦ **GIF (Graphic Interchange Format).** Used to present photographs or artwork that appears in the blank template, these files are stored in the Web site Images subfolder. You can replace these files with your own graphics, using the instructions in the next section.

✦ **JPG (Joint Photographic Experts Group).** Used to present photographs or artwork that appears in the blank template, these files are stored in the Web site Images subfolder. You can replace these files with your own graphics, using the instructions in the next section.

✦ **PSD (Photoshop document).** This is the standard format for graphics created in Adobe Photoshop. Some, but not all, templates in the 1 Hour Web Site family have photographs or artwork originally prepared in Photoshop. The working copies of that artwork are included in GIF or JPG in the Images subfolder of the blank Web site.

The Photoshop files, which are included, are the original, full-size photographs and artwork, and can be useful if you want to make edits and changes to the original material.

Figure 3-10: Template 1140 includes multiple pictures displayed within the layout in both GIF and JPG format.

Templates that contain Photoshop files are included in the source files folder for that template group. This folder contains supporting files that you do not use to create the blank Web site template. Specifically, within the source files folder, the PSD files are stored in a subfolder called src photoshop. Using the folder for template 410 and variations as an example, the file structure looks like this:

```
Chapter 4
    41
        410
        411
        412
        source files
            src flash
            src photoshop
```

Graphic editing software

You can use a variety of commercially available graphic editing software packages to edit the Web site JPG and GIF files. To perform the operations outlined in the next sections, a graphic package must have a feature that can measure and report the exact image size. This feature is essential because it enables you to read the dimensions of any principal or accent illustration in a template. You can then create a blank graphic file or canvas of the exact same dimensions and put your own content into it.

Adobe Photoshop Elements is strongly recommended as the graphic package to use to perform these operations. This program is a streamlined and easy-to-use version of the industry standard graphics editing tool, Adobe Photoshop. It contains a subset of Photoshop features that are ideal for getting started with image editing. The package retails for about $100 U.S. A trial version of Adobe Photoshop Elements is included on the book's CD-ROM.

Note To edit the Photoshop files (.psd) found in the source files subfolder called src photoshop, you must have access to the full version of Adobe Photoshop.

Editing and placing pictures

Image editing operations in the 1 Hour Web Site templates are simple, basic, and easy to perform. These operations enable you to replace the default site logo with your own company or personal logo. You also use these steps to replace default photographs or art in the design with your own graphic content. Figure 3-11 shows a logo displayed in Adobe Photoshop Elements for editing. The following sections reference graphic operations you use for all templates in the 1 Hour Web Site family.

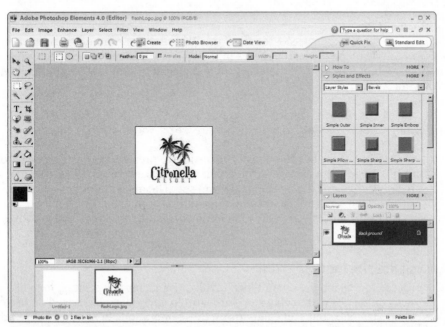

Figure 3-11: The logo for Template 650 is displayed in Adobe Photoshop Elements. This program contains features that enable you to determine the size of image files included with the templates, so you can more accurately replace the images with your own graphic content.

About the site logo

Most templates in the 1 Hour Web Site family include a default logo to animate the design and illustrate how the design can look when a business logo is in place. These are all placeholders, of course, and won't work for your specific business. To complete your Web site, you must replace the default logo with your own content.

Logo replacement options

You have several options for replacing the default logo in a template. The logo is the focal point of the home page design in most instances. It is the logical place in your design to place your business name and identifying graphic signature. When planning to replace the default logo, you have three principal options:

✦ Replace the default logo with your own business logo

✦ Replace the default logo with a graphic file containing the name of your business or organization in text only

✦ Remove the logo from the design by replacing it with a graphic file that is the same color as the logo background

However, before you can replace the default logo with your own logo, company name, or filler graphic, you need to determine and adjust the dimensions of the replacement graphic file.

Logo dimensions

Dimensions for all logos presented in all the Web sites are exactly the same, and reflect the size of the file as it appears in the Web site design. You just edit your graphic content into a file of the exact same dimensions and replace the original with your work.

The dimensions of the standard logo in pixels are 182p side by 153p high. The dimensions of the standard logo in inches are 2.528" wide by 2.125" high.

Screen resolution describes the density of the image presented on the screen. Both GIF and JPG file formats are *bit-mapped*; that is, they are created by a pattern of tiny dots that collectively make up the image you see. The measure of screen resolution is in dots per inch, or dpi. The maximum resolution supported by computer screens is 72 dpi, which is also the resolution of all standard logos and graphics in the templates.

Editing the site logo

The process to replace the default logo involves replacing the existing logo file with your own content. The following steps are written and illustrated based on use of Photoshop Elements, but you can perform these operations in another image editing software with comparable features. This operation assumes that you have copied your desired template file from the CD-ROM to your computer desktop so all files can be edited and saved.

Step 1 – Locate the logo file for your template

The logo files are stored in the images subfolder in the folder each template. Using the following example, note where the images subfolder can be located:

```
620
  images
  includes
```

The filename for the logo is either `flashlogo.gif` or `logo.gif`. If possible, set the file explorer to display thumbnail images of all the graphics in the subfolder or open the file to confirm that it contains the correct logo. This option is found under the View menu in Windows.

Step 2 – Create a logo replacement file

Open Photoshop Elements (or your graphic editing software). Follow these steps to create a blank graphic file that has the identical dimensions to the logo file:

1. Choose File ➪ New ➪ Blank File. The New dialog box opens.

2. In the New dialog box, enter 182 for the Width and 153 for the Height. Change both measurements to pixels. Verify that the resolution is set to 72 pixels/inch, and click OK. A new untitled graphic opens. You can now paste or create content within this file.

3. Choose File ➪ Open to open your chosen graphic file. In the Open dialog box, navigate to the file containing your logo or other artwork. Select the file and click OK. The file opens. You now have a blank image and the logo or graphic file open.

4. Click and drag your mouse from one corner of the image to the opposite corner (from top right to bottom left, for example) to select the entire image.

5. Choose Edit ➪ Copy or press Ctrl+C to copy the graphic or logo.

6. Click the new, blank file window so it becomes the active window.

7. Choose Edit ➪ Paste or press Ctrl+V to paste the copied file. Your logo or graphic should now appear in the blank file. Make any edits to size the logo to fill the available space in the blank file as necessary. You can also elect to enter other content into the blank file; for example, you can use the text entry features to type your business name into the graphic file to create a simple text-only logo.

8. With the untitled file window still active, choose File ➪ Save As. The Save As dialog box opens.

9. In the Save in dropdown menu, navigate to the images folder for your site as placed on your hard drive (not the CD-ROM) and enter the name of the default logo file (`flashlogo.gif` or `logo.gif`). Do not choose a different name. Click OK. When the dialog box appears asking if you want to overwrite the file with the new content, click Yes. This overwrites the generic logo with your own logo or other content.

Editing site pictures and illustrations

The process to replace any of the pictures and illustrations that appear in the site designs is essentially the same as the one you use for logos. The following steps are written and illustrated based on Photoshop Elements, but you can perform these operations in any similar image editing software. Figure 3-11 shows one of the included images from a template opened in Adobe Photoshop Elements for editing.

Step 1 — Locate the picture file

The picture files are stored in the images subfolder, just as logos are, under the blank Web site folder for each template. Using the following example, note where the images subfolder can be located.

```
620
    images
    includes
```

Display the images subfolder in your file explorer or display list. If possible, set the file explorer to display thumbnail images of all the graphics in the subfolder. Pictures may be assigned a variety of filenames in different templates. The principal photograph or artwork appearing on the home page is likely to be named `main.jpg`.

View the graphic files in the images subfolder and decide which files you want to replace with your own. Starting with Step 2, follow the steps for each image you want to replace.

Step 2 — Determine the file dimensions

Open Photoshop Elements (or your graphic editing software). Open the file you want to edit and determine its dimensions. To do this, follow these steps:

1. Choose File ➪ Open. The Open dialog box appears.

2. From the Look in dropdown menu, navigate to the images subfolder for your template and select the file you want to open. Click Open, and the file is displayed.

3. Locate the document dimensions in the bar at the bottom of the image window. You may only see the percentage at which you are viewing the file. If you do not see the dimensions, click and drag the bottom right corner down and out until the window is large enough to show the dimensions.

4. Write down the dimensions for the picture (for example 3.292 inches × 0.917 inches).

Step 3 – Create a picture replacement file

Create a blank graphic file with dimensions that are identical to those of the picture file.

1. Choose File ➪ New ➪ Blank file. The New dialog box appears.

2. Enter the Width and Height as you recorded in the previous set of steps. You may have to change the pixel setting to inches depending on the settings you are using in Photoshop Elements or your image editing software.

3. Verify that the resolution is set to 72 pixels/inch.

4. Click OK. A new, untitled empty graphic opens on your screen. You can now paste or create content within this file.

Step 4 – Enter and edit your content

Now that you have created a blank file that is exactly the same size as the file you want to replace, you can open one or more graphic files containing artwork you want to paste into the blank replacement file or create your own directly in the untitled file. To paste content into the untitled file:

1. Choose File ➪ Open. The Open dialog box appears.

2. Navigate to the location of the artwork you want to use. Select the file, and click Open. The artwork opens.

3. Click and drag your mouse from one corner of the image to the opposite corner (from top right to bottom left, for example) to select the entire image, or click and drag on any portion to select a specific area.

4. Choose Edit ➪ Copy or press Ctrl+C.

5. Click the new, untitled file window to make it the active window.

6. Choose Edit ➪ Paste or press Ctrl+V. Your copied picture material appears in the untitled window. Make any edits to size the picture to fill the available space in the blank file. You may need to copy a smaller or different area to make your artwork fit well into the sized area.

Once you complete these steps, the blank graphic should contain your desired replacement for the site logo that appears on the home page of your Web site.

Step 5 – Save and overwrite your content

Save your edited logo file to replace the default logo in the template Images subfolder by following these steps:

1. Choose File ➪ Save As. The Save As dialog box opens.

2. Use the Save in dropdown menu to navigate the images subfolder for your site.

3. Enter the name of the file you are replacing (such as `main.jpg`) in the File name field. Do not choose a different name. Click OK. When the dialog box appears asking if you want to overwrite the file with the new content, click Yes.

You have now replaced the picture with your own logo or other content.

You may have to experiment with these operations to see what is possible given the artwork or photography and effects you want to integrate. The essential principle of this operation is to simply replace the existing graphic with your own content using the exact same filename. When your site opens up, the code reads and pulls in your content and displays it seamlessly.

✦   ✦   ✦

Templates

General Business Templates

A business must communicate its value to its customer. Consequently, the best business Web sites seek to define their image in ways that reflect the values and interests of their customer base. Some businesses might want to project an image of strength, stability, and longevity, while others might seek to communicate that they are dramatic, innovative, and cutting-edge company.

The general business templates presented in this chapter are designed to clearly present the business name, its tagline or core message, and the principal information defining its products and services. Page links are the next layer of the story of the business, and motivate the reader to access content presented on subpages.

The range of general business templates offers a selection of styles that you can customize to fit a variety of business types and styles; each defines the overall character of the offering and presents a public face to the Web that embodies that character in style and design.

About Business Templates

The mission of each business is to offer products and services based on skills, competencies, and expertise. The general business templates were designed around fictitious companies and serve to showcase different types of businesses with different messages and marketing requirements. Understanding the specifics of each business type—and how your business type fits a template—can help you to more effectively select the template best for your purposes and frame the content you use to carry your message.

Company information

Many companies create a Web presence to establish an identity, brand, and value. The nature of a business might be too complex to conduct over the Web, or the company might simply want to use the Web to be a visible player in the market-place. A company information site is an electronic destination that serves up an interactive brochure that presents the company image and their services to both inform and motivate its customer base.

Successful companies need to reach a broader audience than just its existing cus-tomers. Their sites serve to provide a base of information for secondary but impor-tant audiences, including business partners, suppliers, the press, employment candidates, and recruiters. Company information must be presented to reflect the way the company wants all of these audiences to perceive it, and not just narrowly focused on customer messages.

Product-based business

Product-driven companies need to communicate both the value of the products they sell and the reputation of the company that stands behind the product. For these enterprises, multiple layers of branding must be established — the name of the company, the name of its product lines, and specific product offerings. The goal is to create a unique market space for the company and consistent, authoritative information about its products for customers, retailers, and all others involved in its product marketing and sales channel.

The challenge for product-based businesses is to maintain a distinction between the identity of the company, or the central brand, and that of the products it sells. The company image is a long-term value that should remain consistent and clear in the customer's mind. The products themselves can remain constant or can evolve rapidly in response to changing market conditions.

Service-based business

Service offerings range from the tangible to the intangible. It's one thing to call a plumber to take care of a basic household problem, and quite another to engage more personal services, where offerings are not as urgent and depend on specific customer wants and needs. Discretionary services are driven more by choice than by urgency. Customers must both understand the offering and be motivated to explore their own needs and interests to determine how the offering brings value to them.

Specialty service offerings include those that involve personal attention, care, experience, or transformation such as health and fitness, personal care, counseling, specialized education, and personal growth. Such businesses have a need to market intangible values — comfort, security, and health, to name just a few. Their Web sites must convey a business identity that aligns with these intangible values and then frames service offerings as products that the customer can consider.

Professional practice

All services must, to some extent, demonstrate specific expertise. Some services require a higher level of expert knowledge than others. Professional services demand a greater depth of knowledge in the chosen area, and related insights and abilities to communicate their value to the customer.

Organizations that offer services based on professional practice must not only communicate the extent of their background and knowledge, but also convey the particular approach they bring to the work that differentiates them from competitors. Many professional practice areas, such as health care, legal matters, or financial integrity, are driven by a strong sense of urgency on the part of the customer. In these situations, the professional practice must clearly demonstrate that it has the tools and the people to respond to the customer need.

Business services

Businesses that serve other businesses often think of their customers as clients. Business-to-business, or B2B, offerings must demonstrate credibility, value, and professionalism like all services. The marketing challenge here is not to position and present themselves for the broad general public, but because they serve a smaller subset of business buyers, their offering can undergo a greater level of scrutiny, attention, and review than customer-based businesses do.

Beyond the need to establish the quality of their services, these businesses must articulate the core business value they represent. The appeal to customer interest might address financial and price considerations, but it might also touch on intangibles, such as how a businesses services can help clients be more efficient, effective, and profitable. Typically, B2B services speak in terms of total solutions, coupling the specific service a business offers with intangibles, such as the quality of customer attention and tailoring services to meet specific customer needs.

Tip Instead of navigating from the root of the CD to locate a template, you can click the Templates link in the CD browser application to directly access the chapters on the CD. For faster access, click the Gallery link in the CD browser application to view a listing of all templates. Then click any View Files link to view the files for that template.

Template 410 Company Information

A business site designed to carry company information for a variety of business types, including general company information, company home page, or other business uses.

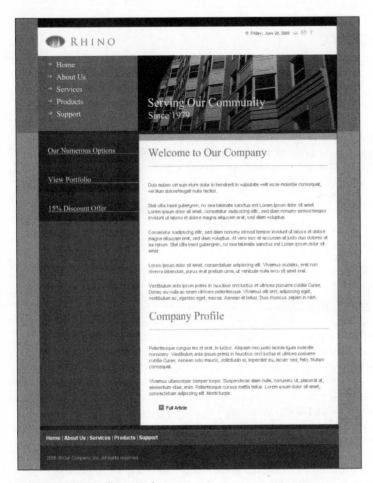

Figure 4-1: Template 410 home

Figure 4-2: Template 410 subpage

Template Developer	Ken Milhous
Filename and Location	CD-ROM: \Templates\Chapter 4\41\410
Variations on this Design	411 412
Site Development Detail	Procedures and supporting information on placing content, links, and Web site images are presented in Chapter 3.

Design Summary

Recommended Use

Best used as a company introduction and electronic brochure that presents the company background and information in the form of short article features and an extended article leading from the home page.

Look and Feel

Built around strong earth tones and black accents, with feature article areas and framing set off in white. This helps the site establish a conservative image for a company in, for example, residential construction and allied fields.

Medium-density layout with use of open space to highlight the article and link selections at the left of the design. The article area is highlighted in a white background with generous white space around the article headings to call attention to them.

Palette is based in browns with the core communication areas accented in black and white. Action item links for primary article content appear as white text on a gradient background, and the lead article appears in white, with headings that pick up and reflect the background color.

Content Plan

Content Plan Overview

Before entering content in your site, make a list of the Web page labels and filenames you will use to build your Web site skeleton. Detailed coverage on building your content plan is presented in Chapter 3.

Subpages

Design supports four subpages that can be linked at the top and bottom navigation bar on the site.

Action Item Pages

Design supports three action item links on the home and subpages. You can use these prominently featured elements as headlines only or as links to subpages containing featured articles or information.

Special Features

Design supports two icons located at the upper right hand corner of the home and subpage layouts.

- Link the Envelope icon to any subpage using the LinkURL1 token.

- Link the Question Mark icon to Frequently Asked Questions (FAQ) page or any subpage using the LinkURL2 token.

Copy the Template

Follow these steps to copy the template to your hard drive:

1. Access the \Templates\Chapter 4\41\410 folder on your CD-ROM.

2. Drag the \410 folder to your desktop or copy and paste the \410 folder to your desktop.

Template Headings and Tags

Figure 4-3: Template 410 home page token reference

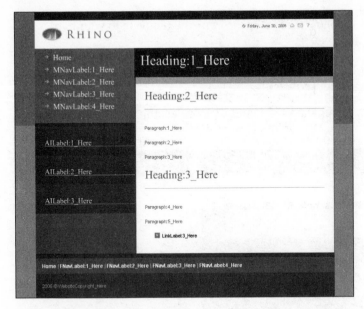

Figure 4-4: Template 410 subpage page token reference

Building Your Site Step-by-Step: 410 Company Information

Building the Site Skeleton

Use the following set of operations to enter the central navigation. Perform the exact same operations within `index.html` and `subpage.html`. Web site navigation and building the site skeleton are presented in Chapter 3.

Note that when opening `index.html` or `subpage.html` in Internet Explorer from your hard drive, a security message may appear. Click for more options, and choose to display the full content so the template displays correctly.

1. Place navigation labels

Review the list of subpage labels and filenames from your content plan. You place the labels for subpage 1 at the top (`MNav`) and bottom (`FNav`) of your page. See Figures 4-3 for home and 4-4 for subpages.

1. Open `index.html` in your text editor.

2. Find `MNavLabel:1_Here` and replace the token with the label for subpage 1.

3. Find `FNavLabel:1_Here` and replace the token with the label for subpage 1.

4. Repeat Steps 2 and 3 for `MNavLabel` and `FNavLabel` 2, 3, and 4.

5. Find `AILabel:1_Here` and replace the token with the label for your first action item. Repeat for `AILabel` 2 and 3.

2. Place navigation links	Review the list of subpage labels and filenames from your content plan. In the following operation, you place the links to the filename for subpage 1 at the top (`MNav`) and bottom (`FNav`) of your page. Enter all filenames in lowercase.

1. Find `MNavURL:1_Here` and replace the token with the filename you selected for subpage 1.

2. Find `FNavURL:1_Here` and replace the token with the filename you selected for subpage 1.

3. Repeat Steps 1 and 2 for `MNavURL` and `FNavURL` 2, 3, 4, and 5 (see Figures 4-3 and 4-4).

    Find `AIURL:1_Here` and replace the token with the filename you selected for action item 1. Repeat for `AIURL` 2 and 3.

3. Place icon references	Place identifying labels and links for the three programmable icons at the top right of the home and subpage. Note that text placed in `LinkLabel` tokens here displays when the user mouses over the icon. The Date and Home icons are already coded for you.

1. Envelope icon label: Find `LinkLabel:1_Here`. Use this icon to link to any page in your site or to your e-mail address. Change the token to the correct text for the desired page or to E-mail, or Send E-mail to denote your e-mail address.

2. Envelope icon link: Find `LinkURL:1_Here` and enter either the filename of the page to which you want to link. If you want to place a link allowing users to e-mail you directly, replace this token with the following text: `Emailto<colon><insert your email address>`. For example: `Emailto:michael@aol.com`.

3. Question Mark icon: Find `LinkLabel:2_Here`. Use this icon to link to any information page, such as an About Us or Help page. Replace the token with the chosen label text for the icon.

4. Question Mark link: Find `LinkURL:2_Here` and replace the token with the filename you chose to link to this icon in your content plan.

4. Place special features

Place the text of the Web site copyright in your pages.

1. Find `WebsiteCopyright:1_Here` and replace the token with your Web site copyright text.

2. Find `LinkURL1:_Here` and replace the token with the filename you chose to link to this icon in your content plan. This token sets the link to the Envelope icon at the top right-hand corner of the page. It links the user directly to your e-mail address. Replace this token with your e-mail address.

3. Find `LinkURL2:_Here` and replace the token with the filename you chose to link to this icon in your content plan. This token sets the link to the Question Mark icon at the top right-hand corner of the page.

4. Save and close `index.html` in your text editor. Do not rename the file.

5. Set up the subpage template

Perform the same set of edits that you completed for `index.html` file on the subpage master template file, `subpage.html`.

1. Open `subpage.html` in your text editor.

2. Return to the beginning of this section ("Building the Site Skeleton"), and start with main Step 1, "Place navigation labels".

3. Complete main Steps 1, 2, and 3 using the `subpage.html` file instead of the `index.html` file.

4. Save `subpage.html` in your text editor. Do not rename the file.

Creating Subpage Files

6. Create subpage files

Use the Save As feature in your text editor to save the `subpage.html` template with the first of the subpage filenames you selected in your content plan. Repeat this to create all subpages listed in your content plan. Save all subpage files to the `\410` folder on your Desktop.

1. Verify that `subpage.html` is open in your text editor.

2. Choose File ➪ Save As or similar from your text editor. In the Save As dialog box, enter the desired filename for the subpage, and click Save.

3. Repeat Step 2 for all subpages in your content plan.

---

7. Display your site

Open your site to check that your labels and pages display correctly.

1. Launch `index.html` from your computer by double-clicking the file name, or choose File ➪ Open (from most browsers) to open it in your browser. An empty home page should appear.

2. Click the navigation links at the top and bottom of the home page and you should see empty subpage pages.

3. Close the empty site skeleton.

Placing Content in the Home Page

8. Edit home page flash tagline

Enter the text for the animated Flash taglines that appears on the home page in `index.html`.

1. Open `flashconfig.xml` in your text editor.

2. Find `Tagline:1_Here` and replace the token with your tagline 1 text.

3. Find `Tagline:2_Here` and replace the token with your tagline 2 text.

4. Save and close `flashconfig.xml`.

9. Place article content

Place content for article headings, paragraph content and links.

1. Find `Heading:1_Here` and replace the token with your heading text.

2. Find `Paragraph:1_Here` and replace the token with your paragraph text. Repeat for `Paragraph` 2 and 3.

3. Find `Heading:2_Here` and replace the token with your heading text.

4. Find `Paragraph:4_Here` and replace the token with your content. Repeat for `Paragraph` 5.

5. Find `LinkLabel:3_Here`. Replace the token text only with your chosen label text for this link (such as "Read More" or "More Information"). You can delete this token if you do not want to use this link.

6. Find `LinkURL:3_Here`. Replace the token with the filename you have selected to be accessed from this link.

7. Save `index.html` in your text editor.

Placing Content in Subpages

Use the following operations to place content into all of your site subpages. Use the subpage token reference (see Figure 4-4) to see the position of the content and label tokens. Repeat this operation to enter content in all of your subpages.

10. Place subpage articles

Place article headings and text in your subpages.

1. Select and open a named subpage for your site in your text editor.

2. Find `Heading:1_Here` and replace the token with your heading 1 text.

3. Find `Heading:2_Here` and replace the token with your heading 2 text.

4. Find `Paragraph:1_Here` and replace the token with your paragraph text. Repeat this action with `Paragraph` 2 and 3.

5. Find `Heading:3_Here` and replace the token with your heading 3 text.

6. Find `Paragraph:4_Here` and replace the tokens with your text. Repeat this action with `Paragraph` 5.

7. Find `LinkLabel:3_Here`. Replace the token with the chosen label text for this link (such as "Read More" or "More Information"). You can delete this token if you do not want to use this link.

8. Find `LinkURL:3_Here`. Replace the token with the filename you have selected to be accessed from this link.

9. Save and close the file when you have finished editing.

Finalizing Your Site

11. Edit site logo and pictures   Turn to Chapter 3 for explanation and procedures to replace the default template logo and images with your own logo and images.

12. Display your Web site   Launch `index.html` from your computer by double-clicking the file name, or choose File ⇨ Open. Check your work in your browser window.

13. Edit and adjust   Make edits to your home page or subpage files in your text editor. Be sure to edit only your content and not to disturb any of the surrounding code.

14. Publish   The basic parameters of what you should provide to your Web hosting company are outlined in Chapter 3. For the specifics on actually posting your live site to the Web, contact your service provide for details.

Variations

Variation 411 Overview   This variation of the design features green accents in the anchor image and the background for the action items. The navigation areas are presented against gray backgrounds. Fonts for the principle headings in the article area are presented in shades of green based on the background color.

See the images in the CD-ROM's Gallery section.

Variation 412 Overview   This version features the anchor image and action item areas presented in complementary shades of gray, with navigation areas on a pastel background with a green tint. Heading fonts in the article areas are colored in pastels to offset them from the paragraph text in black.

See the images in the CD-ROM's Gallery section.

Template 420   Product-Based Business

A business site designed for a manufacturing concern that needs to present its products to both its retail outlets and the end customer.

Figure 4-5: Template 420 home

Figure 4-6: Template 420 subpage

Template Developer	Ken Milhous
Filename and Location	CD-ROM: \Templates\Chapter 4\42\420
Variations on this Design	421 422
Site Development Detail	Procedures and supporting information on placing content, links, and Web site images are presented in Chapter 3.

Design Summary

Recommended Use	Designed to showcase a product, with a strong use of photography throughout the design. The home page features three photographic images: the anchor image, which sets off the site logo, the lead image, which supports dual taglines that fade-in as overlays, and an accent image. The subpage features a main article set off by a sidebar and action item area suitable for presenting details and sales messages.

Look and Feel

Green is the dominant color for the design, presented in the anchor image, the tagline area, and the principal article headline fonts. The white background gives the design an open look with easily readable article areas.

Medium-density layout uses open space to highlight article and link selections at the left of the design. The article area is highlighted in a white background with generous white space around the article headings to call attention to them.

Content Plan

Content Plan Overview

Before entering content in your site, make a list of the Web page labels and filenames you will use to build your Web site skeleton. Detailed coverage on building your content plan is presented in Chapter 3.

Subpages

Design is a catalog layout that supports five subpages that can be linked at the top and bottom navigation bar on the home page. There are five main and footer navigation tokens on the subpage, but one must be reserved as a link to the home. The default form of the layout presents the site design for a clothing manufacturer.

Linked Articles

Design supports two main articles each with a `LinkLabel` to continue the article to a subpage. Subpages offer a single main article with no continuing link. The sidebar and action items areas, however, can both be used to place links to subpages or external sites.

Catalog Detail Pages

Subpage layout in this template supports four links to detail subpages. You can use this feature to create a catalog subpage under the home page and create four product pages linked to it. You can determine how many of these detail pages you want; they are linked to your subpages using the subnavigation (`SNav`) set of tokens.

Special Features

Design supports two special features on the subpage that you need to prepare for:

- Text labels for announcements and offerings (text only).

- Subnavigation labels, each of which supports a link to a subpage or external site.

Copy the Template

Follow these steps to copy the template to your hard drive:

1. Access the `\Templates\Chapter 4\42\420` folder on your CD-ROM.

2. Drag the `\420` folder to your desktop or copy and paste the `\420` folder to your desktop.

Template Headings and Tags

Figure 4-7: Template 420 home page token reference

Figure 4-8: Template 420 subpage page token reference

Building Your Site Step-by-Step: 420 Product-Based Business

Building the Site Skeleton

Use the following set of operations to enter the central navigation. Perform the exact same operations within `index.html` and `subpage.html`. Web site navigation and building the site skeleton are presented in Chapter 3.

Note that when opening `index.html` or `subpage.html` in Internet Explorer from your hard drive, a security message may appear. Click for more options, and choose to display the full content so the template displays correctly.

1. Place navigation labels

Review the list of subpage labels and filenames from your content plan. In the following operation, you place the labels for subpage 1 at the top (`MNav`) and bottom (`FNav`) of your page. See Figures 4-9 for home and 4-10 for subpages.

1. Open `index.html` in your text editor

2. Find `MNavLabel:1_Here` and replace the token with the label for subpage 1. Repeat step for `MNavLabel` 2, 3, and 4.

3. Find `FNavLabel:1_Here` and replace the token with the label for subpage 1. Repeat this step for `FNavLabel` 2, 3, and 4.

---

2. Place navigation links

Review the list of subpage labels and filenames from your content plan. In the following operation, you place the links to the filename for subpage 1 at the top (`MNav`) and bottom (`FNav`) of your page. Enter all filenames in lowercase.

1. Find `MNavURL:1_Here` and replace the token with the filename you selected for subpage 1. Repeat this step for `MNavURL` 2, 3, and 4.

2. Find `FNavURL:1_Here` and replace the token with the filename you selected for subpage 1. Repeat this step for `FNavURL` 2, 3, and 4.

---

3. Place special features

Place the text of the Web site copyright in your pages (see Figures 4-9 and 4-10).

1. Find `WebsiteCopyright:1_Here` and replace the token with your Web site copyright text.

2. Save and close `index.html` in your text editor.

---

4. Set up the subpage template

Perform the same set of edits that you completed for `index.html` file on the subpage master template file, `subpage.html`.

1. Open `subpage.html` in your text editor.

2. Return to the beginning of this section ("Building the Site Skeleton"), and start with main Step 1, "Place navigation label."

3. Complete main Steps 1, 2, and 3 using the `subpage.html` file instead of the `index.html` file.

4. Save `subpage.html` in your text editor. Do not rename the file.

Creating Subpage Files

5. Create subpage files

Use the Save As feature in your text editor to save the `subpage.html` template with the first of the subpage filenames you selected in your content plan. Repeat this to create the four additional new files that match the subpage filenames you selected in your content plan.

Enter filenames exactly as you entered them in the Place navigation links operation (main Step 2). Save all files to the `\420` folder on your desktop.

1. Open `subpage.html` in your text editor.

2. Choose File ➪ Save As or similar from your text editor. Enter the filename you selected for subpage 1, and click OK.

3. Repeat Step 2 for all subpages in your content plan.

6. Display your site

Open your site to check that your labels and pages display correctly.

1. Launch `index.html` from your computer by double-clicking the file name, or choose File ➪ Open (from most browsers) to open it in your browser. An empty home page should appear.

2. Click the navigation links at the top and bottom of the home page and you should see empty subpage pages.

3. Close the site skeleton.

Placing Content in the Home Page

7. Edit home page Flash tagline

Enter the text for the animated Flash taglines that appear on the home page in `index.html`.

1. Open `flashconfig.xml` in your text editor.

2. Find `Tagline:1_Here` and replace the token with your tagline 1 text.

3. Find `Tagline:2_Here` and replace the token with your tagline 2 text.

4. Save and close `flashconfig.xml`.

---

8. Place home page articles

Place the headings and paragraph text for the two article areas on the home page in `index.html` (see Figure 4-9).

1. Open `index.html` in your text editor.

2. Find `Heading:1_Here` and replace the token with your heading text.

3. Find `Paragraph:1_Here` and replace the token with your paragraph text.

4. Find `Heading:2_Here` and replace the token with your heading text.

5. Find `Paragraph:2_Here` and replace the token with your content.

6. Find `LinkLabel:1_Here`. Replace the token with the chosen label text for this link. You can delete this token if you do not want to use this link. Repeat this operation for `LinkLabel` 2.

7. Find `LinkURL:1_Here`. Replace the token with the filename you have selected to be accessed from this link. Repeat this operation for `LinkURL` 2.

8. Save `index.html` in your text editor.

Placing Content in Subpages

Use the following operations to place content into all of your site subpages. Use the subpage token reference (see Figure 4-10) to see the position of the content and label tokens. Repeat this operation to enter content in all of your subpages.

9. Place subpage article	Place leading links and article heading and text in the subpages.

1. Select and open a named subpage for your site in your text editor.

2. Find `LinkLabel:1_Here`. Replace this token with the desired text for the link. Repeat this step for `LinkLabels` 2 and 3.

3. Find `LinkURL:1_Here`. Replace token with the page name or URL destination for the link label. Repeat this step for `LinkURL` 2 and 3.

4. Find `Heading:1_Here` and replace the token with your heading 1 text.

5. Find `Paragraph:1_Here` and replace the token with your paragraph text.

10. Place sidebar content	Place content in the sidebar elements to the left of the page.

1. Find `TextLabel:1_Here`. Replace with the lead text to the sidebar.

2. Find `SNavLabel:1_Here`. Replace this token with the labels to subnavigation links that should appear on this page. Repeat this operation for `SNavLabels` 2, 3, and 4.

3 Find `SNavURL:1_Here`. Replace token with the page name or URL destination for `SNavLabel1`. Repeat this operation for `SNavLabels` 2, 3, and 4.

4. Find `AILabel:1_Here` and replace with the action item text.

5. Find `AIURL:1_Here` and replace with the filename for your link destination.

6. Find `TextLabel:2_Here` and replace with the desired text.

7. Find `LinkLabel:4_Here`. Replace this token with the desired text for the link, such as "Read More."

8. Find `LinkURL:4_Here`. Replace token with the page name or URL destination for the link label.

9. Save and close the file when you have finished editing.

Finalizing Your Site

11. Edit site logo and pictures   Turn to Chapter 3 for explanation and procedures to replace the default template logo and images with your own logo and images.

12. Display your Web site   Launch `index.html` from your computer by double-clicking the file name, or choose File ➪ Open. Check your work in your browser window.

13. Edit and adjust   Make edits by opening up your home page or subpage page files in your text editor and making edits to the content. Be sure to edit only your content and not to disturb any of the surrounding code.

14. Publish   The basic parameters of what you should provide to your Web hosting company are outlined in Chapter 3. For the specifics on actually posting your live site to the Web, contact your service provider for details.

Variations

Variation 421 Overview   The color emphasis in this variation is in yellows and browns, with the anchor image for both home and subpage changed to a desert mountain background. Fonts for main article headings and link labels pick up the yellow color theme.

See the images in the CD-ROM's Gallery section.

Variation 422 Overview   This variation uses a black, white, and gray background, with a different anchor image than the default design — a stylized photo negative as the anchor image for home and subpage. Fonts for main article headings and link labels pick up the green color from the logo.

See the images in the CD-ROM's Gallery section.

Template 430 Service-Based Business

This specialty services site presents a luxury health and fitness center. You can use it to present a variety of health services businesses, such as for businesses that are location-based, such as health clubs, and ones that offer individual health and fitness services.

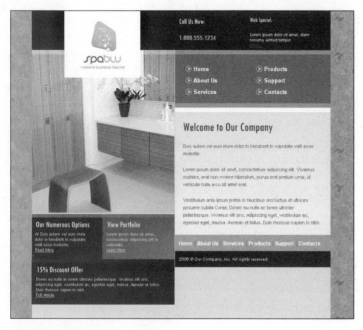

Figure 4-9: Template 430 home

Figure 4-10: Template 430 subpage

Template Developer	Ken Milhous
Filename and Location	CD-ROM: \Templates\Chapter 4\43\430
Variations on this Design	431 432
Site Development Detail	Procedures and supporting information on placing content, links, and Web site images are presented in Chapter 3.

Design Summary

Recommended Use

Template works for a variety of health and fitness businesses. The primary focus of the design is to offer specialized service packages to a core clientele. This design also works for businesses with services for multiple audiences and interests.

Look and Feel

Dominant blue color creates an impression of cool comfort and reinforces the image of water. Offsetting a magenta background for menu items balances the warmth and heat.

Medium-density site featuring a single main article on both the home and subpage layouts. Both home and subpage make extensive use of highlighted feature areas, which offer special packages, and all provide "Learn more" links to article extensions on interior pages.

Content Plan

Content Plan Overview

Before entering content in your site, make a list of the Web page labels and filenames you will use to build your Web site skeleton. Detailed coverage on building your content plan is presented in Chapter 3.

Subpages

Design supports five principal subpages in the main and footer navigation areas for the home and subpage. This layout can support additional subpages that present service details of any kind, as well as background information, contact information, and staff backgrounds. Identify and write down the screen labels and the related filenames.

Sales Offers

The sales offer area leads with action item headings and text you can use for articles or blurbs. You may place links from these areas to principal or additional subpages using the `LinkLabel` and `LinkURL` group of tokens.

Announcements

You can place sales announcements, telephone contact information, addresses, or any other incentive at the top of the home page and subpages using `TextLabel` tokens.

Copy the Template

Follow these steps to copy the template to your hard drive:

1. Access the `\Templates\Chapter 4\43\430` folder on your CD-ROM.

2. Drag the `\430` folder to your desktop or copy and paste the `\430` folder to your desktop.

Template Headings and Tags

Figure 4-11: Template 430 home page token reference

Figure 4-12: Template 430 subpage page token reference

Building Your Site Step-by-Step: 430 Service-Based Business

Building the Site Skeleton

Use the following set of operations to enter the central navigation. Perform the exact same operations within `index.html` and `subpage.html`. Web site navigation and building the site skeleton are presented in Chapter 3.

Note that when opening `index.html` or `subpage.html` in Internet Explorer from your hard drive, a security message may appear. Click for more options, and choose to display the full content so the template displays correctly.

---

1. Place navigation labels

Review the list of subpage labels and filenames from your content plan. In the following operation, you place the labels for subpage 1 at the top (`MNav`) and bottom (`FNav`) of your page. See Figures 4-11 for home and 4-12 for subpages.

1. Open `index.html` in your text editor.

2. Find `MNavLabel:1_Here` and replace the token with the label for subpage 1.

3. Find `FNavLabel:1_Here` and replace the token with the label for subpage 1.

4. Repeat Steps 2 and 3 for `MNavLabel` and `FNavLabel` 2, 3, 4, and 5.

---

2. Place navigation links

Review the list of subpage labels and filenames from your content plan. In the following operation, you place the links to the filename for subpage 1 at the top (`MNav`) and bottom (`FNav`) of your page. Enter all filenames in lowercase.

1. Find `MNavURL:1_Here` and replace the token with the filename you selected for subpage 1.

2. Find `FNavURL:1_Here` and replace the token with the filename you selected for subpage 1.

3. Repeat Steps 1 and 2 for `MNavURL` and `FNavURL` 2, 3, 4, and 5.

---

3. Place sales offers

Place the text for the linked announcements and related linked articles that appear on both home page and subpages.

1. Find `AILabel:1_Here` and replace the token with your sales offer headline. Repeat for `AILabel` 2 and 3.

2. Find `AIParagraph:1_Here` and replace with a short text paragraph under the headline. Repeat for `AIParagraph` 2 and 3.

3. Find `LinkLabel:1_Here` and replace with "Read More" or other text that indicates a link to a subpage. You can delete this token if you don't want to use it. Repeat for `LinkLabel` 2 and 3.

4. Find `LinkURL:1_Here` and replace the filename of the linked page. Repeat for `LinkURL` 2 and 3.

---

4. Place announcements

Place the text for the announcement items, which are text only and not linked, at the top of the home page and subpages.

1. Find `TextLabel:1_Here` and replace the token with your announcement text. Repeat this operation for the `TextLabel` 2, 3, and 4 tokens.

2. Find `LinkLabel:4_Here` and replace with the chosen label text.

3. Find `LinkURL:4_Here` and replace with the filename of the linked page.

---

5. Place special features

Place the text of the Web site copyright in your pages.

1. Find `WebsiteCopyright:1_Here` and replace the token with your Web site copyright text.

2. Save the `index.html` template file in your text editor.

---

6. Set up the subpage template

Perform the same set of edits that you completed for `index.html` file on the subpage master template file, `subpage.html`.

1. Open `subpage.html` in your text editor.

2. Return to the beginning of this section ("Building the Site Skeleton"), and start with main Step 1, "Place navigation labels."

3. Complete main Steps 1, 2, 3, 4, and 5 using the `subpage.html` file instead of the `index.html` file.

4. Save `subpage.html` in your text editor. Do not rename the file.

Creating Subpage Files

7. Create subpage files

Use the Save As feature in your text editor to save the `subpage.html` template with the first of the subpage filenames you selected in your content plan. Repeat this to create all subpages listed in your content plan.

Save all files to the `\430` folder on your Desktop.

1. Verify that `subpage.html` is open in your text editor.

2. Choose File ➪ Save As or similar from your text editor. Enter the filename you selected for subpage 1, and click OK.

3. Repeat Step 2 for all subpages in your content plan.

4. Repeat Step 2 for any linked articles you identified in your content plan.

8. Display your site

Open your site to check that your labels and pages display correctly.

1. Launch `index.html` from your computer by double-clicking the filename, or choose File ➪ Open (from most browsers) to open it in your browser. An empty home page should appear.

2. Click the navigation links at the top and bottom of the home page and you should see an empty subpage page.

3. Close the site skeleton.

Placing Content in the Home Page

9. Place home page articles

Place headings and paragraph text for the two article areas on the home page in `index.html` (see Figure 4-11).

1. Open `index.html` in your text editor.

2. Find `Heading:1_Here` and replace the token with your heading text.

3. Find `Paragraph:1_Here` and replace the token with your paragraph text. Repeat for `Paragraph` 2 and 3.

4. Save and close `index.html`.

Placing Content in Subpages

Use the following operations to place content into all of your site subpages. Use the subpage token reference (see Figure 4-12) to see the position of the content and label tokens. Repeat this operation to enter content in all of your subpages.

---

10. Place subpage article   Place article heading and text in the subpages.

1. Open the subpage file you want to edit.

2. Find `Heading:1_Here` and replace the token with your chosen heading text.

3. Find `Paragraph:1_Here` and replace the token with your chosen paragraph text. Repeat for `Paragraph` 2, 3, 4, and 5.

4. Save and close the subpage files when you are finished.

Finalizing Your Site

11. Edit site logo and pictures   Turn to Chapter 3 for explanation and procedures to replace the default template logo and images with your own logo and images.

12. Display your Web site   Launch `index.html` from your computer by double-clicking the filename, or choose File ➪ Open. Check your work in your browser window.

13. Edit and adjust   Make edits by opening up your home page or subpage page files in your text editor and making edits to the content. Be sure to edit only your content and not to disturb any of the surrounding code.

14. Publish   The basic parameters of what you should provide to your Web hosting company are outlined in Chapter 3. For the specifics on actually posting your live site to the Web, contact your service provide for details.

Variations

Variation 431 Overview	This variation uses shades of brown for the main and footer navigation areas, and is set over a background of beaded water drops on a blue field. See the images in the CD-ROM's Gallery section.
Variation 432 Overview	Set on a steel gray background, this version of the design focuses on rich blues and browns for a darker more conservative look. See the images in the CD-ROM's Gallery section.

Template 440 Professional Practice

A professional practice site designed for business-to-business customers. The site has design features that you can use as company information for almost any business enterprise, and can even adapt for legal, accounting, and consulting firms.

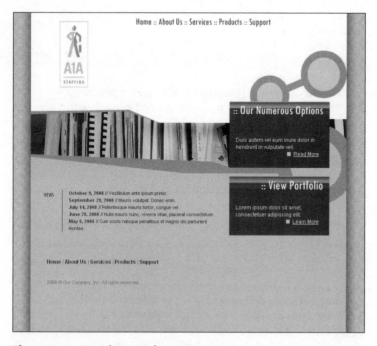

Figure 4-13: Template 440 home

Figure 4-14: Template 440 subpage

Template Developer	Ken Milhous
Filename and Location	CD-ROM: \Templates\Chapter 4\44\440
Variations on this Design	441 442
Site Development Detail	Procedures and supporting information on placing content, links, and Web site images are presented in Chapter 3.

Design Summary

Recommended Use	Template uses a professional services company as the focus example. The open structure of the design and the corporate look and feel make it highly adaptable and usable for a variety of business communication purposes. You can use it as a professional service site or to present individual professional capabilities.

Look and Feel

Template is built around white space at the top leading to content areas in browns and gray. A strong top down, vertical structure carries the eye from the logo on the Home page to a list of news items, and on the subpage a large article area is presented.

Medium- to high-density layout built around sculptured shapes to break up the space. Two prominent action item blocks appear on both Home and Subpages which can be used to present articles or short featured items.

Content Plan

Content Plan Overview

Before entering content in your site, make a list of the Web page labels and filenames you will use to build your Web site skeleton. Detailed coverage on building your content plan is presented in Chapter 3.

Subpages

Supports four subpages that can be linked at the top and bottom navigation bar on the site. The layout is very simple and you can adapt it to just about any business purpose.

News Items

Home page offers five news items that you can link to five additional subpages or any of the core subpages you create. You create these using `TextLabel` tokens for the news announcement and `LinkLabel` and `LinkURL` to create the "Read More" or referral links.

Offer or Announcement Areas

Two announcement areas with linked subpages with headings that appear on both the home page and subpages. Sales offer area leads with action item headings and text that can be used for articles or blurbs. Place links from headings using the `LinkLabel` and `LinkURL` group of tokens.

Copy the Template

Follow these steps to copy the template to your hard drive:

1. Access the \Templates\Chapter 4\44\440 folder on your CD-ROM.

2. Drag the \440 folder to your desktop or copy and paste the \440 folder to your desktop.

Template Headings and Tags

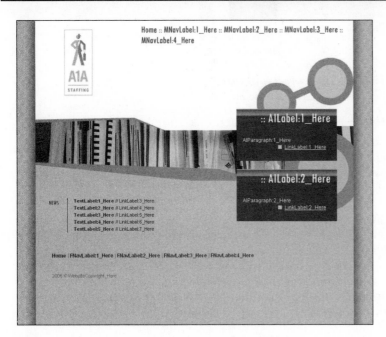

Figure 4-15: Template 440 home page token reference

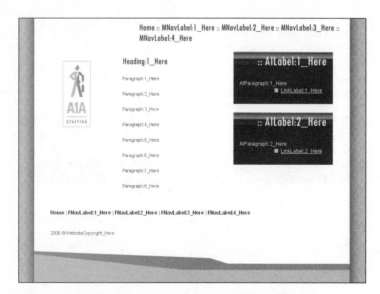

Figure 4-16: Template 440 subpage page token reference

Building Your Site Step-by-Step: 440 Professional Practice

Building the Site Skeleton

Use the following set of operations to enter the central navigation. Perform the exact same operations within `index.html` and `subpage.html`. Web site navigation and building the site skeleton are presented in Chapter 3.

Note that when opening `index.html` or `subpage.html` in Internet Explorer from your hard drive, a security message may appear. Click for more options, and choose to display the full content so the template displays correctly.

---

1. Place navigation labels

Review the list of subpage labels and filenames from your content plan. In the following operation, you place the labels for subpage 1 at the top (`MNav`) and bottom (`FNav`) of your page. See Figure 4-15 for home and 4-16 for subpage.

1. Open `index.html` in your text editor.

2. Find `MNavLabel:1_Here` and replace the token with the label for subpage 1.

3. Find `FNavLabel:1_Here` and replace the token with the label for subpage 1.

4. Repeat Steps 2 and 3 for `MNavLabel` and `FNavLabel` 2, 3 and 4.

---

2. Place navigation links

Review the list of subpage labels and filenames from your content plan. In the following operation, you place the links to the filename for subpage 1 at the top (`MNav`) and bottom (`FNav`) of your page. Enter all filenames in lowercase.

1. Find `MNavURL:1_Here` and replace the token with the filename you selected for subpage 1.

2. Find `FNavURL:1_Here` and replace the token with the filename you selected for subpage 1.

3. Repeat Steps 1 and 2 for `MNavURL` and `FNavURL` 2, 3, and 4.

---

3. Place sales offers

Place text for the linked announcements and related linked articles that appear on both the home page and subpages.

1. Find `AILabel:1_Here` and replace the token with your sales offer headline. Repeat for `AILabel` 2.

2. Find `AIParagraph:1_Here` and replace it with a short text paragraph under the headline. Repeat for `AIParagraph` 2.

3. Find `LinkLabel:1_Here` and replace it with desired text. You can delete this token if you don't want to use it. Repeat for `LinkLabel` 2.

4. Find `LinkURL:1_Here` and replace the filename of the linked page. Repeat for `LinkURL` 2.

---

4. Place special features

Place the text of the Web site copyright in your pages (see Figure 4-15).

1. Find `WebsiteCopyright:1_Here` and replace the token with your Web site copyright text.

2. Save the template file in your text editor.

5. Set up the subpage template

Perform the same set of edits that you completed for `index.html` file on the subpage master template file, `subpage.html`.

1. Open `subpage.html` in your text editor.

2. Return to the beginning of this section ("Building the Site Skeleton"), and start with main Step 1, "Place navigation labels."

3. Complete main Steps 1, 2, 3, and 4 using the `subpage.html` file instead of the `index.html` file.

4. Save `subpage.html` in your text editor. Do not rename the file.

Creating Subpage Files

6. Create subpage files

Use the Save As feature in your text editor to save the `subpage.html` template with the first of the subpage filenames you selected in your content plan. Repeat this to create all subpages listed in your content plan.

Save all files to the `\440` folder on your Desktop.

1. Verify that `subpage.html` is open in your text editor

2. Choose File ➪ Save As or similar from your text editor. Enter the filename you selected for subpage 1, and click OK.

3. Repeat Step 2 for all subpages in your content plan.

4. Repeat Step 2 for any linked articles or catalog detail pages you identified in your content plan.

7. Display your site

Open your site to check that your labels and pages display correctly.

1. Launch `index.html` from your computer by double-clicking the filename, or choose File ➪ Open (from most browsers) to open it in your browser. An empty home page should appear.

2. Click the navigation links at the top and bottom of the home page and you should see empty subpage pages.

3. Close the site skeleton.

Place Content in the Home Page

8. Place home page news items

Place news items and follow on links directly in the home page. See Figure 4-15 for correct placement of News Items.

1. Open `index.html` in your text editor if it isn't already open.

2. Find `TextLabel:1_Here` and replace the token with your news item text. Repeat for `TextLabel` 2, 3, 4, and 5.

3. Find `LinkLabel:3_Here` and replace the token with "Read More" or other transitional text of your choosing. Repeat for `LinkLabel` 4, 5, 6, and 7.

4. Find `LinkURL:3_Here` and replace the token with the filename of the linked subpage. Repeat for `LinkURL` 4, 5, 6, and 7.

5. Save `index.html` in your text editor.

Placing Content in Subpages

Use the following operations to place content into all of your site subpages. Use the subpage token reference (see Figure 4-16) to see the position of the content and label tokens. Repeat this operation to enter content in all of your subpages.

9. Place subpage article

Place article heading and text in the subpages.

1. Select and open a named subpage for your site in your text editor.

2. Find `Heading:1_Here` and replace the token with your heading 1 text.

3. Find `Paragraph:1_Here` and replace the token with your paragraph text.

4. Repeat this action with remaining `Paragraph` tokens 2 through 8. You can delete any of the unwanted or unused `Paragraph` tokens so they do not appear in the page.

5. Save and close the file when you have finished editing.

Finalizing Your Site

10. Edit site logo and pictures   Turn to Chapter 3 for explanation and procedures to replace the default template logo and images with your own logo and images.

11. Display your Web site   Launch `index.html` from your computer by double-clicking the filename, or choose File ➪ Open. Check your work in your browser window.

12. Edit and adjust   Make edits by opening up your home page or subpage page files in your text editor and making edits to the content. Be sure to edit only your content and not to disturb any of the surrounding code.

13. Publish   The basic parameters of what you should provide to your Web hosting company are outlined in Chapter 3. For the specifics on actually posting your live site to the Web, contact your service provide for details.

Variations

Variation 441 Overview   This version of the design features darker gray content area in the Home page, and the anchor image is presented in shades of white and gray. Accent bars at the top of action item blocks are presented in gray.

See the images in the CD-ROM's Gallery section.

Variation 442 Overview   Dark browns dominate this version of the design in the content area on the Home page and in the action item blocks on both Home and subpages. Accent bars at the top of action item blocks are presented in a light brown.

See the images in the CD-ROM's Gallery section.

Template 450 Business Services

An information and sales site designed to present business services offered by individuals and organizations. The layout presents both announcements and multiple article and content areas that detail specific services, background information, and contact information.

Figure 4-17: Template 450 home

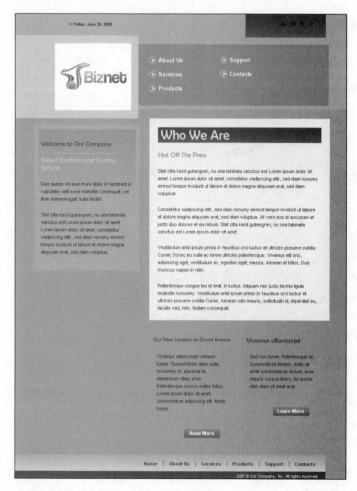

Figure 4-18: Template 450 subpage

Template Developer	Ken Milhous
Filename and Location	CD-ROM: \Templates\Chapter 4\45\450
Variations on This Design	451 452
Site Development Detail	Procedures and supporting information on placing content, links, and Web site images are presented in Chapter 3.

Design Summary

Recommended Use

For content-rich business offerings that need to convey a great deal of information. This site offers many content headlines and information areas, both on the home page and subpages. This layout is ideal for businesses with many offerings to present or information to communicate.

Look and Feel

Design uses a variety of colored accent areas against a turquoise background to set off announcement and article content.

High-density layout that offers a variety of attention-grabbing page features, including featured article areas and additional areas for detail information and links to information subpages.

Content Plan

Content Plan Overview

Before entering content in your site, make a list of the Web page labels and filenames you will use to build your Web site skeleton. Detailed coverage on building your content plan is presented in Chapter 3.

Subpages

Business information layout supports five principal subpages in the main and footer navigation areas plus an embedded Home navigation link. Article headings and text include "Read More" links on both the home page and subpage areas that support additional subpages as needed.

Announcement Areas

Design supports an announcement area to the left of both the home page and subpage. Use these areas to carry key business messages, contact information, or other attention-getting content. The home page announcement area supports two links to subpages, which may be links to principal subpages or freestanding articles.

Article Areas

To maximize the number of impressions per page, this design incorporates three headlined article areas on the home page and another three on the subpage. The three article areas on the home page support subpage links; the two article areas in the subpage layout support links to other subpages.

Special Features

Link icons in this design on the home page and subpage to existing or unique pages that you create using LinkURL tokens:

- Envelope icon

- Magnifying Glass icon

- Question Mark icon

Copy the Template

Follow these steps to copy the template to your hard drive:

1. Access the \Templates\Chapter 4\45\450 folder on your CD-ROM.

2. Drag the \450 folder to your desktop or copy and paste the \450 folder to your desktop.

Template Headings and Tags

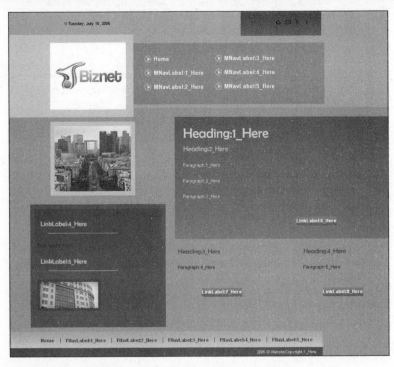

Figure 4-19: Template 450 home page token reference

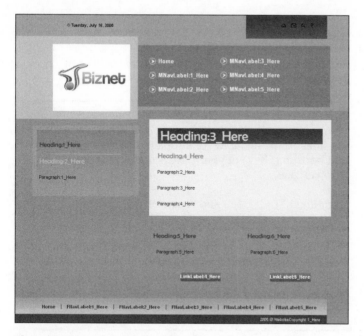

Figure 4-20: Template 450 subpage page token reference

Building Your Site Step-by-Step: 450 Business Services

Building the Site Skeleton

Use the following set of operations to enter the central navigation. Perform the exact same operations within `index.html` and `subpage.html`. Web site navigation and building the site skeleton are presented in Chapter 3.

Note that when opening `index.html` or `subpage.html` in Internet Explorer from your hard drive, a security message may appear. Click for more options, and choose to display the full content so the template displays correctly.

---

1. Place navigation labels

Review the list of subpage labels and filenames from your content plan. In the following operation, you place the labels for subpage 1 at the top (`MNav`) and bottom (`FNav`) of your page. See Figure 4-19 for home and 4-20 for subpages.

1. Open `index.html` in your text editor.

2. Find `MNavLabel:1_Here` and replace the token with the label for subpage 1.

3. Find `FNavLabel:1_Here` and replace the token with the label for subpage 1.

4. Repeat Steps 2 and 3 for `MNavLabel` and `FNavLabel` 2, 3, 4, and 5.

2. Place navigation links

Review the list of subpage labels and filenames from your content plan. In the following operation, you place the links to the filename for subpage 1 at the top (`MNav`) and bottom (`FNav`) of your page. Enter all the filenames in lowercase.

1. Find `MNavURL:1_Here` and replace the token with filename you selected for subpage 1.

2. Find `FNavURL:1_Here` and replace the token with the filename you selected for subpage 1.

3. Repeat Steps 1 and 2 for `MNavURL` and `FNavURL` 2, 3, 4, and 5 (see Figures 4-19 and 4-20).

3. Place icon references

Place identifying labels and links for the three programmable icons at the top right of the home and subpage. Note that text placed in `LinkLabel` tokens here displays when the user mouses over the icon. The Date and Home icons are already coded for you.

1. Envelope icon label: Find `LinkLabel:1_Here`. Use this icon to link to any page in your site or to your e-mail address. Change the token to the correct text for the desired page or to E-mail, or Send E-mail to denote your e-mail address.

2. Envelope icon link: Find `LinkURL:1_Here` and enter either the filename of the page to which you want to link. If you want to place a link allowing users to e-mail you directly, replace this token with the following text: `Emailto<colon><insert your email address>`. For example: `Emailto:michael@aol.com`.

3. Magnifying glass icon: Find `LinkLabel:2_Here`. Use this icon to link to any information page, such as an About Us or Help page. Replace the token with the desired label text for the icon.

4. Magnifying glass link: Find `LinkURL:2_Here` and replace the token with the filename you chose to link to this icon in your content plan.

5. Question Mark icon: Find `LinkLabel:3_Here`. Use this icon to link to any information page, such as an About Us or Help page. Replace the token with the desired label text for the icon.

6. Question Mark link: Find `LinkURL:3_Here` and replace the token with the filename you chose to link to this icon in your content plan.

---

4. Place special features

Enter link destinations for icons appearing at the upper right-hand corner of Home and subpages. Place the text of the Web site copyright in your pages.

1. Find `WebsiteCopyright:1_Here` and replace the token with your Web site copyright text.

2. Save and close the template file in your text editor.

---

5. Set up the subpage template

Perform the same set of edits that you completed for `index.html` file on the subpage master template file, `subpage.html`.

1. Open `subpage.html` in your text editor.

2. Return to the beginning of this section ("Building the Site Skeleton"), and start with main Step 1, "Place navigation labels."

3. Complete main Steps 1, 2, and 3 using the `subpage.html` file instead of the `index.html` file.

4. Save `subpage.html` in your text editor. Do not rename the file.

Creating Subpage Files

6. Create subpage files

Use the Save As feature in your text editor to save the `subpage.html` template with the first of the subpage filenames you selected in your content plan. Repeat this to create all subpages listed in your content plan.

Save all files to the `\450` folder on your Desktop.

1. Verify that `subpage.html` is open in your text editor

2. Choose File ⇨ Save As or similar from your text editor. Enter the filename you selected for subpage 1, and click OK.

3. Repeat Step 2 for all subpages in your content plan.

4. Repeat Step 2 for any linked articles or catalog detail pages you identified in your content plan.

---

7. Display your site   Open your site to check that your labels and pages display correctly.

1. Launch `index.html` from your computer by double-clicking the filename, or choose File ⇨ Open (from most browsers) to open it in your browser. An empty home page should appear.

2. Click the navigation links at the top and bottom of the home page and you should see empty subpage pages.

3. Close the site skeleton.

Placing Content in the Home Page

8. Place home announcement   Place the headings and paragraph text for the two article areas on the home page in `index.html` (see Figure 4-19).

1. Open `index.html` in your text editor.

2. Find `TextLabel:1_Here` and replace the token with announcement text.

3. Find `LinkLabel:4_Here` and replace with label for linked page. You can delete this token if you don't want to use it.

4. Find `LinkURL:4_Here` and replace the filename of the linked page. You can delete this token if you don't want to use it.

5. Repeat Steps 2, 3, and 4 to place the labels and links for `LinkLabel:5_Here` and `LinkURL:5_Here`.

9. Place home main article

Place the headings and paragraph text for the two article areas on the home page in `index.html` (see Figure 4-19).

1. Find `Heading:1_Here` and replace the token with your heading text.

2. Find `Heading:2_Here` and replace the token with your subheading text.

3. Find `Paragraph:1_Here` and replace the token with your content. Repeat Step 3 for `Paragraph` 2 and 3.

4. Find `LinkLabel:6_Here` and replace the token with your chosen label text for this link

5. Find `LinkURL:6_Here` and replace with the desired link destination.

---

10. Place home supporting articles

Place headings, text, and links for articles appearing beneath the main article in the home page.

1. Find `Heading:3_Here` and replace the token with your heading for the information area beneath the main article area.

2. Find `Paragraph:4_Here` and replace the token with your content.

3. Find `LinkLabel:7_Here` and replace the token with your chosen label text for this link.

4. Find `LinkURL:7_Here` and replace with the desired link destination.

5. Find `Heading:4_Here` and replace the token with your heading for the information area beneath the main article area.

6. Find `Paragraph:5_Here` and replace the token with your content.

7. Find `LinkLabel:8_Here` and replace the token with your chosen label text for this link.

8. Find `LinkURL:8_Here` and replace with the desired link destination.

9. Save `index.html` in your text editor.

Placing Content in Subpages

Use the following operations to place content into all of your site subpages. Use the subpage token reference (see Figure 4-20) to see the position of the content and label tokens. Repeat this operation to enter content in all of your subpages.

---

11. Place subpage announcement   Use these steps to place headings and text in the announcement area to the left of the subpage.

1. Select and open a named subpage for your site in your text editor.

2. Find `Heading:1_Here` and replace the token with your heading 1 text.

3. Find `Heading:2_Here` and replace the token with your heading 2 text.

4. Find `Paragraph:1_Here` and replace the token with your paragraph text.

---

12. Place main subpage article   Use these steps to place headings and text for the featured article on the subpage.

1. Find `Heading:3_Here` and replace the token with your heading 3 text.

2. Find `Heading:4_Here` and replace the token with the desired text.

3. Find `Paragraph:2_Here` and replace the tokens with your text. Repeat this action with `Paragraph` 3 and 4.

---

13. Place subpage supporting articles   Place headings, text, and links for articles appearing beneath the main article in the home page.

1. Find `Heading:5_Here` and replace the token with your heading for the information area beneath the main article area.

2. Find `Paragraph:5_Here` and replace the token with your content.

3. Find `LinkLabel:4_Here`. Replace the token with your chosen label text for this link. You can delete this token if you do not want to use this link.

4. Find `LinkURL:4_Here`. Replace the token with your destination page for this link.

5. Find `Heading:6_Here` and replace the token with your heading for the information area beneath the main article area.

6. Find `Paragraph:6_Here` and replace the token with your content.

7. Find `LinkLabel:5_Here` and replace the token with your chosen label text for this link (such as "Read More" or "More Information"). You can delete this token if you do not want to use this link.

8. Find `LinkURL:5_Here`. Replace the token with the destination page for this link.

9. Save and close the file when you have finished editing.

Finalizing Your Site

14. Edit site logo and pictures

Turn to Chapter 3 for explanation and procedures to replace the default template logo and images with your own logo and images.

15. Display your Web site

Launch `index.html` from your computer by double-clicking the filename, or choose File ➪ Open. Check your work in your browser window.

16. Edit and adjust

Make edits by opening up your home page or subpage page files in your text editor and making edits to the content. Be sure to edit only your content and not to disturb any of the surrounding code.

17. Publish

The basic parameters of what you should provide to your Web hosting company are outlined in Chapter 3. For the specifics on actually posting your live site to the Web, contact your service provide for details.

Variations

Variation 451 Overview

This version presents the site with a background in shades of dark and light green. Logo framing remains in a yellow block and left sidebar remains in red. Main navigation is presented against a framed green block and the two supporting articles are presented against a dark green background.

See the images in the CD-ROM's Gallery section.

Variation 452 Overview

In this version, the dominant background color is shades of gray, with a dark gray block as background to the logo, and Main Navigation presented against a dark gray framed area. The main article appears in a bright color shaded block while supporting articles are presented against a light gray background.

See the images in the CD-ROM's Gallery section.

✦   ✦   ✦

Professional Services Templates

Expertise is a valuable commodity in the marketplace. Individuals and organizations that provide business offerings are considered professionals because they base their services on specific expertise, which they often support with industry credentials, certifications, licenses, and other demonstrations of capabilities.

The single most important communications objective for professionals is to establish bona fides and credibility with those who purchase their services. The Web offers an unprecedented opportunity for professionals to establish not only credibility with target audiences, but also to create a compelling and cohesive impression of their practice, their specialties, and their approach to delivering services.

Professional services templates presented in this chapter are designed to offer a showcase for professionals, whether they are individuals, professional practice organizations, or affiliate groups. As a group, these template designs tend to be more simply structured and conservative than other templates in the 1-hour Web site family. They are built around introductory articles and information on the home page and subpage that carry the mission, positioning, and background of the professional practice.

The designs in this chapter share many common design attributes. A design or variation that appears with an example based on one professional practice area, such as a medical Web site, might be equally useful and applicable for a legal practice. What is important is finding the look and feel that reflects the image you want to present and provides the best layout for communicating your content.

About Professional Services Templates

Professional services must establish credible experience, provide an offering relevant to the potential client's needs, and motivate these potential clients to action. When you are developing a Web site for a professional practice, it is important to communicate your message and keep the interests, questions, and concerns of the potential client in mind. A Web page can be your face to the world, defining your values and motivating potential clients to seek consultation.

The professional services templates in this chapter have been designed around fictitious practice organizations that showcase the layout and allow you to more effectively visualize how content will look in the design. The communication challenges faced by professionals are very similar, and the following is a summary of some of the key considerations when developing the content in your Web site.

Establishing credibility

You need to design a professional service Web site to establish credible expertise right from page one. The home page should include a featured article that provides a clear and complete overview of your credibility to practice or ability to provide your services. Some of the information elements that develop your standing include

- ✦ Professional certifications and licenses
- ✦ Years in business
- ✦ Service specialties and expertise
- ✦ Client quotes and testimonials
- ✦ Industry recognition and awards
- ✦ Professional bios for senior professionals and staff
- ✦ Press clippings and news mentions

Each professional area has its own prevailing industry standards for communicating and marketing a practice. Some professional disciplines or service areas are more restrictive than others. When developing the copy for your Web site, it is recommended that you consult recognized professional organizations within your area of specialty for recommendations on the ethical presentation of your practice.

Branding and positioning

Branding and positioning are marketing concepts that are conventionally applied to corporations, small businesses, and consumer product offerings. Reduced to their essence, however, branding and positioning are communication disciplines that focus on simple, effective, and clear communication of a message to an audience, and creating a clear market space for what you have to offer.

When developing your Web site, you should think in terms of presenting your practice's or service's personality. Your mission should define the unique value you bring to your clients, both in the depth of your expertise and how you deliver that expertise. *Branding* for a professional organization boils down to the practice name, perhaps supported by a tagline that expresses areas of specialty or the approach to the work.

Positioning is communicating how you want to be seen by your current and prospective clients. Your position either defines the market space in which you operate or focuses on some quality of your approach to the client. The goal is to set yourself apart from the mass of other professionals and focus on your distinctive value. This doesn't have to be elaborate, overdone, or insincere. Your position should be a focused theme that is reflected throughout your site, in all the headlines and information presentations.

Service detail

Before the advent of the Web, advertising for professional practices and services was often limited to brochures and listings in public and specialty directories. The Web offers both immediate exposure and publishing space. Rather than a short blurb on a handout, you have the ability to expand and present relevant details about your service offerings. The key word is "relevant." Many professional practices have a great deal of experience to present. The risk in presenting too much is that your audience will be overwhelmed and the essential points you want to convey can be buried in detail.

This set of design templates provide subpage designs and link placements that enable you to build pages to carry details about your various service offerings. When you are developing this material, it is vital to keep your client's interests and questions firmly in mind. The more you anticipate client questions and concerns, and reflect them in the way you describe your various services, the more compelling and engaging your Web site will be.

Supporting information

When you are describing your practice and service offerings, it can be useful to include articles or links to external sites that have information that is helpful to your reader. You might decide to include such content directly in your Web site pages — in which case it is always important to give clear attributions to the source of the material. You can also elect to place live links to other sites on the Web that have information of interest to your audience.

These templates include content tokens called *Link Labels*, which always support a related link destination. You can use Link Labels to connect to one of the subpages in your site. You can also use them to link to an external Web site or a specific Web page containing a relevant article or pertinent information.

Tip Instead of navigating from the root of the CD to locate a template, you can click the Templates link in the CD browser application to directly access the chapters on the CD. For faster access, click the Gallery link in the CD browser application to view a listing of all templates. Then click any View Files link to view the files for that template.

Template 510 Physician and Medical Practice

A professional services site designed for a physician, medical practice, or medical products organization. The clean, open design supports a clear presentation of article information as well as featured announcements, headlines, and blurbs in the home page and subpage layouts.

Figure 5-1: Template 510 home page

Figure 5-2: Template 510 subpage

Template Developer	Ken Milhous
Filename and Location	CD-ROM: \Templates\Chapter 5\51\510
Variations on this Design	511 512
Site Development Detail	Procedures and supporting information on placing content, links, and Web site images are presented in Chapter 3.

Design Summary

Recommended Use

Information and practice information for doctors, medical practitioners, or medical products. Use the home page featured article to present introductory and background information and present links to featured information articles using action items or sidebar headings and text.

Look and Feel

Layout is clear and simple, built around shades of blue over white, and accented by gray. Pages are open, readable, and make good use of white space to set off content.

Medium-density layout that features information articles in both the home page and subpage layouts. Sidebar headings and action items can be used as text labels or links to subpages.

Content Plan

Content Plan Overview

Before entering content in your site, make a list of the Web page labels and filenames you will use to build your Web site skeleton. Detailed coverage on building your content plan is presented in Chapter 3.

Subpages

Design is a business information layout that supports five principal subpages plus an embedded home link. Identify and write down the screen labels and the related filenames.

Action Item Pages

Design supports three action item links on the home page and subpages. These prominently featured elements can be used as headlines only, or as links to subpages containing featured articles or information.

Sidebars

Design supports a sidebar area on the subpage, with two major headings, each supported by paragraph text, and link labels.

Special Features

Design supports several special features that you need to prepare for.

- Envelope icon

- Question Mark icon

Copy the Template

Follow these steps to copy the template to your hard drive:

1. Access the \Templates\Chapter 5\51\510 folder on your CD-ROM.

2. Drag the \510 folder to your desktop or copy and paste the \510 folder to your desktop.

Template Headings and Tags

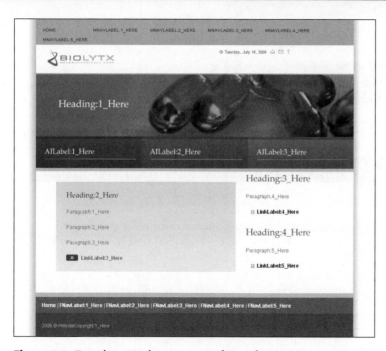

Figure 5-3: Template 510 home page token reference

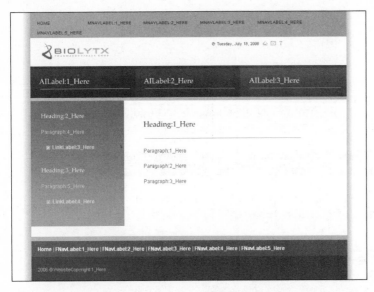

Figure 5-4: Template 510 subpage page token reference

Building Your Site Step-by-Step: 510 Physician and Medical Practice

Building the Site Skeleton

Use the following set of operations to enter the central navigation. Perform the exact same operations within `index.html` and `subpage.html`. Web site navigation and building the site skeleton are presented in Chapter 3.

Note that when opening `index.html` or `subpage.html` in Internet Explorer from your hard drive, a security message may appear. Click for more options, and choose to display the full content so the template displays correctly.

1. Place navigation labels	Review the list of subpage labels and filenames from your content plan. You place the labels for subpage 1 at the top (`MNav`) and bottom (`FNav`) of your page. See Figures 5-3 for home and 5-4 for subpages.

1. Open `index.html` in your text editor.

2. Find `MNavLabel:1_Here` and replace the token with the label for subpage 1.

3. Find `FNavLabel:1_Here` and replace the token with the label for subpage 1. |

4. Repeat Steps 2 and 3 for `MNavLabel` and `FNavLabel` 2, 3, 4, and 5 (see Figure 5-3).

5. Find `AILabel:1_Here` and replace the token with the desired label text. Repeat this step for `AILabel` 2 and 3.

---

2. Place navigation links

Review the list of subpage labels and filenames from your content plan. In the following operation, you place the links to the filename for subpage 1 at the top (`MNav`) and bottom (`FNav`) of your page. Enter all filenames in lowercase.

1. Find `MNavURL:1_Here` and replace the token with the filename you selected for subpage 1.

2. Find `FNavURL:1_Here` and replace the token with the filename you selected for subpage 1.

3. Repeat Steps 1 and 2 for `MNavURL` and `FNavURL` 2, 3, 4, and 5 (see Figure 5-3).

4. Find `AIURL:1_Here` and replace the token with the filename of the link destination. Repeat this step for `AIRUL` 2 and 3.

---

3. Place icon references

Place identifying labels and links for the three programmable icons at the top right of the home and subpage. Note that text placed in `LinkLabel` tokens here displays when the user mouses over the icon. The Date and Home icons are already coded for you.

1. Envelope icon label: Find `LinkLabel:1_Here`. Use this icon to link to any page in your site or to your e-mail address. Change the token to the correct text for the desired page or to E-mail, or Send E-mail to denote your e-mail address.

2. Envelope icon link: Find `LinkURL:1_Here` and enter the filename of the page to which you want to link. If you want to place a link allowing users to e-mail you directly, replace this token with the following text: `Emailto<colon><insert your email address>`. For example: `Emailto:michael@aol.com`.

3. Question Mark icon: Find `LinkLabel:3_Here`. Use this icon to link to any information page, such as an About Us or Help page. Replace the token with the desired label text for the icon.

4. Question Mark link: Find `LinkURL:3_Here` and replace the token with the filename you chose to link to this icon in your content plan.

4. Place special features	Place the text of the Web site copyright in your pages (see Figure 5-3).

1. Find `WebsiteCopyright:1_Here` and replace the token with your Web site copyright text.

2. Save and close the template file in your text editor.

5. Set up the subpage template	Perform the same set of edits that you completed for the `index.html` file on the subpage master template file, `subpage.html`.

1. Open `subpage.html` in your text editor.

2. Return to the beginning of this section ("Building the Site Skeleton"), and start with main Step 1, "Place navigation labels."

3. Complete main Steps 1, 2, and 3 using the `subpage.html` file instead of the `index.html` file.

4. Save `subpage.html` in your text editor. Do not rename the file.

Creating Subpage Files

6. Create subpage files	Use the Save As feature in your text editor to save the `subpage.html` template with the first of the subpage filenames you selected in your content plan. Repeat this to create all subpages listed in your content plan.

Save all files to the `\510` folder on your desktop.

1. Verify that `subpage.html` is open in your text editor.

2. Choose File ➪ Save As or similar from your text editor. Enter the filename you selected for subpage 1, and click OK.

3. Repeat Step 2 for all subpages in your content plan.

4. Repeat Step 2 for any linked articles or catalog detail pages you identified in your content plan.

7. Display your site

Open your site to check that your labels and pages display correctly.

1. Launch `index.html` from your computer by double-clicking the filename, or choose File ➪ Open (from most browsers) to open it in your browser. An empty home page should appear.

2. Click the navigation links at the top and bottom of the home page and you should see empty subpage pages.

3. Close the empty site skeleton.

Placing Content in the Home Page

8. Place home feature elements

Place page headings, other headings, and paragraph text for the featured article in `index.html` (see Figure 5-3).

1. Open `index.html` in your text editor.

2. Find `Heading:1_Here` and replace the token with your heading text.

3. Find `Heading:2_Here` and replace the token with your heading text.

4. Find `Paragraph:1_Here` and replace the token with your paragraph text.

5. Repeat Step 3 for `Paragraph` 2 and 3.

6. Find `LinkLabel:3_Here`. Replace the token with the label text for this link. You can delete this token if you do not want to use this link.

7. Find `LinkURL:3_Here`. Replace the token with the filename you have selected to be accessed from this link.

9. Place home sidebar articles

Place headings and paragraph text for the two sidebar articles in `index.html` (see Figure 5-3).

1. Find `Heading:3_Here` and replace the token with your heading text.

2. Find `Paragraph:4_Here` and replace the token with your paragraph text.

3. Find `LinkLabel:4_Here`. Replace the token with the label text for this link. You can delete this token if you do not want to use this link.

4. Find `LinkURL:4_Here`. Replace the token with the filename you have selected to be accessed from this link.

5. Find `Heading:4_Here` and replace the token with your heading text.

6. Find `Paragraph:5_Here` and replace the token with your paragraph text.

7. Find `LinkLabel:5_Here`. Replace the token with the label text for this link. You can delete this token if you do not want to use this link.

8. Find `LinkURL:5_Here`. Replace the token with the filename you have selected to be accessed from this link.

9. Save `index.html` in your text editor.

Placing Content in Subpages

Use the following operations to place content into all of your site subpages. Use the subpage token reference (see Figure 5-4) to see the position of the content and label tokens. Repeat this operation to enter content in all of your subpages.

10. Place subpage articles	Place article headings and text in your subpages.

1. Open the selected subpage in your text editor.

2. Find `Heading:1_Here` and replace the token with your heading text.

3. Find `Paragraph:1_Here` and replace the token with your paragraph text. Repeat for `Paragraph` 2 and 3.

11. Place subpage sidebar articles	Place headings and paragraph text for the two sidebar articles in `index.html` (see Figure 5-4).

1. Find `Heading:2_Here` and replace the token with your heading text.

2. Find `Paragraph:4_Here` and replace the token with your paragraph text.

3. Find `LinkLabel:3_Here`. Replace the token with the label text for this link .You can delete this token if you do not want to use this link.

4. Find `LinkURL:3_Here`. Replace the token with the filename you have selected to be accessed from this link.

5. Find `Heading:3_Here` and replace the token with your heading text.

6. Find `Paragraph:5_Here` and replace the token with your paragraph text.

7. Find `LinkLabel:4_Here`. Replace the token with the label text for this link. You can delete this token if you do not want to use this link.

8. Find `LinkURL:4_Here`. Replace the token with the filename you have selected to be accessed from this link.

9. Save and close the file when you have finished editing.

Finalizing Your Site

12. Edit site logo and pictures Turn to Chapter 3 for explanation and procedures to replace the default template logo and images with your own logo and images.

13. Display your Web site Launch `index.html` from your computer by double-clicking the filename, or choose File ⇨ Open. Check your work in your browser window.

14. Edit and adjust Make edits by opening up your home page or subpage page files in your text editor and making edits to the content. Be sure to edit only your content and not to disturb any of the surrounding code.

15. Publish The basic parameters of what you should provide to your Web hosting company are outlined in Chapter 3. For the specifics on actually posting your live site to the Web, contact your service provide for details.

Variations

Variation 511 Overview This version of the site emphasizes dominant yellow accent areas with black background for the heading area and brown accents for footer navigation. The anchor image is an abstract with strong yellow accents.

See the images in the CD-ROM's Gallery section.

Variation 512 Overview   This variation emphasizes shades of yellow, red, and orange in the Main Navigation and title areas of the home page, supported with shades of gray and black accenting content areas in the home and subpages.

See the images in the CD-ROM's Gallery section.

Template 520 Attorney and Legal Services

A professional services site designed for an attorney, a legal practice, or other legal services or resource firm. The design presents a clean, business-like image with lively colors and allows for clarity in presenting information, announcements, and notices to the reader.

Figure 5-5: Template 520 home page

Figure 5-6: Template 520 subpage

Template Developer	Ken Milhous
Filename and Location	CD-ROM: \Templates\Chapter 5\52\520
Variations on this Design	521 522
Site Development Detail	Procedures and supporting information on placing content, links, and Web site images are presented in Chapter 3.

Design Summary

Recommended Use

Practice site is designed for use by law offices and attorneys. The design can be used for other legal applications, such as legal resource networks or community legal groups. The simple and clean design can also be adapted for other business or professional practice uses.

Look and Feel

Clear layout is built around a balance between blues and gray with orange accents for sidebars and navigation features.

Medium- to low-density layout featuring information articles in both the home page and subpage layouts. Sidebar headings and action items can be used as text labels or links to subpages. The subpage layout is uncluttered and ideal for article presentation.

Content Plan

Content Plan Overview

Before entering content in your site, make a list of the Web page labels and filenames you will use to build your Web site skeleton. Detailed coverage on building your content plan is presented in Chapter 3.

Subpages

Design is a catalog layout that supports five subpages that can be linked at the top and bottom navigation bar on the site plus a built-in home link. Identify and write down the screen labels and the related filenames.

Article Areas

To maximize the number of impressions per page, this design incorporates three headlined article areas on the home page and another three on the subpage. Three article areas on the home page support subpage links; two article areas in the subpage layout support links to other subpages.

Sidebars

Design supports a sidebar area on both the home page and subpages, with two major headings, paragraph text, and link-through tags on the home page, and a single heading that supports two links to supporting pages.

Copy the Template

Follow these steps to copy the template to your hard drive:

1. Access the `\Templates\Chapter 5\52\520` folder on your CD-ROM.

2. Drag the `\520` folder to your desktop or copy and paste the `\520` folder to your desktop.

Template Headings and Tags

Figure 5-7: Template 520 home page token reference

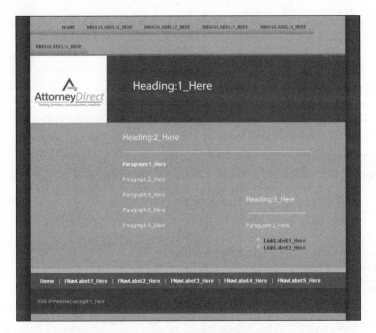

Figure 5-8: Template 520 subpage page token reference

Building Your Site Step-by-Step: 520 Attorney and Legal Services

Building the Site Skeleton

Use the following set of operations to enter the central navigation. Perform the exact same operations within `index.html` and `subpage.html`. Web site navigation and building the site skeleton are presented in Chapter 3.

Note that when opening `index.html` or `subpage.html` in Internet Explorer from your hard drive, a security message may appear. Click for more options, and choose to display the full content so the template displays correctly.

---

1. Place navigation labels

Review the list of subpage labels and filenames from your content plan. You place the labels for subpage 1 at the top (`MNav`) and bottom (`FNav`) of your page. See Figures 5-7 for home and 5-8 for subpages.

1. Open `index.html` in your text editor.

2. Find `MNavLabel:1_Here` and replace the token with the label for subpage 1.

3. Find `FNavLabel:1_Here` and replace the token with the label for subpage 1.

4. Repeat Steps 2 and 3 for `MNavLabel` and `FNavLabel` 2, 3, 4, and 5.

---

2. Place navigation links

Review the list of subpage labels and filenames from your content plan. In the following operation, you will place the links to the filename for subpage 1 at the top (`MNav`) and bottom (`FNav`) of your page. Enter all filenames in lowercase.

1. Find `MNavURL:1_Here` and replace the token with the filename you selected for subpage 1.

2. Find `FNavURL:1_Here` and replace the token with the filename you selected for subpage 1.

3. Repeat Steps 1 and 2 for `MNavURL` and `FNavURL` 2, 3, 4, and 5 (see Figure 5-7).

---

3. Place special features

Place the text of the Web site copyright in your pages. (see Figure 5-7).

1. Find `Tagline:1_Here` and replace the token with your practice summary content, which appears directly underneath the sample logo in the design.

2. Find `WebsiteCopyright:1_Here` and replace the token with your Web site copyright text.

3. Save and close the template file in your text editor.

---

4. Set up the subpage template

Perform the same set of edits that you completed for the `index.html` file on the subpage master template file, `subpage.html`.

1. Open `subpage.html` in your text editor.

2. Return to the beginning of this section ("Building the Site Skeleton"), and start with main Step 1, "Place navigation labels."

3. Complete main Steps 1, 2, and 3 using the `subpage.html` file instead of the `index.html` file.

4. Save `subpage.html` in your text editor. Do not rename the file.

Creating Subpage Files

5. Create subpage files   Use the Save As feature in your text editor to save the `subpage.html` template with the first of the subpage filenames you selected in your content plan. Repeat this to create all subpages listed in your content plan.

Save all subpage files to the \520 folder on your desktop.

1. Verify that `subpage.html` is open in your text editor.

2. Choose File ➪ Save As or similar from your text editor. Enter the filename you selected for subpage 1, and click OK.

3. Repeat Step 2 for all subpages in your content plan.

4. Repeat Step 2 for any linked articles or catalog detail pages you identified in your content plan.

---

6. Display your site   Open your site to check that your labels and pages display correctly.

1. Launch `index.html` from your computer by double-clicking the filename, or choose File ➪ Open (from most browsers) to open it in your browser. An empty home page should appear.

2. Click the navigation links at the top and bottom of the home page and you should see empty subpage pages.

3. Close the empty site skeleton.

Placing Content in the Home Page

7. Place home feature article   Place the headings and paragraph text for the featured article in `index.html` (see Figure 5-7).

1. Open `index.html` in your text editor.

2. Find `Heading:1_Here` and replace the token with your heading text.

3. Find `Paragraph:1_Here` and replace the token with your paragraph text. Repeat for `Paragraph` 2 and 3.

4. Find `LinkLabel:1_Here`. Replace the token with the label text for this link (such as "Read More" or "More Information"). You can delete this token if you do not want to use this link.

5. Find `LinkURL:1_Here`. Replace the token with the filename you have selected to be accessed from this link.

---

8. Place home sidebar articles

Place the headings and paragraph text for the two sidebar articles in `index.html` (see Figure 5-7).

1. Find `Heading:2_Here` and replace the token with your heading text.

2. Find `Paragraph:4_Here` and replace the token with your paragraph text.

3. Find `LinkLabel:2_Here`. Replace the token with the label text for this link. You can delete this token if you do not want to use this link.

4. Find `LinkURL:2_Here`. Replace the token with the filename you have selected to be accessed from this link.

5. Find `Heading:3_Here` and replace the token with your heading text.

6. Find `Paragraph:5_Here` and replace the token with your paragraph text.

7. Find `LinkLabel:3_Here`. Replace the token with the label text for this link. You can delete this token if you do not want to use this link.

8. Find `LinkURL:3_Here`. Replace the token with the filename you have selected to be accessed from this link.

9. Save `index.html` in your text editor.

Placing Content in Subpages

Use the following operations to place content into all of your site subpages. Use the subpage token reference (see Figure 5-8) to see the position of the content and label tokens. Repeat this operation to enter content in all of your subpages.

9. Place subpage articles	Place article headings and text in your subpages.

1. Open the selected subpage in your text editor.

2. Find `Heading:1_Here` and replace the token with the title for this subpage.

3. Find `Heading:2_Here` and replace the token with your heading text.

4. Find `Paragraph:1_Here` and replace the token with your paragraph text. Repeat for `Paragraph` 2, 4, 5, and 6. You can delete unused `Paragraph` tokens.

10. Place subpage sidebar articles	Place headings and paragraph text for the sidebar heading. Use the dual `LinkLabel` feature to link to two different pages of interest that relate to the headline.

1. Find `Heading:3_Here` and replace the token with your heading text.

2. Find `Paragraph:3_Here` and replace the token with your paragraph text.

3. Find `LinkLabel:1_Here`. Replace the token with the label text for this link .You can delete this token if you do not want to use this link.

4. Find `LinkURL:1_Here`. Replace the token with the filename you have selected to be accessed from this link.

5. Find `LinkLabel:2_Here`. Replace the token with the label text for this link. You can delete this token if you do not want to use this link.

6. Find `LinkURL:2_Here`. Replace the token with the filename you have selected to be accessed from this link.

7. Save and close the file when you have finished editing.

Finalizing Your Site

11. Edit site logo and pictures   Turn to Chapter 3 for explanation and procedures to replace the default template logo and images with your own logo and images.

12. Display your Web site   Launch `index.html` from your computer by double-clicking the filename, or choose File ➪ Open. Check your work in your browser window.

13. Edit and adjust   Make edits by opening up your home page or subpage page files in your text editor and making edits to the content. Be sure to edit only your content and not to disturb any of the surrounding code.

14. Publish   The basic parameters of what you should provide to your Web hosting company are outlined in Chapter 3. For the specifics on actually posting your live site to the Web, contact your service provide for details.

Variations

Variation 521 Overview   This variation features content areas in blue and gray and is placed against an orange background.

See the images in the CD-ROM's Gallery section.

Variation 522 Overview   In this version, all content areas are presented in shades of gray.

See the images in the CD-ROM's Gallery section.

Template 530 Accountant

A professional services site designed for an accounting practice, a tax accountant, or a financial management company.

Figure 5-9: Template 530 home page

Figure 5-10: Template 530 subpage

Template Developer	Ken Milhous
Filename and Location	CD-ROM: \Templates\Chapter 5\53\530
Variations on this Design	531 532
Site Development Detail	Procedures and supporting information on placing content, links, and Web site images are presented in Chapter 3.

Design Summary

Recommended Use

Accounting practice site is designed to provide depth for dense information and includes a featured article and sidebar on the home page focusing on special services that action item links support. Links and depth are ideal for businesses with many special services or customer education articles to present.

Look and Feel

Browns and darker colors in the framing areas suggest the ambience of a conservative business office. Article content is presented on white and brown or gray shades that accent the content. An animated tagline appears at the top when the site is launched. The look is very conservative and businesslike.

Medium- to high-density layout that features principal article areas surrounded by sidebar headings and special article links.

Content Plan

Content Plan Overview

Before entering content in your site, make a list of the Web page labels and filenames you will use to build your Web site skeleton. Detailed coverage on building your content plan is presented in Chapter 3.

Flash Heading

Site features an animated tagline in the home page and the upper navigation bar is presented in Flash.

Subpages

Design is a catalog layout that supports three subpages that can be linked at the top and bottom navigation bar on the site, plus a built-in home link. Identify and write down the screen labels and the related filenames.

Action Items

Home page layout features three action item links that are best used as lead articles, service offerings, or client-type areas that immediately engage readers and take them to points of interest in the content.

Article Areas

Home page and subpage layouts are built around a featured article supported by sidebars with two New Item article headings and related text and links.

Sidebars   Design supports a sidebar area on both the home pages and subpages, with two major headings, paragraph text, and link-through tags on the home page, and a single heading that supports two links to supporting pages.

Copy the Template   Follow these steps to copy the template to your hard drive:

1. Access the `\Templates\Chapter 5\53\530` folder on your CD-ROM.

2. Drag the `\530` folder to your desktop or copy and paste the `\530` folder to your desktop.

Template Headings and Tags

Figure 5-11: Template 530 home page token reference

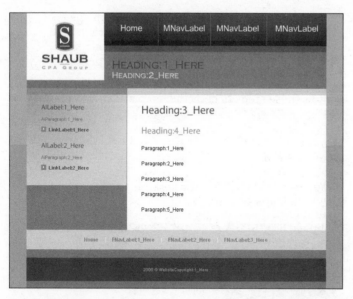

Figure 5-12: Template 530 subpage page token reference

Building Your Site Step-by-Step: 530 Accountant

Setting Up Flash Content

1. Place flash elements

Enter the text for the animated Flash taglines that appear on the home page.

Review the list of subpage labels and filenames from your content plan. Place the labels and links for the main navigation elements (MNav) into the flash configuration file.

1. Open flashconfig.xml in your text editor.

2. Find Tagline:1_Here and replace the token with your tagline 1 text. Repeat for Tagline 2.

3. Find MNavLabel:1_Here and replace the token with the label for subpage 1. Repeat for MNavLabel 2 and 3.

4. Find MNavURL:1_Here and replace the token with the filename you selected for subpage 1. Repeat for MNavURL 2 and 3.

5. Save and close flashconfig.xml.

Building the Site Skeleton

Use the following set of operations to enter the central navigation. Perform the exact same operations within `index.html` and `subpage.html`. Web site navigation and building the site skeleton are presented in Chapter 3.

Note that when opening `index.html` or `subpage.html` in Internet Explorer from your hard drive, a security message may appear. Click for more options, and choose to display the full content so the template displays correctly.

---

2. Place footer navigation

Review the list of subpage labels and filenames from your content plan. Place the labels and links for the footer navigation elements (`FNav`) in both home and subpage files. See Figures 5-11 and 5-12.

1. Open `index.html` in your text editor.

2. Find `FNavLabel:1_Here` and replace the token with the label for subpage 1. Repeat for `FNavLabel` 2 and 3.

3. Find `FNavURL:1_Here` and replace the token with the filename you selected for subpage 1. Repeat the operation for `FNavURL` 2 and 3.

---

3. Place special features

Place the text of the Web site copyright in your pages.

1. Find `WebsiteCopyright:1_Here` and replace the token with your Web site copyright text.

2. Save and close `index.html` in your text editor.

---

4. Set up the subpage template

Perform the same set of edits that you completed for the `index.html` file on the subpage master template file, `subpage.html`.

1. Open `subpage.html` in your text editor.

2. Return to the beginning of this section ("Building the Site Skeleton"), and start with main Step 1, "Place navigation labels."

3. Complete main Steps 2, 3, and 4 using the `subpage.html` file instead of the `index.html` file.

4. Save `subpage.html` in your text editor. Do not rename the file.

Creating Subpage Files

5. Create subpage files

Use the Save As feature in your text editor to save the `subpage.html` template with the first of the subpage filenames you selected in your content plan. Repeat this to create all subpages listed in your content plan.

Save all subpage files to the `\530` folder on your desktop.

1. Verify that `subpage.html` is open in your text editor.

2. Choose File ➪ Save As or similar from your text editor. Enter the filename you selected for subpage 1, and click OK.

3. Repeat Step 2 for all subpages in your content plan.

4. Repeat Step 2 for any linked articles or catalog detail pages you identified in your content plan.

6. Display your site

Open your site to check that your labels and pages display correctly.

1. Launch `index.html` from your computer by double-clicking the filename, or choose File ➪ Open (from most browsers) to open it in your browser. An empty home page should appear.

2. Click the navigation links at the top and bottom of the home page and you should see empty subpage pages.

3. Close the empty site skeleton.

Placing Content in the Home Page

7. Place home action items

Place headings and paragraph text for the featured action items in `index.html` (see Figure 5-11).

1. Open `index.html` in your text editor.

2. Find `AILabel:1_Here` and replace the token with your action item heading text. Repeat for `AILabel` 2 and 3.

3. Find `AIParagraph:1_Here` and replace the token with your action item paragraph text. Repeat for `AIParagraph` 2 and 3.

4. Find `LinkLabel:1_Here` and replace the token with the "Read More," or other title, for the action item link. Repeat for `LinkLabel` 2 and 3.

5. Find `LinkURL:1_Here` and replace the token with the destination filename for the action item link. Repeat for `LinkURL` 2 and 3.

---

8. Place home feature article

Place the headings and paragraph text for the featured article in `index.html` (see Figure 5-11).

1. Find `Heading:1_Here` and replace the token with your heading text.

2. Find `Paragraph:1_Here` and replace the token with your paragraph text.

3. Repeat Step 2 for `Paragraph` 2, 3, 4, and 5. You can delete these tokens if you don't use them.

4. Find `LinkLabel:6_Here`. Replace the token with the label text for this link (such as "Read More" or "More Information"). You can delete this token if you do not want to use this link.

5. Find `LinkURL:6_Here`. Replace the token with the filename you have selected to be accessed from this link.

---

9. Place home sidebar articles

Place the headings and paragraph text for the two sidebar articles in `index.html` (see Figure 5-11).

1. Find `AILabel:4_Here` and replace the token with your heading text.

2. Find `AIParagraph:4_Here` and replace the token with your paragraph text.

3. Find `LinkLabel:4_Here`. Replace the token with the label text for this link. You can delete this token if you do not want to use this link.

4. Find `LinkURL:4_Here`. Replace the token with the filename you have selected to be accessed from this link.

5. Find `AILabel:5_Here` and replace the token with your heading text.

6. Find `AIParagraph:5_Here` and replace the token with your paragraph text.

7. Find `LinkLabel:5_Here`. Replace the token with the label text for this link. You can delete this token if you do not want to use this link.

8. Find `LinkURL:5_Here`. Replace the token with the filename you have selected to be accessed from this link.

9. Save `index.html` in your text editor.

Placing Content in Subpages

Use the following operations to place content into all of your site subpages. Use the subpage token reference (see Figure 5-12) to see the position of the content and label tokens. Repeat this operation to enter content in all of your subpages.

10. Place subpage articles   Place article headings and text in your subpages.

1. Open the selected subpage in your text editor.

2. Find `Heading:1_Here` and replace the token with the title or message statement for this subpage.

3. Find `Heading:2_Here` and replace the token with the subtitle or message statement for this subpage text.

4. Find `Heading:3_Here` and replace the token with the article main title.

5. Find `Heading:4_Here` and replace the token with the article subtitle.

6. Find `Paragraph:1_Here` and replace the token with your paragraph text.

7. Repeat Step 6 for `Paragraph` 2, 3, 4, and 5 tokens. You can delete unused `Paragraph` tokens.

11. Place sidebar articles

Place headings and paragraph text for the two sidebar articles in `index.html` (see Figure 5-12).

1. Find `AILabel:1_Here` and replace the token with your action item heading text. Repeat for `AILabel` 2.

2. Find `AIParagraph:1_Here` and replace the token with your paragraph text. Repeat for `AIParagraph` 2.

3. Find `LinkLabel:1_Here`. Replace the token with the label text for this link. You can delete this token if you do not want to use this link.

4. Find `LinkURL:1_Here`. Replace the token with the filename you have selected to be accessed from this link.

5. Find `LinkLabel:2_Here`. Replace the token with the label text for this link. You can delete this token if you do not want to use this link.

6. Find `LinkURL:2_Here`. Replace the token with the filename you have selected to be accessed from this link.

7. Save and close the file when you have finished editing.

Finalizing Your Site

12. Edit site logo and pictures

Turn to Chapter 3 for explanation and procedures to replace the default template logo and images with your own logo and images.

13. Display your Web site

Launch `index.html` from your computer by double-clicking the filename, or choose File ➪ Open. Check your work in your browser window.

14. Edit and adjust

Make edits by opening up your home page or subpage page files in your text editor and making edits to the content. Be sure to edit only your content and not to disturb any of the surrounding code.

15. Publish

The basic parameters of what you should provide to your Web hosting company are outlined in Chapter 3. For the specifics on actually posting your live site to the Web, contact your service provider for details.

Variations

Variation 531 Overview	This colorful variation of the design is built around shades of blue and pink for the navigation, headline, and sidebar areas.
	See the images in the CD-ROM's Gallery section.
Variation 532 Overview	In this version of the design, the main title area and action items are shown against shades of gray, with sidebar and navigation areas presented in shades of yellow.
	See the images in the CD-ROM's Gallery section.

Template 540 Consultant

A professional services site designed for a consulting practice or specialty business services firm.

Figure 5-13: Template 540 home

Figure 5-14: Template 540 subpage

Template Developer	Ken Milhous
Filename and Location	CD-ROM: `\Templates\Chapter 5\54\540`
Variations on this Design	541 542
Site Development Detail	Procedures and supporting information on placing content, links, and Web site images are presented in Chapter 3.

Design Summary

Recommended Use

Featured version of this template is designed around a marketing services firm; consulting individuals or organizations can adapt the design to their needs. The design makes use of strong colors, featured text, and sidebar presentations to carry information, special offers, and content links in an engaging and stylish manner.

Look and Feel

Floral background sets the tone for the lighter and darker shades of color in the framing and content presentation areas.

Medium-density layout that features principal article areas surrounded by sidebar headings and special article links.

Content Plan

Content Plan Overview

Before entering content in your site, make a list of the Web page labels and filenames you will use to build your Web site skeleton. Detailed coverage on building your content plan is presented in Chapter 3.

Subpages

Design is a catalog layout that supports four subpages that can be linked at the top and bottom navigation bar on the site. Identify and write down the screen labels and the related filenames.

Article Areas

To maximize the number of impressions per page, this design incorporates three headlined article areas on the home page and another three on the subpage. Three article areas on the home page support subpage links; two article areas in the subpage layout support links to other subpages.

Sidebars

Design supports a sidebar area on both the home page and subpages, with two major headings, paragraph text, and link-through tags on the home page, and a single heading that supports two links to supporting pages.

Copy the Template

Follow these steps to copy the template to your hard drive:

1. Access the `\Templates\Chapter 5\54\540` folder on your CD-ROM.

2. Drag the `\540` folder to your desktop or copy and paste the `\540` folder to your desktop.

Template Headings and Tags

Figure 5-15: Template 540 home page token reference

Figure 5-16: Template 540 subpage page token reference

Building Your Site Step-by-Step: 540 Consultant

Building the Site Skeleton

Use the following set of operations to enter the central navigation. Perform the exact same operations within `index.html` and `subpage.html`. Web site navigation and building the site skeleton are presented in Chapter 3.

Note that when opening `index.html` or `subpage.html` in Internet Explorer from your hard drive, a security message may appear. Click for more options, and choose to display the full content so the template displays correctly.

---

1. Place navigation labels

Review the list of subpage labels and filenames from your content plan. You place the labels for subpage 1 at the top (`MNav`) and bottom (`FNav`) of your page. See Figures 5-15 for home and 5-16 for subpages.

1. Open `index.html` in your text editor.

2. Find `MNavLabel:1_Here` and replace the token with the label for subpage 1.

3. Find `FNavLabel:1_Here` and replace the token with the label for subpage 1.

4. Repeat Steps 2 and 3 for `MNavLabel` and `FNavLabel` 2, 3, and 4.

---

2. Place navigation links

Review the list of subpage labels and filenames from your content plan. In the following operation, you place the links to the filename for subpage 1 at the top (`MNav`) and bottom (`FNav`) of your page. Enter all filenames in lowercase.

1. Find `MNavURL:1_Here` and replace the token with the filename you selected for subpage 1.

2. Find `FNavURL:1_Here` and replace the token with the filename you selected for subpage 1.

3. Repeat Steps 1 and 2 for `MNavURL` and `FNavURL` 2, 3, and 4 (see Figure 5-15).

---

3. Place special features

Place the text of the Web site copyright in your pages and special features.

1. Find `WebsiteCopyright:1_Here` and replace the token with your Web site copyright text.

2. Find `Tagline:1_Here` and replace with the desired site tagline.

3. Save and close the template file in your text editor.

---

4. Set up the subpage template

Perform the same set of edits that you completed for the `index.html` file on the subpage master template file, `subpage.html`.

1. Open `subpage.html` in your text editor.

2. Return to the beginning of this section ("Building the Site Skeleton"), and start with main Step 1, "Place navigation labels."

3. Complete main Steps 1, 2, and 3 using the `subpage.html` file instead of the `index.html` file.

4. Save `subpage.html` in your text editor. Do not rename the file.

Creating Subpage Files

5. Create subpage files

Use the Save As feature in your text editor to save the `subpage.html` template with the first of the subpage filenames you selected in your content plan. Repeat this to create all subpages listed in your content plan.

Save all subpage files to the `\540` folder on your desktop.

1. Verify that `subpage.html` is open in your text editor.

2. Choose File ⇨ Save As or similar from your text editor. Enter the filename you selected for subpage 1, and click OK.

3. Repeat Step 2 for all subpages in your content plan.

4. Repeat Step 2 for any linked articles or catalog detail pages you identified in your content plan.

6. Display your site

Open your site to check that your labels and pages display correctly.

1. Launch `index.html` from your computer by double-clicking the filename, or choose File ⇨ Open (from most browsers) to open it in your browser. An empty home page should appear.

2. Click the navigation links at the top and bottom of the home page and you should see empty subpage pages.

3. Close the empty site skeleton.

Placing Content in Home Page

7. Place home feature article

Place the headings and paragraph text for the featured article in `index.html` (see Figure 5-15).

1. Open the `index.html` in your text editor.

2. Find `Heading:1_Here` and replace the token with your heading text.

3. Find `Heading:2_Here` and replace the token with your heading text.

4. Find `Paragraph:1_Here` and replace the token with your paragraph text.

5. Repeat Step 4 for `Paragraph` 2 and 3. You can delete these tokens if you don't use them.

6. Find `LinkLabel:3_Here`. Replace the token with the label text for this link (such as "Read More" or "More Information"). You can delete this token if you do not want to use this link.

7. Find `LinkURL:3_Here`. Replace the token with the filename you have selected to be accessed from this link.

---

8. Place home sidebar articles   Place the headings and paragraph text for the two sidebar articles in `index.html` (see Figure 5-15).

1. Find `AILabel:1_Here` and replace the token with your action item text.

2. Find `AIURL:1_Here` and replace the token with your action item link text.

3. Find `TextLabel:1_Here` and replace the token with your label text.

4. Find `LinkLabel:1_Here`. Replace the token with the label text for this link .You can delete this token if you do not want to use this link.

5. Find `LinkURL:1_Here`. Replace the token with the filename you have selected to be accessed from this link.

6. Save `index.html` in your text editor.

Placing Content in Subpages

Use the following operations to place content into all of your site subpages. Use the subpage token reference (see Figure 5-16) to see the position of the content and label tokens. Repeat this operation to enter content in all of your subpages.

---

9. Place subpage feature article

Place headings and paragraph text for the featured article in you selected subpage.

1. Open the selected subpage in your text editor.

2. Find `Heading:1_Here` and replace the token with your heading text.

3. Find `Heading:2_Here` and replace the token with your heading text.

4. Find `Paragraph:1_Here` and replace the token with your paragraph text.

5. Repeat Step 4 for `Paragraph` 2 and 3. You can delete these tokens if you don't use them.

---

10. Place sidebar articles

Place the headings and paragraph text for the two sidebar articles in `index.html` (see Figure 5-16).

1. Find `AILabel:1_Here` and replace the token with your action item text. Repeat for `AILabel` 2.

2. Find `AIURL:1_Here` and replace the token with the filename for your action item link. Repeat for `AIRUL` 2.

3. Find `TextLabel:1_Here` and replace the token with your label text. Repeat for `TextLabel` 2.

4. Find `LinkLabel:1_Here`. Replace the token with the label text for this link. You can delete this token if you do not want to use this link. Repeat for `LinkLabel` 2.

5. Find `LinkURL:1_Here`. Replace the token with the filename you have selected to be accessed from this link. Repeat for `LinkURL` 2.

6. Save and close the file when you have finished editing.

Finalizing Your Site

11. Edit site logo and pictures   Turn to Chapter 3 for explanation and procedures to replace the default template logo and images with your own logo and images.

12. Display your Web site   Launch `index.html` from your computer by double-clicking the file name, or choose File ➪ Open. Check your work in your browser window.

13. Edit and adjust   Make edits by opening up your home page or subpage page files in your text editor and making edits to the content. Be sure to edit only your content and not to disturb any of the surrounding code.

14. Publish   The basic parameters of what you should provide to your Web hosting company are outlined in Chapter 3. For the specifics on actually posting your live site to the Web, contact your service provide for details.

Variations

Variation 541 Overview   The design is presented with emphasis on brown accents and a different shade for content areas.

See the images in the CD-ROM's Gallery section.

Variation 542 Overview   The design is presented with emphasis on brown accents and a muted green for content areas.

See the images in the CD-ROM's Gallery section.

✦   ✦   ✦

Retail Business Templates

Retail business is based in the art of communicating value to a customer. Regardless of what product or service you may be selling, the key to success is in your ability to communicate both the value of the offering and your credibility, as an individual or an organization, to deliver the value.

The challenge begins by understanding your target customers and what they consider important. Customer perceptions of what value means can include the price of a product, its quality and the related purchase experience, the selection, and other factors. What products your customers consider high priority and lower priority also factors into any transaction. Your Web site is an important tool for shaping your customers' perceptions of their own needs and how your business can meet them.

Retail business template designs in this chapter feature models for a bank, an auto dealership, a restaurant, a grocery store, and a hotel. Each of these businesses creates a distinct value relationship with their customers, and the sites present a look and layout to develop that relationship. These are not, however, the only sites in the 1-hour Web site family that you can use to present retail businesses. What is important when making your selection is understanding the interests of your customers and the message you want to convey to them.

Presenting a Retail Business

From the outset, your site must both establish your business clearly in the customer's mind and provide a clear and direct explanation of the products and services you have to offer. In an age of e-commerce and the Internet, customers expect to look before they leap. They won't necessarily come running down to your store unless you give them a good, compelling reason to do so.

Once their interest is engaged, customers always have questions. Here is yet another of the singular advantages the Web offers — it gives you a clear and an inexpensive means to anticipate and address customer questions. As you develop your site content, you should make an effort to continually test your material with current customers and other associates to identify the kind of questions that customers need answered to get involved and do business with you.

Your business identity

Your business must have a clear identity in the customer's mind. Establishing who you are and what you do is a cornerstone of the customer credibility that is essential for attracting and keeping customers. Some of the information elements that develop your business identity include

✦ Product selection or service range

✦ Expertise in delivering products and services

✦ Pricing

✦ Years in business

✦ Product delivery and customer service approach

✦ Product support, service, and repair

✦ Satisfaction guarantees

✦ Quotes and recommendations from satisfied customers

Each business must meet customer expectations in different ways. A hotel and an auto dealership might seem to be radically different businesses, operating in different worlds. But the common denominator for both of these operations is the quality of, and attention to, customer service — whether that service is delivering a clean, comfortable room or providing a quality car at a reasonable price, with a fair and attentive sales process. By establishing your identity clearly on your Web site, you create the foundation for a customer sale.

Branding and positioning

Branding is the art of making your business identity memorable. *Positioning* is how you set yourself apart from other competing businesses.

Your brand is made up of many elements that have an impact on the customer. The business name and logo and your place of business, if you have a store, all are very visible expressions of your brand. But a more subtle and telling form of your brand is how consistently you communicate your approach to the customer on your Web site and in direct interactions with customers when they visit you or interact with you on the phone.

Your brand might be based on key values such as experience, quality of service, product quality, and other values. It's not enough just to say these things; you need to demonstrate them. If you want to make a case for experience, use your site to demonstrate it with quotes from satisfied customers and detailed product information, or clearly and proactively anticipate customer concerns and questions.

Positioning is an element of your brand communication effort. To attract customers, you want them to feel they get something from you they won't get from your competitors. So your positioning might turn on specialized services you offer, or your fast product delivery, or particular, demonstrable claims to product quality. You want the customer to identify your business with something unique and desirable. Your Web site is a powerful tool to communicate that message and make that impression.

Retail offerings

Your credibility relies on the quality, range, and perceived value of the products or services you offer. Your site should include the essential information about the products you sell or the services you offer to develop customer interest.

When developing your site content, pay close attention to what the customer needs to know about the products you are offering. If you provide too little detail, customers might be confused, or worse, look at somebody else's site to find more information before they spend their money. If you provide too much information, what's really important can be buried in a mass of detail.

Inspire to action

Your Web site does not stand alone; it is part of your company sales process. The *sales process* is really the set of steps you and the customer take that lead to a transaction. Usually a Web site fits at the very beginning of the sales process for both new and existing customers. They come to the site to get information and make initial decisions about what they want to buy. The Web site, in other words, covers the initial contact and information steps in your sales process.

You should pay attention to how your sales process works and what you want customers to do after they have visited your site. Do you want them to call you on the phone or visit the store? Do you want them to buy something now, through the Web? Whatever that action is, you should include information and notes to inspire them to take action. For example, many of the sites in this chapter include action items and text label elements in the design. It is usually best to use these elements to present contact information or incentives and special sale offerings that motivate the user to take action.

Taking action is the name of the game. Your retail business Web site is not a passive brochure or a billboard. It is an active tool for the customer to explore to get answers to questions and make decisions. Give your customers the information they need and you're on your way to success.

Tip   Instead of navigating from the root of the CD to locate a template, you can click the Templates link in the CD browser application to directly access the chapters on the CD. For faster access, click the Gallery link in the CD browser application to view a listing of all templates. Then click any View Files link to view the files for that template.

Template 610 Bank or Financial Institution

A financial services site that blends conservative business imagery with bright color accents to create an open and friendly design to frame a variety of financial service or other business offerings.

Figure 6-1: Template 610 home page

Figure 6-2: Template 610 subpage page

Template Developer	Ken Milhous
Filename and Location	CD-ROM: \Templates\Chapter 6\61\610
Variations on this Design	611 612
Site Development Detail	Procedures and supporting information on placing content, links, and Web site images are presented in Chapter 3.

Design Summary

Recommended Use	Financial or professional business site designed to present background information, service offerings, and other details. It is a simple, declarative design built around large article and sidebar blocks, with a conservative look and feel. The model for this design is a bank, but it is equally applicable for any financial, professional, or general business application.

Look and Feel

Built around shades of gray and green with white accent areas for articles, this design presents a conservative image with lively colors to attract the eye. The home page presents a principal and sidebar article with action item headings and text to present special topics of interest that can be developed in linked subpages.

Layout is medium to high density, depending on the length of articles presented. Sidebar areas are simple, featuring tokens for a heading and paragraph link, which you can delete on the home page or subpage to create a simpler and more focused page display.

Content Plan

Content Plan Overview

Before entering content in your site, make a list of the Web page labels and filenames you will use to build your Web site skeleton. Detailed coverage on building your content plan is presented in Chapter 3.

Subpages

Layout is an informational, content-rich presentation that supports five subpages, including a dedicated home link, plus four programmable navigation bar labels at the top and bottom. Identify and write down the screen labels and the related filenames you plan to use for these.

Action Item Pages

Design supports two action item links on the home page and subpages. You can use these prominently featured elements as headlines only or to carry supporting paragraph text.

Sidebars

This design supports a sidebar area on both the home page and subpage, with one heading, a paragraph text area, and a link to subpages.

Copy the Template

Follow these steps to copy the template to your hard drive:

1. Access the \Templates\Chapter 6\61\610 folder on your CD-ROM.

2. Drag the \610 folder to your desktop or copy and paste the \610 folder to your desktop.

Template Headings and Tags

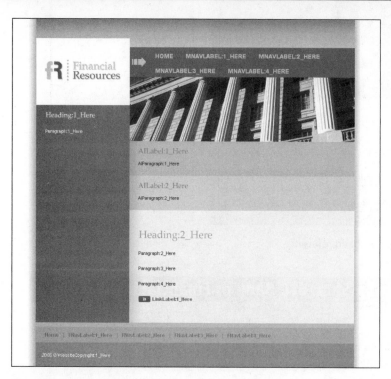

Figure 6-3: Template 610 home page token reference

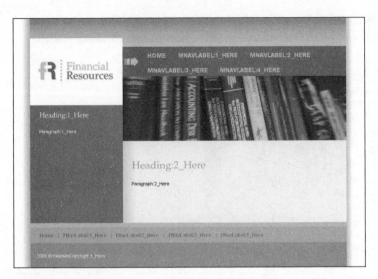

Figure 6-4: Template 610 subpage token reference

Building Your Site Step-by-Step: 610 Bank or Financial Institution

Building the Site Skeleton

Use the following set of operations to enter the central navigation. Perform the exact same operations within index.html and subpage.html. Web site navigation and building the site skeleton are presented in Chapter 3.

Note that when opening index.html or subpage.html in Internet Explorer from your hard drive, a security message may appear. Click for more options, and choose to display the full content so the template displays correctly.

1. Place navigation labels	Review the list of subpage labels and filenames from your content plan. You place the labels for subpage 1 at the top (MNav) and bottom (FNav) of your page. See Figures 6-3 for home and 6-4 for subpages.

1. Open index.html in your text editor.

2. Find MNavLabel:1_Here and replace the token with the label for subpage 1.

3. Find `FNavLabel:1_Here` and replace the token with the label for subpage 1.

4. Repeat Steps 2 and 3 for `MNavLabel` and `FNavLabel` 2, 3, and 4.

---

2. Place navigation links

Review the list of subpage labels and filenames from your content plan. In the following operation, you place the links to the filename for subpage 1 at the top (`MNav`) and bottom (`FNav`) of your page. Enter all filenames in lowercase.

1. Find `MNavURL:1_Here` and replace the token with the filename you selected for subpage 1.

2. Find `FNavURL:1_Here` and replace the token with the filename you selected for subpage 1.

3. Repeat Steps 1 and 2 for `MNavURL` and `FNavURL` 2, 3, and 4.

---

3. Place special features

Place the text of the Web site copyright in your pages.

1. Find `WebsiteCopyright:1_Here` and replace the token with your Web site copyright text.

2. Save and close `index.html` in your text editor.

---

4. Set up the subpage template

Perform the same set of edits that you completed for the `index.html` file on the subpage master template file, `subpage.html`.

1. Open `subpage.html` in your text editor.

2. Return to the beginning of this section ("Building the Site Skeleton"), and start with main Step 1, "Place navigation labels."

3. Complete main Steps 1, 2, and 3 using the `subpage.html` file instead of the `index.html` file.

4. Save `subpage.html` in your text editor. Do not rename the file.

Creating Subpage Files

5. Create subpage files

Use the Save As feature in your text editor to save the `subpage.html` template with the first of the subpage filenames you selected in your content plan. Repeat this to create all subpages listed in your content plan.

Save all files to the `\610` folder on your desktop.

1. Verify that `subpage.html` is open in your text editor.

2. Choose File ⇨ Save As or similar from your text editor. Enter the filename you selected for subpage 1, and click OK.

3. Repeat Step 2 for all subpages in your content plan.

4. Repeat Step 2 for any linked articles or catalog detail pages you identified in your content plan.

6. Display your site

Open your site to check that your labels and pages display correctly.

1. Launch `index.html` from your computer by double-clicking the filename, or choose File ⇨ Open (from most browsers) to open it in your browser. An empty home page should appear.

2. Click the navigation links at the top and bottom of the home page and you should see empty subpage pages.

3. Close the empty site skeleton.

Placing Content in the Home Page

7. Place home action items

Place the headings and paragraph text for the featured article in `index.html` (see Figure 6-3).

1. Open `index.html` in your text editor.

2. Find `AILabel:1_Here` and replace the token with your action item heading text. Repeat for `AILabel` 2.

3. Find `AIURL:1_Here` and replace the token with the filename for the action item link. Repeat for `AIURL` 2.

4. Find `AIParagraph:1_Here` and replace the token with your action item paragraph text. Repeat for `AIParagraph` 2.

8. Place home feature article

Place the headings and paragraph text for the featured article in `index.html`.

1. Find `Heading:2_Here` and replace the token with your heading text.

2. Find `Paragraph:2_Here` and replace the token with your paragraph text.

3. Repeat Step 2 for `Paragraph` 3 and 4.

4. Find `LinkLabel:1_Here`. Replace the token with your chosen label text for this link (such as "Read More" or "More Information"). You can delete this token if you do not want to use this link.

5. Find `LinkURL:1_Here`. Replace the token with the filename you have selected to be accessed from this link.

9. Place home sidebar articles

Place the headings and paragraph text for the two sidebar articles in `index.html` (see Figure 6-3).

1. Find `Heading:1_Here` and replace the token with your heading text.

2. Find `Paragraph:1_Here` and replace the token with your paragraph text.

3. Save `index.html` in your text editor.

Placing Content in Subpages

Use the following operations to place content into all of your site subpages. Use the subpage token reference (see Figure 6-4) to see the position of the content and label tokens. Repeat this operation to enter content in all of your subpages.

10. Place subpage feature article

Place the headings and paragraph text for the featured article in `subpage.html` (see Figure 6-4).

1. Open the selected subpage in your text editor.

2. Find `Heading:2_Here` and replace the token with your heading text.

3. Find `Paragraph:2_Here` and replace the token with your paragraph text.

| **11. Place subpage sidebar articles** | Place the headings and paragraph text for the two sidebar articles in your selected subpage file. |

1. Find `Heading:1_Here` and replace the token with your heading text.

2. Find `Paragraph:1_Here` and replace the token with your paragraph text.

3. Save and close the file when you have finished editing.

Finalizing Your Site

12. Edit site logo and pictures	Turn to Chapter 3 for explanation and procedures to replace the default template logo and images with your own logo and images.
13. Display your Web site	Launch `index.html` from your computer by double-clicking the filename, or choose File ⇨ Open. Check your work in your browser window.
14. Edit and adjust	Make edits by opening up your home page or subpage page files in your text editor and making edits to the content. Be sure to edit only your content and not to disturb any of the surrounding code.
15. Publish	The basic parameters of what you should provide to your Web hosting company are outlined in Chapter 3. For the specifics on actually posting your live site to the Web, contact your service provider for details.

Variations

| **Variation 611 Overview** | This version presents the design in variations of gray, black, and white. |

See the images in the CD-ROM's Gallery section.

| **Variation 612 Overview** | This variation presents the site with navigation and framing accents in shades of pink against gray and white content areas. |

See the images in the CD-ROM's Gallery section.

Template 620 Restaurant

A retail business site designed to present a restaurant or other food service offering. Strong use of headings and featured item links is designed for announcements and product detail.

Figure 6-5: Template 620 home page

Figure 6-6: Template 620 subpage

Template Developer	Ken Milhous
Filename and Location	CD-ROM: \Templates\Chapter 6\62\620
Variations on this Design	621 622
Site Development Detail	Procedures and supporting information on placing content, links, and Web site images are presented in Chapter 3.

Design Summary

Recommended Use	Retail food service site uses iconography to establish a sense of place in the anchor photograph on both the home page and subpages, with evocative natural background imagery to create an appetizing presentation. Use this site for a restaurant, food service, grocery, or food delivery business.

Look and Feel

Bright colors accent the design, with yellow shades that are dominant in the background and picked up in framing areas. Color accents in background areas of black, red, and green create a warm, sharp impression, and content areas are strongly delineated.

Layout is medium density, with a strong emphasis on stylish headlines to bring attention to products and specialty items on the menu. The home page and subpages feature a principal article with multiple display headlines, as well as a boxed link area, to bring special attention to products of interest.

Content Plan

Content Plan Overview

Before entering content in your site, make a list of the Web page labels and filenames you will use to build your Web site skeleton. Detailed coverage on building your content plan is presented in Chapter 3.

Subpages

The display layout focuses on headlines and links that support five subpages, including a dedicated home link plus four programmable navigation bar labels at the top and bottom. Identify and write down the screen labels and the related filenames.

Sidebars

This design supports a sidebar area on both the home page and subpages, with two links and supporting text items that are suitable for short focused presentations of topics of interest, which link to subpages offering expanded presentations of the content.

Copy the Template

Follow these steps to copy the template to your hard drive:

1. Access the `\Templates\Chapter 6\62\620` folder on your CD-ROM.

2. Drag the `\620` folder to your desktop or copy and paste the `\620` folder to your desktop.

Template Headings and Tags

Figure 6-7: Template 620 home page token reference

Figure 6-8: Template 620 subpage token reference

Building Your Site Step-by-Step: 620 Restaurant

Building the Site Skeleton

Use the following set of operations to enter the central navigation. Perform the exact same operations within `index.html` and `subpage.html`. Web site navigation and building the site skeleton are presented in Chapter 3.

Note that when opening `index.html` or `subpage.html` in Internet Explorer from your hard drive, a security message may appear. Click for more options, and choose to display the full content so the template displays correctly.

---

1. Place navigation labels

Review the list of subpage labels and filenames from your content plan. You place the labels for subpage 1 at the top (`MNav`) and bottom (`FNav`) of your page. See Figures 6-7 for home and 6-8 for subpages.

1. Open `index.html` in your text editor.

2. Find `MNavLabel:1_Here` and replace the token with the label for subpage 1.

3. Find `FNavLabel:1_Here` and replace the token with the label for subpage 1.

4. Repeat Steps 2 and 3 for `MNavLabel` and `FNavLabel` 2, 3, and 4.

---

2. Place navigation links

Review the list of subpage labels and filenames from your content plan. In the following operation you will place the links to the filename for subpage 1 at the top (`MNav`) and bottom (`FNav`) of your page. Enter all filenames in lowercase.

1. Find `MNavURL:1_Here` and replace the token with the filename you selected for subpage 1.

2. Find `FNavURL:1_Here` and replace the token with the filename you selected for subpage 1.

3. Repeat Steps 1 and 2 for `MNavURL` and `FNavURL` 2, 3, and 4.

---

3. Place special features

Place the text of the Web site copyright in your pages.

1. Find `WebsiteCopyright:1_Here` and replace the token with your Web site copyright text.

2. Save and close `index.html` in your text editor.

---

4. Set up the subpage template

Perform the same set of edits that you completed for the `index.html` file on the subpage master template file, `subpage.html`.

1. Open `subpage.html` in your text editor.

2. Return to the beginning of this section ("Building the Site Skeleton"), and start with main Step 1, "Place navigation labels."

3. Complete main Steps 1, 2, and 3 using the `subpage.html` file instead of the `index.html` file.

4. Save `subpage.html` in your text editor. Do not rename the file.

Creating Subpage Files

5. Create subpage files

Use the Save As feature in your text editor to save the `subpage.html` template with the first of the subpage filenames you selected in your content plan. Repeat this to create all subpages listed in your content plan.

Save all files to the `\620` folder on your desktop.

1. Verify that `subpage.html` is open in your text editor.

2. Choose File ➪ Save As or similar from your text editor. Enter the filename you selected for subpage 1, and click OK.

3. Repeat Step 2 for all subpages in your content plan.

4. Repeat Step 2 for any linked articles or catalog detail pages you identified in your content plan.

6. Display your site

Open your site to check that your labels and pages display correctly.

1. Launch `index.html` from your computer by double-clicking the filename, or choose File ➪ Open (from most browsers) to open it in your browser. An empty home page should appear.

2. Click the navigation links at the top and bottom of the home page and you should see empty subpage pages.

3. Close the empty site skeleton.

Placing Content in the Home Page

7. Place home headings and article

Place the headings and paragraph text for the featured article in `index.html` (see Figure 6-7).

1. Open `index.html` in your text editor.

2. Find `Heading:1_Here` and replace the token with your heading text. Repeat this operation for `Heading` 2, 3, and 4.

3. Find `Paragraph:1_Here` and replace the token with your paragraph text. Repeat this operation for `Paragraph` 2 and 3.

4. Find `LinkLabel:1_Here`. Replace the token with the label text for this link (such as "Read More" or "More Information"). You can delete this token if you do not want to use this link.

5. Find `LinkURL:1_Here`. Replace the token with the filename you have selected to be accessed from this link.

---

8. Place home sidebar articles

Place the headings and paragraph text for the two sidebar articles in `index.html` (see Figure 6-7).

1. Find `LinkLabel:2_Here` and replace the token with your heading text. Repeat for `LinkLabel` 3.

2. Find `LinkURL:2_Here` and replace the token with the name of the linked subpage. Repeat for `LinkURL` 3.

3. Find `TextLabel:1_Here` and replace the token with your paragraph text. Repeat for `TextLabel` 2.

4. Save `index.html` in your text editor.

Placing Content in Subpages

Use the following operations to place content into all of your site subpages. Use the subpage token reference (see Figure 6-8) to see the position of the content and label tokens. Repeat this operation to enter content in all of your subpages.

---

9. Place subpage feature article

Place the headings and paragraph text for the featured article in `subpage.html` (see Figure 6-8).

1. Open the selected subpage in your text editor.

2. Find `Heading:1_Here` and replace the token with your heading text.

3. Find `Heading:2_Here` and replace the token with your heading text.

4. Find `Paragraph:1_Here` and replace the token with your paragraph text.

10. Place subpage sidebar articles	Place the headings and paragraph text for the two sidebar articles in `subpage.html`.

1. Find `LinkLabel:1_Here` and replace the token with your heading text. Repeat for `LinkLabel` 2.

2. Find `LinkURL:1_Here` and replace the token with the name of the linked subpage. Repeat for `LinkURL` 2.

3. Find `TextLabel:1_Here` and replace the token with your paragraph text. Repeat for `TextLabel` 2.

4. Save and close the file when you have finished editing.

Finalizing Your Site

11. Edit site logo and pictures	Turn to Chapter 3 for explanation and procedures to replace the default template logo and images with your own logo and images.
12. Display your Web site	Launch `index.html` from your computer by double-clicking the filename, or choose File ⇨ Open. Check your work in your browser window.
13. Edit and adjust	Make edits by opening up your home page or subpage page files in your text editor and making edits to the content. Be sure to edit only your content and not to disturb any of the surrounding code.
14. Publish	The basic parameters of what you should provide to your Web hosting company are outlined in Chapter 3. For the specifics on actually posting your live site to the Web, contact your service provider for details.

Variations

Variation 621 Overview	This variation presents the design on a textured turquoise background with red and gray accents in the navigation and framing areas.
	See the images in the CD-ROM's Gallery section.

Variation 622 Overview   In this version the design is presented against a dark textured background, with shades of turquoise used in the framing and navigation areas.

See the images in the CD-ROM's Gallery section.

Template 630 Auto Dealer

An automotive retail site designed to showcase dealers of new and used cars as well as other automotive products and services.

Figure 6-9: Template 630 home page

Figure 6-10: Template 630 subpage

Template Developer	Ken Milhous
Filename and Location	CD-ROM: \Templates\Chapter 6\63\630
Variations on this Design	631 632
Site Development Detail	Procedures and supporting information on placing content, links, and Web site images are presented in Chapter 3.

Design Summary

Recommended Use

Automotive sales and product site is designed to present detailed information and special offerings on both the home page and subpages. This design is focused on retail business concerns focused on engaging the customer with offerings and inspiring immediate action.

Look and Feel

Background in shades of yellow creates a strong and bright look, with accents from the anchor photograph and the strongly contrasting action item block that sets off customer announcements such as special offerings, incentive messages, and contact information.

Medium-density layout features a single article area on home pages and subpages, with special emphasis upon action item announcements. A special tagline overprinting the anchor photograph appears in the home page, and you can customize it as a heading on each of the subpages.

Content Plan

Content Plan Overview

Before entering content in your site, make a list of the Web page labels and filenames you will use to build your Web site skeleton. Detailed coverage on building your content plan is presented in Chapter 3.

Subpages

Display layout focuses on action items that support six subpages, including a dedicated home link plus five programmable navigation bar labels at the top and bottom. Identify and write down the screen labels and the related filenames you will use.

Feature Article

A feature article appears on both the home page and subpages, with a continuing link from the home page.

Tagline and Page Head

A tagline with link appears as an overlay to the anchor photograph on the home page. The same construction is available on each subpage as a heading, and you can uniquely assign it to each subpage.

Action Items

Action items appear as a highlighted block on both the home page and subpages, with three action item headings, each supporting a paragraph of text and Link Label.

Copy the Template

Follow these steps to copy the template to your hard drive:

1. Access the \Templates\Chapter 6\63\630 folder on your CD-ROM.

2. Drag the \630 folder to your desktop or copy and paste the \630 folder to your desktop.

Template Headings and Tags

Figure 6-11: Template 630 home page token reference

Figure 6-12: Template 630 subpage token reference

Building Your Site Step-by-Step: 630 Auto Dealer

Building the Site Skeleton

Use the following set of operations to enter the central navigation. Perform the exact same operations within index.html and subpage.html. Web site navigation and building the site skeleton are presented in Chapter 3.

Note that when opening index.html or subpage.html in Internet Explorer from your hard drive, a security message may appear. Click for more options, and choose to display the full content so the template displays correctly.

| **1. Place navigation labels** | Review the list of subpage labels and filenames from your content plan. You place the labels for subpage 1 at the top (`MNav`) and bottom (`FNav`) of your page. See Figures 6-11 for home and 6-12 for subpages. |

1. Open `index.html` in your text editor.

2. Find `MNavLabel:1_Here` and replace the token with the label for subpage 1.

3. Find `FNavLabel:1_Here` and replace the token with the label for subpage 1.

4. Repeat Steps 2 and 3 for `MNavLabel` and `FNavLabel` 2, 3, 4, and 5.

| **2. Place navigation links** | Review the list of subpage labels and filenames from your content plan. In the following operation you place the links to the filename for subpage 1 at the top (`MNav`) and bottom (`FNav`) of your page. Enter all filenames in lowercase. |

1. Find `MNavURL:1_Here` and replace the token with filename you selected for subpage 1.

2. Find `FNavURL:1_Here` and replace the token with the filename you selected for subpage 1.

3. Repeat Steps 1 and 2 for `MNavURL` and `FNavURL` 2, 3, 4, and 5.

| **3. Place action items** | Place the headings and paragraph text for the featured action items (see Figures 6-11 and 6-12). |

You can program action items separately for the home page and subpages. In that event, perform these operations individually for the home page and subpages.

1. Find `AILabel:1_Here` and replace the token with your action item heading text. Repeat for `AILabel` 2 and 3.

2. Find `AIURL:1_Here` and replace the token with the filename for the action item link. Repeat for `AIURL` 2 and 3.

3. Find `AIParagraph:1_Here` and replace the token with your action item paragraph text. Repeat for `AIParagraph` 2 and 3.

4. Find `LinkLabel:1_Here` and replace the token with the "Read More" or another title of your choosing for the action item link. Repeat for `LinkLabel` 2 and 3.

5. Find `LinkURL:1_Here` and replace the token with the destination filename for the action item link. Repeat for `LinkURL` 2 and 3.

---

4. Place special features

Place the text of the Web site copyright in your pages.

1. Find `WebsiteCopyright:1_Here` and replace the token with your Web site copyright text.

2. Save and close `index.html` in your text editor.

---

5. Set up the subpage template

Perform the same set of edits that you completed for the `index.html` file on the subpage master template file, `subpage.html`.

1. Open `subpage.html` in your text editor.

2. Return to the beginning of this section ("Building the Site Skeleton"), and start with main Step 1, "Place navigation labels."

3. Complete main Steps 1, 2, 3, and 4 using the `subpage.html` file instead of the `index.html` file.

4. Save `subpage.html` in your text editor. Do not rename the file.

Creating Subpage Files

6. Create subpage files

Use the Save As feature in your text editor to save the `subpage.html` template with the first of the subpage filenames you selected in your content plan. Repeat this to create all subpages listed in your content plan.

Save all files to the `\630` folder on your desktop.

1. Verify that `subpage.html` is open in your text editor.

2. Choose File ➪ Save As or similar from your text editor. Enter the filename you selected for subpage 1, and click OK.

3. Repeat Step 2 for all subpages in your content plan.

4. Repeat Step 2 for any linked articles or catalog detail pages you identified in your content plan.

---

7. Display your site　　Open your site to check that your labels and pages display correctly.

1. Launch `index.html` from your computer by double-clicking the filename, or choose File ⇨ Open (from most browsers) to open it in your browser. An empty home page should appear.

2. Click the navigation links at the top and bottom of the home page and you should see empty subpage pages.

3. Close the empty site skeleton.

Placing Content in the Home Page

8. Place home tagline and link　　Place the headings and paragraph text for the featured article in `index.html` (see Figure 6-11).

1. Open `index.html` in your text editor.

2. Find `Tagline:1_Here` and replace the token with your tagline text.

3. Find `LinkLabel:5_Here`. Replace the token with the label text for this link.

4. Find `LinkURL:5_Here`. Replace the token with the filename you have selected to be accessed from this link.

---

9. Place home article　　Place the headings and paragraph text for the featured article in `index.html`.

1. Find `Heading:1_Here` and replace the token with your heading text.

2. Find `Paragraph:1_Here` and replace the token with your paragraph text. Repeat this operation for `Paragraph` 2 and 3.

3. Find `LinkLabel:4_Here`. Replace the token with the label text for this link (such as "Read More" or "More Information"). You can delete this token if you do not want to use this link.

4. Find `LinkURL:4_Here`. Replace the token with the filename you have selected to be accessed from this link.

5. Save `index.html` in your text editor.

Placing Content in Subpages

Use the following operations to place content into all of your site subpages. Use the subpage token reference (see Figure 6-12) to see the position of the content and label tokens. Repeat this operation to enter content in all of your subpages.

---

10. Place subpage tagline and link

Place the headings and paragraph text for the featured article in the selected subpage (see Figure 6-12).

1. Open the selected subpage in your text editor.

2. Find `Tagline:1_Here` and replace the token with your tagline text.

3. Find `LinkLabel:4_Here` and replace the token with the label text for this link.

4. Find `LinkURL:4_Here`. Replace the token with the filename you have selected to be accessed from this link.

---

11. Place subpage articles

Place article headings and text in your subpages.

1. Find `Heading:1_Here` and replace the token with your heading text. Repeat this operation for `Heading` 2, 3, and 4.

2. Find `Paragraph:1_Here` and replace the token with your paragraph text. Repeat this operation for `Paragraph` 2 and 3.

3. Save and close the file when you have finished editing.

Finalizing Your Site

12. Edit site logo and pictures   Turn to Chapter 3 for explanation and procedures to replace the default template logo and images with your own logo and images.

13. Display your Web site   Launch `index.html` from your computer by double-clicking the filename, or choose File ➪ Open. Check your work in your browser window.

14. Edit and adjust   Make edits by opening up your home page or subpage page files in your text editor and making edits to the content. Be sure to edit only your content and not to disturb any of the surrounding code.

15. Publish   The basic parameters of what you should provide to your Web hosting company are outlined in Chapter 3. For the specifics on actually posting your live site to the Web, contact your service provider for details.

Variations

Variation 631 Overview   This version presents the design against a light blue background and a totally different logo and anchor image to be used as a birth announcement site.

See the images in the CD-ROM's Gallery section.

Variation 632 Overview   This variation presents the default design against a dark blue background, with a pastel yellow content presentation area.

See the images in the CD-ROM's Gallery section.

Template 640 Grocery or General Retail

A general retail site that you can adapt to present any retail business, including grocery products, hardware, or any store or Web store offering.

Figure 6-13: Template 640 home page

Figure 6-14: Template 640 subpage

Template Developer	Ken Milhous
Filename and Location	CD-ROM: \Templates\Chapter 6\64\640
Variations on this Design	641 642
Site Development Detail	Procedures and supporting information on placing content, links, and Web site images are presented in Chapter 3.

Design Summary

Recommended Use

This design is a blank slate; it uses no anchor photographs and is oriented around a feature and supporting articles. You can adapt it to any retail business application.

Look and Feel

The site is simply presented in shades of blue, with a strong deep blue background, a blue-white gradient background for article presentation, and deep blue accent buttons for principal page links.

This medium- to high-density layout features identical home page and subpage layouts with three article areas each. You can delete tokens for heading and paragraph links on the home page or subpages to scale the density of the content presented and focus on fewer articles if desired.

Content Plan

Content Plan Overview

Before entering content in your site, make a list of the Web page labels and filenames you will use to build your Web site skeleton. Detailed coverage on building your content plan is presented in Chapter 3.

Subpages

It is a basic retail information layout that supports six subpages, including a dedicated home link plus five programmable navigation bar labels at the top and bottom. Identify and write down the screen labels and the related filenames.

Articles

The design supports three levels of article headings, with a feature article and two supporting articles with progressively smaller font size and positioning. Article headings and text areas are positioned and presented identically on the home page and subpages.

Copy the Template

Follow these steps to copy the template to your hard drive:

1. Access the \Templates\Chapter 6\64\640 folder on your CD-ROM.

2. Drag the \640 folder to your desktop or copy and paste the \640 folder to your desktop.

Template Headings and Tags

Figure 6-15: Template 640 home page token reference

Figure 6-16: Template 640 subpage token reference

Building Your Site Step-by-Step: 640 Grocery or General Retail

Building the Site Skeleton

Use the following set of operations to enter the central navigation. Perform the exact same operations within index.html and subpage.html. Web site navigation and building the site skeleton are presented in Chapter 3.

Note that when opening index.html or subpage.html in Internet Explorer from your hard drive, a security message may appear. Click for more options, and choose to display the full content so the template displays correctly.

---

1. Place navigation labels

Review the list of subpage labels and filenames from your content plan. You place the labels for subpage 1 at the top (MNav) and bottom (FNav) of your page. See Figures 6-15 for home and 6-16 for subpages.

1. Open index.html in your text editor.

2. Find MNavLabel:1_Here and replace the token with the label for subpage 1.

3. Find `FNavLabel:1_Here` and replace the token with the label for subpage 1.

4. Repeat Steps 2 and 3 for `MNavLabel` and `FNavLabel` 2, 3, 4, and 5.

---

2. Place navigation links

Review the list of subpage labels and filenames from your content plan. In the following operation you place the links to the filename for subpage 1 at the top (`MNav`) and bottom (`FNav`) of your page. Enter all filenames in lowercase.

1. Find `MNavURL:1_Here` and replace the token with filename you selected for subpage 1.

2. Find `FNavURL:1_Here` and replace the token with the filename you selected for subpage 1.

3. Repeat Steps 1 and 2 for `MNavURL` and `FNavURL` 2, 3, 4, and 5.

---

3. Place special features

Place the text of the Web site copyright in your pages.

1. Find `WebsiteCopyright:1_Here` and replace the token with your Web site copyright text.

2. Save and close `index.html` in your text editor.

---

4. Set up the subpage template

Perform the same set of edits that you completed for the `index.html` file on the subpage master template file, `subpage.html`.

1. Open `subpage.html` in your text editor.

2. Return to the beginning of this section ("Building the Site Skeleton"), and start with main Step 1, "Place navigation labels."

3. Complete main Steps 1, 2, and 3 using the `subpage.html` file instead of the `index.html` file.

4. Save `subpage.html` in your text editor. Do not rename the file.

Creating Subpage Files

5. Create subpage files

Use the Save As feature in your text editor to save the `subpage.html` template with the first of the subpage filenames you selected in your content plan. Repeat this to create all subpages listed in your content plan.

Save all files to the `\640` folder on your desktop.

1. Verify that `subpage.html` is open in your text editor.

2. Choose File ➪ Save As or similar from your text editor. Enter the filename you selected for subpage 1, and click OK.

3. Repeat Step 2 for all subpages in your content plan.

4. Repeat Step 2 for any linked articles or catalog detail pages you identified in your content plan.

6. Display your site

Open your site to check that your labels and pages display correctly.

1. Launch `index.html` from your computer by double-clicking the filename, or choose File ➪ Open (from most browsers) to open it in your browser. An empty home page should appear.

2. Click the navigation links at the top and bottom of the home page and you should see empty subpage pages.

3. Close the empty site skeleton.

Placing Content in the Home Page

7. Place home article

Place the headings and paragraph text for the articles in `index.html` (see Figure 6-15). Note that only Heading 2 accepts a link to a subpage.

1. Open `index.html` in your text editor.

2. Find `Heading:1_Here` and replace the token with your heading text. Repeat for `Heading` 2, 3, and 4.

3. Find `Paragraph:1_Here` and replace the token with your paragraph text. Repeat this operation for `Paragraph` 2, 3, and 4.

4. Find `LinkLabel:1_Here` and replace the token with the label text for this link. Repeat for `LinkLabel` 2.

5. Find `LinkURL:1_Here` and replace the token with the filename you have selected to be accessed from this link. Repeat for `LinkURL` 2.

6. Save `index.html` in your text editor.

Placing Content in Subpages

Use the following operations to place content into all of your site subpages. Use the subpage token reference (see Figure 6-16) to see the position of the content and label tokens. Repeat this operation to enter content in all of your subpages.

---

8. Place subpage articles   Place article headings and text in your subpages.

1. Open the selected subpage in your text editor.

2. Find `Heading:1_Here` and replace the token with your heading text. Repeat for `Heading` 2.

3. Find `Paragraph:1_Here` and replace the token with your paragraph text. Repeat this operation for `Paragraph` 2.

4. Find `LinkLabel:1_Here` and replace the token with the label text for this link.

5. Find `LinkURL:1_Here` and replace the token with the filename you have selected to be accessed from this link.

6. Find `Heading:3_Here` and place the text for the article at the right side of the page.

7. Find `Paragraph:3_Here` and place the related text for `Heading` 3.

8. Save and close the file when you have finished editing.

Finalizing Your Site

9. Edit site logo and pictures

Turn to Chapter 3 for explanation and procedures to replace the default template logo and images with your own logo and images.

10. Display your Web site

Launch `index.html` from your computer by double-clicking the filename, or choose File ➪ Open. Check your work in your browser window.

11. Edit and adjust

Make edits by opening up your home page or subpage page files in your text editor and making edits to the content. Be sure to edit only your content and not to disturb any of the surrounding code.

12. Publish

The basic parameters of what you should provide to your Web hosting company are outlined in Chapter 3. For the specifics on actually posting your live site to the Web, contact your service provider for details.

Variations

Variation 641 Overview

In this variation, the site is presented against a steel gray gradient with pink text display and shades of pink in the main navigation area.

See the images in the CD-ROM's Gallery section.

Variation 642 Overview

This version uses green as the dominant color for the background, font color and main navigation area.

See the images in the CD-ROM's Gallery section.

Template 650 Hospitality — Hotel or Motel

A hospitality industry site designed to present a hotel or motel offering. You can easily adapt this design to use for other travel-related business, such as a travel agency, restaurant, or local attraction, such as a museum or an entertainment venue.

Figure 6-17: Template 650 home page

Figure 6-18: Template 650 subpage

Template Developer	Ken Milhous
Filename and Location	CD-ROM: \Templates\Chapter 6\65\650
Variations on this Design	651 652
Site Development Detail	Procedures and supporting information on placing content, links, and Web site images are presented in Chapter 3.

Design Summary

Recommended Use	Hospitality site focused on presenting announcements, sales incentives, and topics of customer interest in an eye-catching way. The home page is designed to engage the reader with strongly presented topics and offerings that can be developed in subpages.
Look and Feel	Background in shades of yellow and orange is offset by the colorful anchor photograph. The look is open and light, bright and warm. Medium-density layout features two article areas on the home page that support dominant action item announcement areas, and three icon-enhanced article areas on the subpage that support the hospitality industry theme.

Content Plan

Content Plan Overview	Before entering content in your site, make a list of the Web page labels and filenames you will use to build your Web site skeleton. Detailed coverage on building your content plan is presented in Chapter 3.
Subpages	Display layout focused on action items that support five subpages, including a dedicated home link plus four programmable navigation bar labels at the top and bottom. Identify and write down the screen labels and the related filenames.
Articles	Home features two article areas supporting the action item lead block, and the subpage features three boxed article areas.
Action Items	Action items appear as a highlighted block on the home page only, with three action item headings, each supporting a paragraph of text and Link Label.

Copy the Template

Follow these steps to copy the template to your hard drive:

1. Access the `\Templates\Chapter 6\65\650` folder on your CD-ROM.

2. Drag the `\650` folder to your desktop or copy and paste the `\650` folder to your desktop.

Template Headings and Tags

Figure 6-19: Template 650 home page token reference

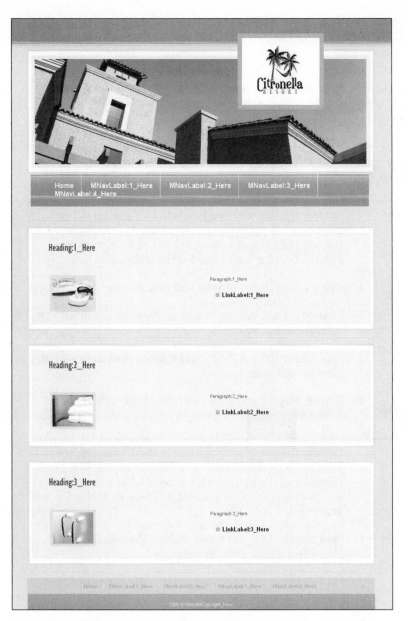

Figure 6-20: Template 650 subpage token reference

Building Your Site Step-by-Step: 650 Hospitality — Hotel or Motel

Building the Site Skeleton

Use the following set of operations to enter the central navigation. Perform the exact same operations within `index.html` and `subpage.html`. Web site navigation and building the site skeleton are presented in Chapter 3.

Note that when opening `index.html` or `subpage.html` in Internet Explorer from your hard drive, a security message may appear. Click for more options, and choose to display the full content so the template displays correctly.

---

1. Place navigation labels

Review the list of subpage labels and filenames from your content plan. You place the labels for subpage 1 at the top (`MNav`) and bottom (`FNav`) of your page. See Figures 6-19 for home and 6-20 for subpages.

1. Open `index.html` in your text editor.

2. Find `MNavLabel:1_Here` and replace the token with the label for subpage 1.

3. Find `FNavLabel:1_Here` and replace the token with the label for subpage 1.

4. Repeat Steps 2 and 3 for `MNavLabel` and `FNavLabel` 2, 3, and 4.

---

2. Place navigation links

Review the list of subpage labels and filenames from your content plan. In the following operation you place the links to the filename for subpage 1 at the top (`MNav`) and bottom (`FNav`) of your page. Enter all filenames in lowercase.

1. Find `MNavURL:1_Here` and replace the token with filename you selected for subpage 1.

2. Find `FNavURL:1_Here` and replace the token with the filename you selected for subpage 1.

3. Repeat Steps 1 and 2 for `MNavURL` and `FNavURL` 2, 3, and 4.

---

3. Place special features

Place the text of the Web site copyright in your pages.

1. Find `WebsiteCopyright:1_Here` and replace the token with your Web site copyright text.

2. Save and close `index.html` in your text editor.

4. Set up the subpage template

Perform the same set of edits that you completed for the `index.html` file on the subpage master template file, `subpage.html`.

1. Open `subpage.html` in your text editor.

2. Return to the beginning of this section ("Building the Site Skeleton"), and start with main Step 1, "Place navigation labels."

3. Complete main Steps 1, 2, and 3 using the `subpage.html` file instead of the `index.html` file.

4. Save `subpage.html` in your text editor. Do not rename the file.

Creating Subpage Files

5. Create subpage files

Use the Save As feature in your text editor to save the `subpage.html` template with the first of the subpage filenames you selected in your content plan. Repeat this to create all subpages listed in your content plan.

Save all files to the `\650` folder on your desktop.

1. Verify that `subpage.html` is open in your text editor.

2. Choose File ⇨ Save As or similar from your text editor. Enter the filename you selected for subpage 1, and click OK.

3. Repeat Step 2 for all subpages in your content plan.

4. Repeat Step 2 for any linked articles or catalog detail pages you identified in your content plan.

6. Display your site

Open your site to check that your labels and pages display correctly.

1. Launch `index.html` from your computer by double-clicking the filename, or choose File ⇨ Open (from most browsers) to open it in your browser. An empty home page should appear.

2. Click the navigation links at the top and bottom of the home page and you should see empty subpage pages.

3. Close the empty site skeleton.

Placing Content in the Home Page

7. Place action items

Place the action item headings and paragraph text for the featured article in `index.html` (see Figure 6-19).

1. Open `index.html` in your text editor.

2. Find `AILabel:1_Here` and replace the token with your action item heading text. Repeat for `AILabel` 2 and 3.

3. Find `AIURL:1_Here` and replace the token with the filename for the action item link. Repeat for `AIURL` 2 and 3.

4. Find `AIParagraph:1_Here` and replace the token with your action item paragraph text. Repeat for `AIParagraph` 2 and 3.

5. Find `LinkLabel:1_Here` and replace the token with the "Read More" or another title for the action item link. Repeat for `LinkLabel` 2 and 3.

6. Find `LinkURL:1_Here` and replace the token with the destination filename for the action item link. Repeat for `LinkURL` 2 and 3.

8. Place home articles

Place the headings and paragraph text for the featured article in `index.html` (see Figure 6-19).

1. Find `Heading:1_Here` and replace the token with your heading text.

2. Find `Paragraph:1_Here` and replace the token with your paragraph text. Repeat this operation for `Paragraph` 2 and 3.

3. Find `LinkLabel:4_Here`. Replace the token with the label text for this link (such as "Read More" or "More Information"). You can delete this token if you do not want to use this link.

4. Find `LinkURL:4_Here`. Replace the token with the filename you have selected to be accessed from this link.

5. Find `Heading:2_Here` and replace the token with your heading text.

6. Find `Paragraph:4_Here` and replace the token with your paragraph text. Repeat this operation for `Paragraph` 5 and 6.

7. Find `LinkLabel:5_Here`. Replace the token with the label text for this link (such as "Read More" or "More Information"). You can delete this token if you do not want to use this link.

8. Find `LinkURL:5_Here`. Replace the token with the filename you have selected to be accessed from this link.

9. Save `index.html` in your text editor.

Placing Content in Subpages

Use the following operations to place content into all of your site subpages. Use the subpage token reference (see Figure 6-20) to see the position of the content and label tokens. Repeat this operation to enter content in all of your subpages.

---

9. Place subpage articles   Place article headings and text in your subpages.

1. Open the selected subpage in your text editor.

2. Find `Heading:1_Here` and replace the token with your heading text. Repeat for `Heading` 2 and 3.

3. Find `Paragraph:1_Here` and replace the token with your paragraph text. Repeat for `Paragraph` 2 and 3.

4. Find `LinkLabel:1_Here` and replace the token with the label text for this link. Repeat for `LinkLabel` 2 and 3.

5. Find `LinkURL:1_Here` and replace the token with the filename you have selected to be accessed from this link. Repeat for `LinkURL` 2 and 3.

6. Save and close the file when you have finished editing.

Finalizing Your Site

10. Edit site logo and pictures   Turn to Chapter 3 for explanation and procedures to replace the default template logo and images with your own logo and images.

11. Display your Web site   Launch `index.html` from your computer by double-clicking the filename, or choose File ➪ Open. Check your work in your browser window.

12. Edit and adjust   Make edits by opening up your home page or subpage page files in your text editor and making edits to the content. Be sure to edit only your content and not to disturb any of the surrounding code.

13. Publish   The basic parameters of what you should provide to your Web hosting company are outlined in Chapter 3. For the specifics on actually posting your live site to the Web, contact your service provider for details.

Variations

Variation 651 Overview   In this version, the navigation bar and framing areas are presented in muted earth tones of brown and gray.

See the images in the CD-ROM's Gallery section.

Variation 652 Overview   This variation presents the design on a pastel gray background with shades of brown used in the navigation areas.

See the images in the CD-ROM's Gallery section.

✦   ✦   ✦

Non-Profit Organization Templates

Non-profit organizations are businesses on a mission. Often these enterprises are organizations that have been set up to generate civic, social, or political influence. They need a business structure to collect and spend money to create an impact and meet the mission they were designed to accomplish.

The starting point for most non-profit organizations is to clearly establish their mission and their credibility to pursue it. This creates the foundation for building a community of interested individuals that may include members, partners, affiliates, contributors, or clients if the organization offers services. Many non-profits are also information authorities who make it their business to know more about their mission than anybody else and to draw involvement from those seeking this experience.

Non-Profit Organization Templates

Non-profit organization templates are designed to present both the organization mission and its information in an engaging way. The templates included in this chapter present sites that are modeled on civic organizations, lobbying organizations, political parties, religious institutions, and communities of special interest. As diverse as these examples are, they all share the need to communicate their purpose and get other people involved.

When selecting a template for a non-profit group from the 1 Hour Web Site family, it's important to keep both the organization identity and the interests of its constituents in mind. Keep in mind that templates in Chapters 10 and 11 that were designed for businesses information publishing or communities can offer the right look for presenting the organization message as well.

Presenting a non-profit organization

Many of the fundamental communication requirements for businesses also apply to non-profit organizations. Each must establish credibility through proven expertise and a clear focus on its mission. Those who read the site must believe that the group is grounded, serious, and able to realize its goals.

Unlike many businesses, however, non-profit organizations are seeking involvement as well as money from supporters, not customers. The public cannot be sold something they don't fundamentally believe in; rather, they seek organizations that are aligned with their existing personal beliefs and commitments. People are drawn to non-profits for a plethora of personal and professional reasons. Therefore, it is of vital importance that the Web site for a non-profit focus on its core beliefs, experience, personal passions, and larger sense of the goal that motivates involvement.

Detailing the mission

Non-profit organization Web sites must make the mission crystal clear right on the home page. By establishing a clear identity, goals, and credibility with potential constituents, the organization lays the foundation for future dialog. Some of the key elements that establish a non-profit organization include

✦ A clearly stated organizational mission

✦ Programs

✦ Organizational goals and objectives

✦ An approach and organizational activities

✦ Years in operation

✦ Statements by executives, directors, and prominent members

✦ Members or affiliated groups

✦ Member involvement activities

✦ Press clippings and news mentions

Each organization must clearly establish its mission so that its key constituents and partners can recognize its value and become involved in its work.

Organization objectives

Where businesses speak in terms of branding and positioning, non-profit organizations often think and act in terms of their underlying message and transformational goals. What do a lobbying group and a church have in common? At one level, each organization operates based on a belief in shared goals.

It is essential for the non-profit organization to make its objectives and purpose clear throughout its Web site. Communicating objectives occurs on three distinct levels. First, what is the high-level vision and beliefs that all potential supporters can identify with? Second, how does the organization translate those beliefs into practical action? And finally, how can individuals and organizations that share this world view or approach become involved in the life of the organization?

Combined, these three questions give form to the communications tasks for any non-profit. When building your Web site content, be mindful of these three important factors and present information that helps readers understand that they are interrelated. Constituents may understand the message more clearly through practical goals or personal involvement than simply a broad and possibly amorphous or intangible mission statement.

Constituents, allies, and rivals

Non-profit organizations by their very nature must convey their message to many different populations.

A non-profit organization operating in civic and political work has to deal with many audiences. Members or allied organizations that support its work represent only one facet of the communication challenge. Neutral or critical observers can include the press, other (possibly competitive) advocacy groups, interested business organizations, and political analysts. Business partners, such as fund-raising organizations, sponsors, or contributors, might have another point of view.

A Web site for a non-profit organization is a highly effective tool for advancing the organization's work through clear and global communication. Given the range of audiences and interests involved, it can be strategically important for an organization to create Web pages that address not only its core audience, but also those, like the press or politicians, who are critically assessing the organization's work.

Levels of involvement

The non-profit seeks involvement from people and other organizations to continue its work. That involvement can be an exchange of money or resources — membership subscriptions, contributions, alliance with partners, and in-kind contributions of service, to name a few. Beyond purely financial concerns, the fundamental goal of the non-profit is to continually build, develop, and retain its core supporters. Whether they are individual members, volunteers, political contacts, or organization sponsors, all represent the lifeblood of the organization.

When developing your non-profit organization Web site, pay particular attention to personal and organizational involvement. The Web is an active, participatory medium, and it is an ideal way to both engage attention and action. Don't just stick articles in a page; ask the readers to e-mail you with comments or requests for additional material that interests them. Provide clear pathways for them to communicate their support for what you are doing. Shared beliefs and goals are one thing, but taking action is what moves the mission.

Tip   Instead of navigating from the root of the CD to locate a template, you can click the Templates link in the CD browser application to directly access the chapters on the CD. For faster access, click the Gallery link in the CD browser application to view a listing of all templates. Then click any View Files link to view the files for that template.

Template 710 Civic Organizations

Non-profit organization sites are designed to present civic organizations or companies working on public business. This design can be adapted to any non-profit or public content, including governmental organizations, citizen action groups, or political organizations.

Figure 7-1: Template 710 home page

Figure 7-2: Template 710 subpage

Template Developer	Ken Milhous
Filename and Location	CD-ROM: `\Templates\Chapter 7\71\710`
Variations on this Design	711 712
Site Development Detail	Procedures and supporting information on placing content, links, and Web site images are presented in Chapter 3.

Design Summary

Recommended Use

Civic organization site is shown as a public works firm, but you can use the design for any information-rich content. The home page is densely laid out with an emphasis on action items of interest, which are reflected on subpages. The subpages are designed to present individual articles.

Look and Feel

Design is built on shades of blue and gray accented by highlighted background areas for action items and white framing borders around article areas.

Medium- to low-density design is built to emphasize action item announcements or points of interest with article areas supporting the prominent navigation bar and action item areas. Subpages feature a dominant single article heading and text.

Content Plan

Content Plan Overview

Before entering content in your site, make a list of the Web page labels and filenames you will use to build your Web site skeleton. Detailed coverage on building your content plan is presented in Chapter 3.

Subpages

A display layout focused on action item that support four subpages, including a dedicated home link plus three programmable navigation bar labels at the top and bottom. Identify and write down the screen labels and the related filenames.

Articles

The home page features two article areas supporting the action item lead block and the subpage features a single article area with a prominent headline and featured illustration within the article block.

Action Items

Action items appear as a highlighted block on the home and subpages with three action item headings, each supporting a paragraph of text and Link Label.

Copy the Template

Follow these steps to copy the template to your hard drive:

1. Access the \Templates\Chapter 7\71\710 folder on your CD-ROM.

2. Drag the \710 folder to your desktop or copy and paste the \710 folder to your desktop.

Template Headings and Tags

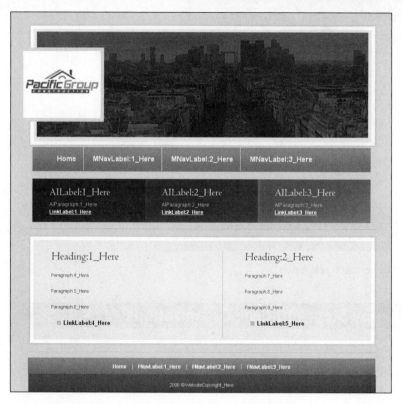

Figure 7-3: Template 710 home page token reference

Figure 7-4: Template 710 subpage token reference

Building Your Site Step-by-Step: 710 Civic Organizations

Building the Site Skeleton

Use the following set of operations to enter the central navigation. Perform the exact same operations within `index.html` and `subpage.html`. Web site navigation and building the site skeleton are presented in Chapter 3.

Note that when opening `index.html` or `subpage.html` in Internet Explorer from your hard drive, a security message may appear. Click for more options, and choose to display the full content so the template displays correctly.

1. Place navigation labels

Review the list of subpage labels and filenames from your content plan. You place the labels for subpage 1 at the top (MNav) and bottom (FNav) of your page. See Figures 7-3 for home and 7-4 for subpages.

1. Open index.html in your text editor.

2. Find MNavLabel:1_Here and replace the token with the label for subpage 1.

3. Find FNavLabel:1_Here and replace the token with the label for subpage 1.

4. Repeat Steps 2 and 3 for MNavLabel and FNavLabel 2, 3, and 4.

2. Place navigation links

Review the list of subpage labels and filenames from your content plan. In the following operation you place the links to the filename for subpage 1 at the top (MNav) and bottom (FNav) of your page. Enter all filenames in lowercase.

1. Find MNavURL:1_Here and replace the token with filename you selected for subpage 1.

2. Find FNavURL:1_Here and replace the token with the filename you selected for subpage 1.

3. Repeat Steps 1 and 2 for MNavURL and FNavURL 2, 3, and 4.

3. Place action items

Place the headings and paragraph text for the featured article in index.html.

1. Find AILabel:1_Here and replace the token with your action item heading text. Repeat for AILabel 2 and 3.

2. Find AIParagraph:1_Here and replace the token with your action item paragraph text. Repeat for AIParagraph 2 and 3.

3. Find LinkLabel:1_Here and replace the token with the "Read More" or other title for the action item link. Repeat with LinkLabel 2 and 3.

4. Find LinkURL:1_Here and replace the token with the destination filename for the action item link. Repeat with LinkURL 2 and 3.

4. Place special features	Place the text of the Web site copyright in your pages.

1. Find `WebsiteCopyright:1_Here` and replace the token with your Web site copyright text.

2. Save and close `index.html` in your text editor.

5. Set up the subpage	Perform the same set of edits that you completed for the `index.html` file on the subpage master template file, `subpage.html`.

1. Open `subpage.html` in your text editor.

2. Return to the beginning of this section ("Building the Site Skeleton"), and start with main Step 1, "Place navigation labels."

3. Complete main Steps 1, 2, 3, and 4 using the `subpage.html` file instead of the `index.html` file.

4. Save `subpage.html` in your text editor. Do not rename the file.

Creating Subpage Files

6. Create subpage files	Use the Save As feature in your text editor to save the `subpage.html` template with the first of the subpage filenames you selected in your content plan. Repeat this to create all subpages listed in your content plan.

Save all files to the \710 folder on your desktop.

1. Verify that `subpage.html` is open in your text editor.

2. Choose File ➪ Save As or similar from your text editor. Enter the filename you selected for subpage 1, and click OK.

3. Repeat Step 2 for all subpages in your content plan.

4. Repeat Step 2 for any linked articles or catalog detail pages you identified in your content plan.

7. Display your site

Open your site to check that your labels and pages display correctly.

1. Launch index.html from your computer by double-clicking the filename, or choose File ➪ Open (from most browsers) to open it in your browser. An empty home page should appear.

2. Click the navigation links at the top and bottom of the home page and you should see empty subpage pages.

3. Close the empty site skeleton.

Placing Content in the Home Page

8. Place home article

Place the headings and paragraph text for the featured article in index.html (see Figure 7-3).

1. Open index.html in your text editor.

2. Find Heading:1_Here and replace the token with your heading text.

3. Find Paragraph:1_Here and replace the token with your paragraph text. Repeat this operation for Paragraph 2 and 3.

4. Find LinkLabel:4_Here. Replace the token with the label text for this link (such as "Read More" or "More Information"). You can delete this token if you do not want to use this link.

5. Find LinkURL:4_Here. Replace the token with the filename you have selected to be accessed from this link.

6. Find Heading:2_Here and replace the token with your heading text.

7. Find Paragraph:4_Here and replace the token with your paragraph text. Repeat this operation for Paragraph 5 and 6.

8. Find `LinkLabel:5_Here`. Replace the token with the label text for this link (such as "Read More" or "More Information"). You can delete this token if you do not want to use this link.

9. Find `LinkURL:5_Here`. Replace the token with the filename you have selected to be accessed from this link.

10. Save `index.html` in your text editor.

Placing Content in Subpages

Use the following operations to place content into all of your site subpages. Use the subpage token reference (see Figure 7-4) to see the position of the content and label tokens. Repeat this operation to enter content in all of your subpages.

9. Place subpage articles   Place article headings and text in your subpages.

1. Open the selected subpage in your text editor.

2. Find `Heading:1_Here` and replace the token with your heading text.

3. Find `Paragraph:1_Here` and replace the token with your paragraph text. Repeat this operation with `Paragraph` 2 and 3.

4. Find `LinkLabel:4_Here` and replace the token with the label text for this link.

5. Find `LinkURL:4_Here` and replace the token with the filename you have selected to be accessed from this link.

6. Save and close the file when you have finished editing.

Finalizing Your Site

10. Edit site logo and pictures

Turn to Chapter 3 for explanation and procedures to replace the default template logo and images with your own logo and images.

11. Display your Web site

Launch index.html from your computer by double-clicking the filename, or choose File ⇨ Open. Check your work in your browser window.

12. Edit and adjust

Make edits by opening up your home page or subpage page files in your text editor and making edits to the content. Be sure to edit only your content and not to disturb any of the surrounding code.

13. Publish

The basic parameters of what you should provide to your Web hosting company are outlined in Chapter 3. For the specifics on actually posting your live site to the Web, contact your service provide for details.

Variations

Variation 711 Overview

This version uses a blue gray background and brown gradient accents to present principal action items.

See the images in the CD-ROM's Gallery section.

Variation 712 Overview

In this variation, the design is presented against a pastel muted yellow with brown and gray accents through the design.

See the images in the CD-ROM's Gallery section.

Template 720 Lobbying Group

Non-profit organization sites are designed to present a lobbying group or other civic organization. This design embodies a conservative, professional services look and feel, and you can easily adapt it for professional services uses, including law, accounting, or business services.

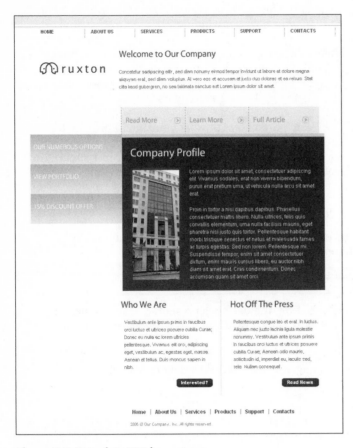

Figure 7-5: Template 720 home page

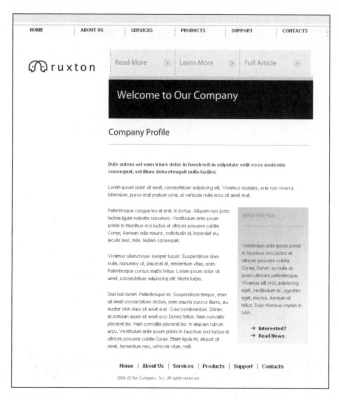

Figure 7-6: Template 720 subpage

Template Developer	Ken Milhous
Filename and Location	CD-ROM: `\Templates\Chapter 7\72\720`
Variations on this Design	721 722
Site Development Detail	Procedures and supporting information on placing content, links, and Web site images are presented in Chapter 3.

Design Summary

Recommended Use

Design is information intensive, both with links to topics and announcements as well as to article text blocks. The home page is designed to pack as much content as possible on the screen, both as featured articles and as links to topics of interest. It is best used for business or civic applications that are content intensive and seek to engage the audience with many areas of interest.

Look and Feel

White background sets off an open area for content display, with a heavily featured article offset in a deep blue background on the home page, and the same color recurring as an article heading on the subpage.

Medium- to high-density design is centered on topic links through Link Labels and action items (on the home page only.) The home page is high density with four article blocks, and subpages make use of white space to set off a single article with a principal heading and subhead. Sidebar accents on both the home page and subpages support links on featured content.

Content Plan

Content Plan Overview

Before entering content in your site, make a list of the Web page labels and filenames you will use to build your Web site skeleton. Detailed coverage on building your content plan is presented in Chapter 3.

Subpages

High-density display information layout focuses on action items and links that support six subpages, including a dedicated home link plus five programmable navigation bar labels at the top and bottom. Identify and write down the screen labels and the related filenames.

Articles

Home page features four article areas supporting the action item lead block, and the subpage features a single article area with a prominent headline and featured illustration within the article block.

Sidebar Accent

Small sidebar accent area appears on the subpage, which is ideal for presenting links to external sites of interest related to the featured article.

Action Items

Action items appear as a highlighted block on the home page only with three highlighted Link Label headings that recur on the subpages as well.

Copy the Template

Follow these steps to copy the template to your hard drive:

1. Access the \Templates\Chapter 7\72\720 folder on your CD-ROM.

2. Drag the \720 folder to your desktop or copy and paste the \720 folder to your desktop.

Template Headings and Tags

Figure 7-7: Template 720 home page token reference

Figure 7-8: Template 720 subpage token reference

Building Your Site Step-by-Step: 720 Lobbying Group

Building the Site Skeleton

Use the following set of operations to enter the central navigation. Perform the exact same operations within `index.html` and `subpage.html`. Web site navigation and building the site skeleton are presented in Chapter 3.

Note that when opening `index.html` or `subpage.html` in Internet Explorer from your hard drive, a security message may appear. Click for more options, and choose to display the full content so the template displays correctly.

---

1. Place navigation labels

Review the list of subpage labels and filenames from your content plan. You place the labels for subpage 1 at the top (`MNav`) and bottom (`FNav`) of your page. See Figures 7-7 for home and 7-8 for subpages.

1. Open `index.html` in your text editor.

2. Find `MNavLabel:1_Here` and replace the token with the label for subpage 1.

3. Find `FNavLabel:1_Here` and replace the token with the label for subpage 1.

4. Repeat Steps 2 and 3 for `MNavLabel` and `FNavLabel` 2, 3, 4, and 5.

---

2. Place navigation links

Review the list of subpage labels and filenames from your content plan. In the following operation you place the links to the filename for subpage 1 at the top (`MNav`) and bottom (`FNav`) of your page. Enter all filenames in lowercase.

1. Find `MNavURL:1_Here` and replace the token with the filename you selected for subpage 1.

2. Find `FNavURL:1_Here` and replace the token with the filename you selected for subpage 1.

3. Repeat Steps 1 and 2 for `MNavURL` and `FNavURL` 2, 3, 4, and 5.

---

3. Place link label buttons

Place text and links for the link label buttons that appear on the home page and subpages (see Figures 7-7 and 7-8).

1. Find `LinkLabel:1_Here` and replace the token with your action item heading text.

2. Find `LinkURL:1_Here` and replace the token with the destination filename for the action item link.

3. Repeat Steps 1 and 2 for `LinkLabel` and `LinkURL` 2 and 3.

---

4. Place special features

Place the text of the Web site copyright in your pages.

1. Find `WebsiteCopyright:1_Here` and replace the token with your Web site copyright text.

2. Save and close `index.html` in your text editor.

5. Set up the subpage template

Perform the same set of edits that you completed for the `index.html` file on the subpage master template file, `subpage.html`.

1. Open `subpage.html` in your text editor.

2. Return to the beginning of this section ("Building the Site Skeleton"), and start with main Step 1, "Place navigation labels."

3. Complete main Steps 1, 2, 3, and 4 using the `subpage.html` file instead of the `index.html` file.

4. Save `subpage.html` in your text editor. Do not rename the file.

Creating Subpage Files

6. Create subpage files

Use the Save As feature in your text editor to save the `subpage.html` template with the first of the subpage filenames you selected in your content plan. Repeat this to create all subpages listed in your content plan.

Save all files to the `\720` folder on your desktop.

1. Verify that `subpage.html` is open in your text editor.

2. Choose File ➪ Save As or similar from your text editor. Enter the filename you selected for subpage 1, and click OK.

3. Repeat Step 2 for all subpages in your content plan.

4. Repeat Step 2 for any linked articles or catalog detail pages you identified in your content plan.

7. Display your site

Open your site to check that your labels and pages display correctly.

1. Launch `index.html` from your computer by double-clicking the filename, or choose File ➪ Open (from most browsers) to open it in your broswer. An empty home page should appear.

2. Click the navigation links at the top and bottom of the home page and you should see empty subpage pages.

3. Close the empty site skeleton.

Placing Content in the Home Page

8. Place action items

Place action item labels and links to subpages in `index.html` (see Figure 7-7).

1. Open `index.html` in your text editor.

2. Find `AILabel:1_Here` and replace the token with your action item heading text. Repeat for `AILabel` 2 and 3.

3. Find `AIURL:1_Here` and replace the token with the destination filename for the action item link. Repeat for `AIURL` 2 and 3.

9. Place home articles

Place the headings and paragraph text for the articles in `index.html`.

1. Find `Heading:1_Here` and replace the token with your heading text.

2. Find `Paragraph:1_Here` and replace the token with your paragraph text.

3. Find `Heading:2_Here` and replace the token with your heading text.

4. Find `Paragraph:2_Here` and replace the token with your paragraph text.

5. Find `Heading:3_Here` and replace the token with your heading text.

6. Find `Paragraph:3_Here` and replace the token with your paragraph text.

7. Find `LinkLabel:4_Here`. Replace the token with the label text for this link.

8. Find `LinkURL:4_Here`. Replace the token with the filename you have selected to be accessed from this link.

9. Find `Heading:4_Here` and replace the token with your heading text.

10. Find `Paragraph:4_Here` and replace the token with your paragraph text.

11. Find `LinkLabel:5_Here`. Replace the token with the label text for this link.

12. Find `LinkURL:5_Here`. Replace the token with the filename you have selected to be accessed from this link.

13. Save `index.html` in your text editor.

Placing Content in Subpages

Use the following operations to place content into all of your site subpages. Use the subpage token reference (see Figure 7-8) to see the position of the content and label tokens. Repeat this operation to enter content in all of your subpages.

10. Place subpage articles	Place article headings and text in your subpages.

1. Open the selected subpage in your text editor.

2. Find `Heading:1_Here` and replace the token with your main heading text.

3. Find `Heading:2_Here` and replace the token with your subheading text.

4. Find `Paragraph:1_Here` and replace the token with your paragraph text. Repeat this operation with `Paragraph` 2, 4, 5, and 6.

11. Place sidebar accent	Place the heading text, paragraph copy, and links for the shaded sidebar accent area on the subpage. Note that this layout accepts two links. You can use them to link to another page in the site or to external sites that have information of interest.

1. Find `Heading:3_Here` and replace the token with your subheading text.

2. Find `Paragraph:3_Here` and replace the token with your paragraph text.

3. Find `LinkLabel:4_Here` and replace the token with the label text for this link.

4. Find `LinkURL:4_Here` and replace the token with the filename you have selected to be accessed from this link.

5. Find `LinkLabel:5_Here` and replace the token with the label text for this link.

6. Find `LinkURL:5_Here` and replace the token with the filename you have selected to be accessed from this link.

7. Save and close the file when you have finished editing.

8. Click to activate `index.html`. (You may need to single- or double-click your mouse to activate the file.)

9. View your completed site in your browser. Close the browser when you have completed your review.

Finalizing Your Site

12. Edit site logo and pictures
Turn to Chapter 3 for explanation and procedures to replace the default template logo and images with your own logo and images.

13. Display your Web site
Launch `index.html` from your computer by double-clicking the filename, or choose File ➪ Open. Check your work in your browser window.

14. Edit and adjust
Make edits by opening up your home page or subpage page files in your text editor and making edits to the content. Be sure to edit only your content and not to disturb any of the surrounding code.

15. Publish
The basic parameters of what you should provide to your Web hosting company are outlined in Chapter 3. For the specifics on actually posting your live site to the Web, contact your service provider for details.

Variations

Variation 721 Overview
In this version the principal content block on the Home is presented in black with gray accents for action items.

See the images in the CD-ROM's Gallery section.

Variation 722 Overview
This variation presents the principal content area on the Home in a deep shade of red that is picked up in Link displays. Action items are presented in gray accent backgrounds.

See the images in the CD-ROM's Gallery section.

Template 730 Fund Raising

Civic non-profit Web sites are designed for political fundraising or civic action groups. The design features identical home page and subpage layouts and can be adapted to any civic or poltiical use.

Figure 7-9: Template 730 home page

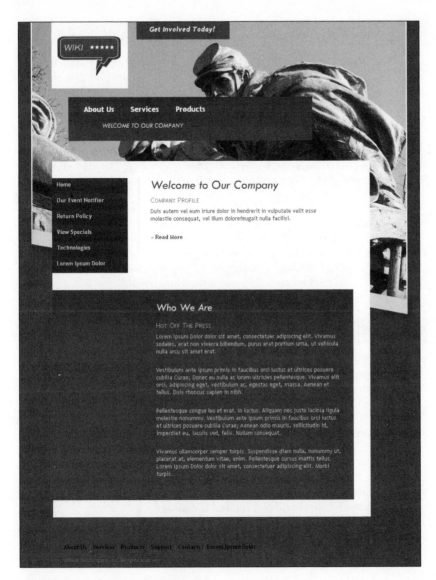

Figure 7-10: Template 730 subpage

Template Developer	Ken Milhous
Filename and Location	CD-ROM: `\Templates\Chapter 7\73\730`
Variations on this Design	731 732
Site Development Detail	Procedures and supporting information on placing content, links, and Web site images are presented in Chapter 3.

Design Summary

Recommended Use

Design engages the reader with a tagline at the very top of both the home page and subpages and frames two principal article areas with links to areas within the site. It is best used for information-intensive applications to engage community building and fundraising.

Look and Feel

Dark background sets off a dynamic design built around rectangular frames in white, blue, and black. The design is blunt and draws attention, with article areas clearly set off from one another.

Medium- to high-density design places main navigation items both at the top and side of the home page and subpages, with special emphasis on the first three items shown at the top. The tagline is a special feature of this design that is used to place a political theme or other message prominently on each page of the site.

Content Plan

Content Plan Overview

Before entering content in your site, make a list of the Web page labels and filenames you will use to build your Web site skeleton. Detailed coverage on building your content plan is presented in Chapter 3.

Subpages

Design supports six subpages. The first three main navigation items are featured with special emphasis at the top of the design, six main navigation items appear at the left in a sidebar, and the first five are featured as footer navigation at the bottom. Identify and write down the screen labels and the related filenames.

Articles

Home page and subpages feature two article areas, each with links at the end.

Copy the Template

Follow these steps to copy the template to your hard drive:

1. Access the \Templates\Chapter 7\73\730 folder on your CD-ROM.

2. Drag the \730 folder to your desktop or copy and paste the \730 folder to your desktop.

Template Headings and Tags

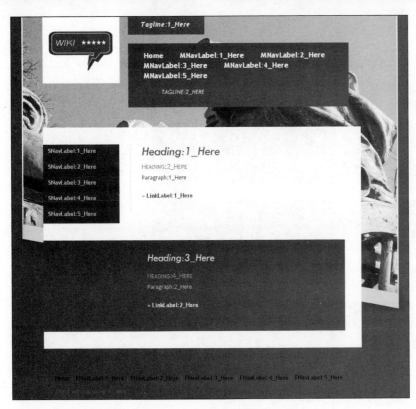

Figure 7-11: Template 730 home page token reference

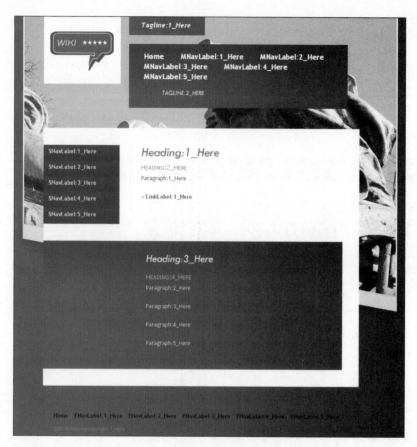

Figure 7-12: Template 730 subpage token reference

Building Your Site Step-by-Step: 730 Fund Raising Websites

Building the Site Skeleton

Use the following set of operations to enter the central navigation. Perform the exact same operations within `index.html` and `subpage.html`. Web site navigation and building the site skeleton are presented in Chapter 3.

Note that when opening `index.html` or `subpage.html` in Internet Explorer from your hard drive, a security message may appear. Click for more options, and choose to display the full content so the template displays correctly.

1. Place navigation labels

Review the list of subpage labels and filenames from your content plan. You place the labels for subpage 1 at the top (`MNav`) and bottom (`FNav`) of your page. See Figures 7-11 for home and 7-12 for subpages.

1. Open `index.html` in your text editor.

2. Find `MNavLabel:1_Here` and replace the token with the label for subpage 1.

3. Find `FNavLabel:1_Here` and replace the token with the label for subpage 1.

4. Repeat Steps 2 and 3 for `MNavLabel` and `FNavLabel` 2, 3, 4, and 5.

2. Place navigation links

Review the list of subpage labels and filenames from your content plan. In the following operation you will place the links to the filename for subpage 1 at the top (`MNav`) and bottom (`FNav`) of your page. Enter all filenames in lowercase.

1. Find `MNavURL:1_Here` and replace the token with the filename you selected for subpage 1.

2. Find `FNavURL:1_Here` and replace the token with the filename you selected for subpage 1.

3. Repeat Steps 1 and 2 for `MNavURL` and `FNavURL` 2, 3, 4, and 5.

3. Place sidebar elements

Use the sidebar's five subnavigation labels and links to link to any of your subpages.

You can enter these elements here so they are the same on home and subpage. If you want to set up the sidebar to be different on your home and various subpages, perform these steps when you edit those individual pages.

1. Find `SNavLabel:1_Here` and replace the token with the desired label text.

2. Find `FNavURL:1_Here` and replace the token with the filename of the link destination.

3. Repeat Steps 1 and 2 for `SNavURL` and `SNavURL` 2, 3, 4, and 5.

4. Place special features
           Place the text of the Tagline and Web site copyright in your pages.

1. Find `Tagline:1_Here` and replace the token with your page tagline text.

2. Find `Tagline:2_Here` and replace the token with your page tagline text. If you elect to enter a different tagline for your home and subpages, perform this operation when editing the individual pages.

3. Find `WebsiteCopyright:1_Here` and replace the token with your Web site copyright text.

4. Save and close `index.html` in your text editor.

5. Set up the subpage template
           Perform the same set of edits that you completed for the `index.html` file on the subpage master template file, `subpage.html`.

1. Open `subpage.html` in your text editor.

2. Return to the beginning of this section ("Building the Site Skeleton"), and start with main Step 1, "Place navigation labels."

3. Complete main Steps 1, 2, and 3 using the `subpage.html` file instead of the `index.html` file.

4. Save `subpage.html` in your text editor. Do not rename the file.

Creating Subpage Files

6. Create subpage files
           Use the Save As feature in your text editor to save the `subpage.html` template with the first of the subpage filenames you selected in your content plan. Repeat this to create all subpages listed in your content plan.

Save all files to the \730 folder on your desktop.

1. Verify that `subpage.html` is open in your text editor.

2. Choose File ➪ Save As or similar from your text editor. Enter the filename you selected for subpage 1, and click OK.

3.   Repeat Step 2 for all subpages in your content plan.

4.   Repeat Step 2 for any linked articles or catalog detail pages you identified in your content plan.

---

7. Display your site

Open your site to check that your labels and pages display correctly.

1.   Launch index.html from your computer by double-clicking the filename, or choose File ⇨ Open (from most browsers) to open it in your broswer. An empty home page should appear.

2.   Click the navigation links at the top and bottom of the home page and you should see empty subpage pages.

3.   Close the empty site skeleton.

Placing Content in the Home Page

8. Place home articles

Place headings and paragraph text for the articles in index.html (see Figure 7-11).

1.   Open index.html in your text editor.

2.   Find Heading:1_Here and replace the token with your heading text.

3.   Find Heading:2_Here and replace the token with your heading text.

4.   Find Paragraph:1_Here and replace the token with your paragraph text.

5.   Find LinkLabel:1_Here and replace the token with the label text for this link.

6.   Find LinkURL:1_Here and replace the token with the filename you have selected to be accessed from this link.

7.   Find Heading:3_Here and replace the token with your heading text.

8.   Find Heading:4_Here and replace the token with your heading text.

9. Find `Paragraph:2_Here` and replace the token with your paragraph text.

10. Find `LinkLabel:2_Here` and replace the token with the label text for this link.

11. Find `LinkURL:2_Here` and replace the token with the filename you have selected to be accessed from this link.

12. Save `index.html` in your text editor.

Placing Content in Subpages

Use the following operations to place content into all of your site subpages. Use the subpage token reference (see Figure 7-12) to see the position of the content and label tokens. Repeat this operation to enter content in all of your subpages.

9. Place subpage articles   Place article headings and text in your subpages.

1. Open the selected subpage in your text editor.

2. Find `Heading:1_Here` and replace the token with your heading text.

3. Find `Heading:2_Here` and replace the token with your heading text.

4. Find `Paragraph:1_Here` and replace the token with your paragraph text.

5. Find `LinkLabel:1_Here` and replace the token with the label text for this link.

6. Find `LinkURL:1_Here` and replace the token with the filename you have selected to be accessed from this link.

7. Find `Heading:3_Here` and replace the token with your heading text.

8. Find `Heading:4_Here` and replace the token with your heading text.

9. Find `Paragraph:2_Here` and replace the token with your paragraph text. Repeat for `Paragraph` 3, 4, and 5.

10. Save and close the file when you have finished editing.

11. Click to activate index.html. (You may need to single or double-click your mouse to activate the file.)

12. View your completed site in your browser. Close the browser when you have completed your review.

Finalizing Your Site

10. Edit site logo and pictures

Turn to Chapter 3 for explanation and procedures to replace the default template logo and images with your own logo and images.

11. Display your Web site

Launch index.html from your computer by double-clicking the filename, or choose File ⇨ Open. Check your work in your browser window.

12. Edit and adjust

Make edits by opening up your home page or subpage page files in your text editor and making edits to the content. Be sure to edit only your content and not to disturb any of the surrounding code.

13. Publish

The basic parameters of what you should provide to your Web hosting company are outlined in Chapter 3. For the specifics on actually posting your live site to the Web, contact your service provider for details.

Variations

Variation 731 Overview

This variation presents the design with navigation and content areas in deep shades of red over a dark gray background. A floral photograph replaces the anchor image in the default design.

See the images in the CD-ROM's Gallery section.

Variation 732 Overview

In this version, the dominant color for navigation and article presentation areas are green gradients with the design presented over a dark gray background. The anchor image is a desert scene.

See the images in the CD-ROM's Gallery section.

Template 740 Church

Churches or religious organizations have a Web site that is designed to project a serene and relaxing presence. Fonts and imagery have a softer look and feel and the impression is very distinctly different from a business or community organization site.

Figure 7-13: Template 740 home page

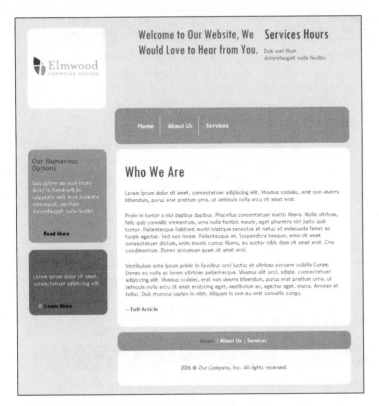

Figure 7-14: Template 740 subpage

Template Developer	Ken Milhous
Filename and Location	CD-ROM: \Templates\Chapter 7\74\740
Variations on this Design	741 742
Site Development Detail	Procedures and supporting information on placing content, links, and Web site images are presented in Chapter 3.

Design Summary

Recommended Use

Distinctive font display for headings in this site establishes an otherworldly mood and presentation from first glance. This site is best used as an institutional and community site for a religious or spiritual group, either built around a community house of worship or an online community.

Look and Feel

Design is built around a series of color accent areas within a soft off-white background. The goal is to create a welcoming and calming site presence, enhanced through the use of the distinctive headline display.

Design is best used as a medium- to low-density layout to create the most engaging impression. This site features a unique page heading configuration that allows you to place two headings and supporting text at the top of the page, which can be present on all pages or customized for each one. As a common feature of all pages, this design element lets you place the key messages of your group consistently throughout the design.

Content Plan

Content Plan Overview

Before entering content in your site, make a list of the Web page labels and filenames you will use to build your Web site skeleton. Detailed coverage on building your content plan is presented in Chapter 3.

Subpages

Design two programmable main and footer navigation links with a dedicated home link. Identify and write down the screen labels and the related filenames.

Theme Headings

Use Heading 1 and Heading 2 elements with paragraph text as recurring theme elements across all pages (the default operation) or enter text for them individually on each page with key messages or inspirational content.

Action Item Blocks

Action item sidebar accent areas are included, one on the home page and two on the subpages. You can enter action item 1 across all pages in the home page and subpage or enter both separately on the home page and on individual subpages (the default operation for this site).

Articles

In addition to the top page headings, there are two article areas on the home page and one featured article on the subpage layout, each of which contain continuing links.

Copy the Template

Follow these steps to copy the template to your hard drive:

1. Access the `\Templates\Chapter 7\74\740` folder on your CD-ROM.

2. Drag the `\740` folder to your desktop or copy and paste the `\740` folder to your desktop.

Template Headings and Tags

Figure 7-15: Template 740 home page token reference

Figure 7-16: Template 740 subpage token reference

Building Your Site Step-by-Step: 740 Church

Building the Site Skeleton

Use the following set of operations to enter the central navigation. Perform the exact same operations within `index.html` and `subpage.html`. Web site navigation and building the site skeleton are presented in Chapter 3.

Note that when opening `index.html` or `subpage.html` in Internet Explorer from your hard drive, a security message may appear. Click for more options, and choose to display the full content so the template displays correctly.

1. Place navigation labels

Review the list of subpage labels and filenames from your content plan. You place the labels for subpage 1 at the top (MNav) and bottom (FNav) of your page. See Figures 7-15 for home and 7-16 for subpages.

1. Open `index.html` in your text editor.

2. Find `MNavLabel:1_Here` and replace the token with the label for subpage 1.

3. Find `FNavLabel:1_Here` and replace the token with the label for subpage 1.

4. Repeat Steps 2 and 3 for `MNavLabel` and `FNavLabel` 2.

2. Place navigation links

Review the list of subpage labels and filenames from your content plan. In the following operation you will place the links to the filename for subpage 1 at the top (MNav) and bottom (FNav) of your page. Enter all filenames in lowercase.

1. Find `MNavURL:1_Here` and replace the token with filename you selected for subpage 1.

2. Find `FNavURL:1_Here` and replace the token with the filename you selected for subpage 1.

3. Repeat Steps 1 and 2 for `MNavURL` and `FNavURL` 2.

3. Place theme headings

This operation enables you to place the same theme message and supporting text across every page of your site. You have the option to apply these steps individually to the home page and individual subpages if you want to present different themes at the top of the page design.

1. Find `Heading:1_Here` and replace the token with your page tagline text.

2. Find `Heading:2_Here` and replace the token with your page tagline text.

3. Find `Paragraph:1_Here` and replace the token with your page tagline text.

4. Place special features

The logo in this template includes a mouse over image label. When the mouse is placed over the image, this label appears. The image label should carry a message associated with the logo. Note that if you do not replace this token, the text of the token appears when you mouse over the image. Also place Web site copyright for both home and subpage.

1. Find `ImageLabel:1_Here` and replace with desired content for the mouse over image label. Place the text of the Web site copyright in your pages.

2. Find `WebsiteCopyright:1_Here` and replace the token with your Web site copyright text.

3. Save and close `index.html` in your text editor.

5. Set up the subpage template

Perform the same set of edits that you completed for the `index.html` file on the subpage master template file, `subpage.html`.

1. Open `subpage.html` in your text editor.

2. Return to the beginning of this section ("Building the Site Skeleton"), and start with main Step 1, "Place navigation labels."

3. Complete main Steps 1, 2, 3, and 4 using the `subpage.html` file instead of the `index.html` file.

4. Save `subpage.html` in your text editor. Do not rename the file.

Creating Subpage Files

6. Create subpage files

Use the Save As feature in your text editor to save the `subpage.html` template with the first of the subpage filenames you selected in your content plan. Repeat this to create all subpages listed in your content plan.

Save all files to the `\740` folder on your desktop.

1. Verify that `subpage.html` is open in your text editor.

2. Choose File ➪ Save As or similar from your text editor. Enter the filename you selected for subpage 1, and click OK.

3. Repeat Step 2 for all subpages in your content plan.

4. Repeat Step 2 for any linked articles or catalog detail pages you identified in your content plan.

---

7. Display your site

Open your site to check that your labels and pages display correctly.

1. Launch `index.html` from your computer by double-clicking the filename, or choose File ➪ Open (from most browsers) to open it in your broswer. An empty home page should appear.

2. Click the navigation links at the top and bottom of the home page and you should see empty subpage pages.

3. Close the empty site skeleton.

Placing Content in the Home Page

8. Place home action items

Place the headings and paragraph text for the featured article in `index.html` (see Figure 7-15).

1. Open `index.html` in your text editor.

2. Find `AILabel:1_Here` and replace the token with your action item heading text.

3. Find `AIURL:1_Here` and replace the token with the filename for the action item link.

4. Find `AIParagraph:1_Here` and replace the token with your action item paragraph text.

5. Find `LinkLabel:1_Here` and replace the token with the "Read More" or another title of your choosing for the action item link.

6. Find `LinkURL:1_Here` and replace the token with the destination filename for the action item link.

---

9. Place home articles

Place the headings and paragraph text for the articles in `index.html` (see Figure 7-15).

1. Find `Heading:3_Here` and replace the token with your heading text.

2. Find `Paragraph:2_Here` and replace the token with your paragraph text.

3. Find `LinkLabel:2_Here` and replace the token with the label text for this link.

4. Find `LinkURL:2_Here` and replace the token with the filename you have selected to be accessed from this link.

5. Find `Heading:4_Here` and replace the token with your heading text.

6. Find `Paragraph:3_Here` and replace the token with your paragraph text.

7. Find `LinkLabel:3_Here` and replace the token with the label text for this link.

8. Find `LinkURL:3_Here` and replace the token with the filename you have selected to be accessed from this link.

9. Save `index.html` in your text editor.

Placing Content in Subpages

Use the following operations to place content into all of your site subpages. Use the subpage token reference (see Figure 7-16) to see the position of the content and label tokens. Repeat this operation to enter content in all of your subpages.

10. Place subpage action items   Place the headings and paragraph text for the featured article in the selected subpage.

1. Open the selected subpage in your text editor.

2. Find `AILabel:1_Here` and replace the token with your action item heading text. Repeat for `AILabel` 2.

3. Find AIURL:1_Here and replace the token with the filename for the action item link. Repeat for `AIURL` 2.

4. Find `AIParagraph:1_Here` and replace the token with your action item paragraph text. Repeat for `AIParagraph` 2.

5. Find `LinkLabel:1_Here` and replace the token with the "Read More" or another title of your choosing for the action item link. Repeat for `LinkLabel` 2.

6. Find `LinkURL:1_Here` and replace the token with the destination filename for the action item link. Repeat for `LinkURL` 2.

11. Place subpage article	Place the headings and paragraph text for the articles in the selected subpage.

1. Find `Heading:3_Here` and replace the token with your heading text.

2. Find `Paragraph:2_Here` and replace the token with your paragraph text.

3. Find `LinkLabel:3_Here` and replace the token with the label text for this link.

4. Find `LinkURL:3_Here` and replace the token with the filename you have selected to be accessed from this link.

5. Save and close the file when you have finished editing.

Finalizing Your Site

12. Edit site logo and pictures	Turn to Chapter 3 for explanation and procedures to replace the default template logo and images with your own logo and images.
13. Display your Web site	Launch `index.html` from your computer by double-clicking the filename, or choose File ➪ Open. Check your work in your browser window.
14. Edit and adjust	Make edits by opening up your home page or subpage page files in your text editor and making edits to the content. Be sure to edit only your content and not to disturb any of the surrounding code.
15. Publish	The basic parameters of what you should provide to your Web hosting company are outlined in Chapter 3. For the specifics on actually posting your live site to the Web, contact your service provide for details.

Variations

Variation 741 Overview	In this version of the design, the background and principal navigation areas are presented as shades of green.

See the images in the CD-ROM's Gallery section. |
| **Variation 742 Overview** | This variation uses dark green navigation areas and a light green sidebar over a solid gray background.

See the images in the CD-ROM's Gallery section. |

Template 750 Communities of Interest

A speciality site is designed to showcase communities of interest locally or across the Web. You can adapt the design to present any community of common interest, including cultural, informational, political, or action groups.

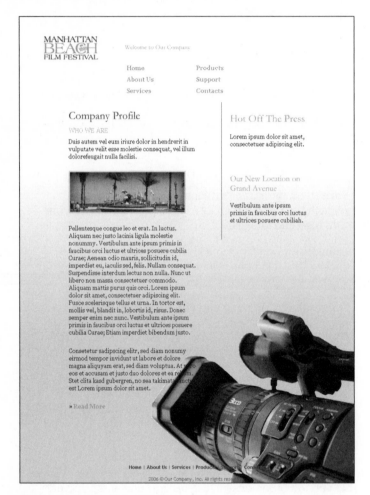

Figure 7-17: Template 750 home page

Figure 7-18: Template 750 subpage

Template Developer	Ken Milhous
Filename and Location	CD-ROM: `\Templates\Chapter 7\75\750`
Variations on this Design	751 752
Site Development Detail	Procedures and supporting information on placing content, links, and Web site images are presented in Chapter 3.

Design Summary

Recommended Use

A simple and expansive design to present content of interest to a community. You can easily adapt this design for any community interest purpose or content.

Look and Feel

The design is built around a series of colored font headings over a gradient gray background. The visual presentation is simple and unobtrusive, and the audience's attention is drawn to the headlines and content articles feature.

A medium- to low-density layout, this design features a feature article with color emphasis in the heading font and supporting articles in the home page and a single article in the subpage. The theme heading at the top of the page can be used to carry a group tagline or key message.

Content Plan

Content Plan Overview

Before entering content in your site, make a list of the Web page labels and filenames you will use to build your Web site skeleton. Detailed coverage on building your content plan is presented in Chapter 3.

Subpages

This design supports a dedicated home link and five principal subpages. Identify and write down the screen labels and the related filenames.

Theme Heading

You can use Heading 1 as a recurring theme element across all pages (the default operation) or enter text for it individually on each page with key messages or inspirational content.

Articles

In addition to the top page heading, there is a feature article with links and two supporting articles on the home page, and a single featured article on the subpage. Featured articles in this design offer multiple headings to create main and subheading text leading into the article.

Copy the Template

Follow these steps to copy the template to your hard drive:

1. Access the \Templates\Chapter 7\75\750 folder on your CD-ROM.

2. Drag the \750 folder to your desktop or copy and paste the \750 folder to your desktop.

Template Headings and Tags

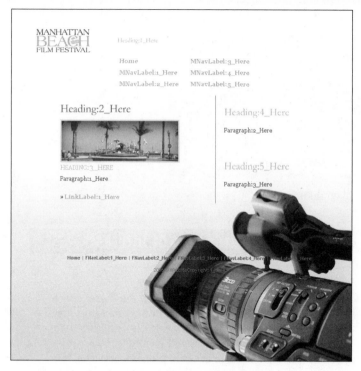

Figure 7-19: Template 750 home page token reference

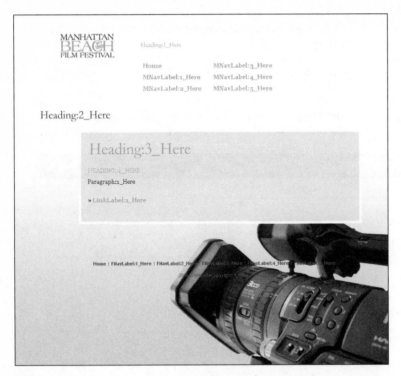

Figure 7-20: Template 750 subpage token reference

Building Your Site Step-by-Step: 750 Communities of Interest

Building the Site Skeleton

Use the following set of operations to enter the central navigation. Perform the exact same operations within `index.html` and `subpage.html`. Web site navigation and building the site skeleton are presented in Chapter 3.

Note that when opening `index.html` or `subpage.html` in Internet Explorer from your hard drive, a security message may appear. Click for more options, and choose to display the full content so the template displays correctly.

1. Place navigation labels	Review the list of subpage labels and filenames from your content plan. You place the labels for subpage 1 at the top (MNav) and bottom (FNav) of your page. See Figures 7-19 for home and 7-20 for subpages.

1. Open `index.html` in your text editor.

2. Find `MNavLabel:1_Here` and replace the token with the label for subpage 1.

3. Find `FNavLabel:1_Here` and replace the token with the label for subpage 1.

4. Repeat Steps 2 and 3 for `MNavLabel` and `FNavLabel` 2, 3, 4, and 5. |
| **2. Place navigation links** | Review the list of subpage labels and filenames from your content plan. In the following operation you place the links to the filename for subpage 1 at the top (MNav) and bottom (FNav) of your page. Enter all filenames in lowercase.

1. Find `MNavURL:1_Here` and replace the token with the filename you selected for subpage 1.

2. Find `FNavURL:1_Here` and replace the token with the filename you selected for subpage 1.

3. Repeat Steps 1 and 2 for `MNavURL` and `FNavURL` 2, 3, 4, and 5. |
| **3. Place theme heading** | This operation enables you to place the same theme message and supporting text across every page of your site. You have the option to apply this step individually to the home page and individual subpages if you want to present different themes at the top of the page design.

1. Find `Heading:1_Here` and replace the token with your page tagline text. |

4. Place special features	Place the text of the Web site copyright in your pages.

1. Find `WebsiteCopyright:1_Here` and replace the token with your Web site copyright text.

2. Save and close `index.html` in your text editor.

5. Set up the subpage template	Perform the same set of edits that you completed for the `index.html` file on the subpage master template file, `subpage.html`.

1. Open `subpage.html` in your text editor.

2. Return to the beginning of this section ("Building the Site Skeleton"), and start with main Step 1, "Place navigation labels."

3. Complete main Steps 1, 2, 3, and 4 using the `subpage.html` file instead of the `index.html` file.

4. Save `subpage.html` in your text editor. Do not rename the file.

Creating Subpage Files

6. Create subpage files	Use the Save As feature in your text editor to save the `subpage.html` template with the first of the subpage filenames you selected in your content plan. Repeat this to create all subpages listed in your content plan.
	Save all files to the \750 folder on your desktop.

1. Verify that `subpage.html` is open in your text editor.

2. Choose File ➪ Save As or similar from your text editor. Enter the filename you selected for subpage 1, and click OK.

3. Repeat Step 2 for all subpages in your content plan.

4. Repeat Step 2 for any linked articles or catalog detail pages you identified in your content plan.

7. Display your site

Open your site to check that your labels and pages display correctly.

1. Launch `index.html` from your computer by double-clicking the filename, or choose File ⇨ Open (from most browsers) to open it in your broswer. An empty home page should appear.

2. Click the navigation links at the top and bottom of the home page and you should see empty subpage pages.

3. Close the empty site skeleton.

Placing Content in the Home Page

8. Place home articles

Place the headings and paragraph text for the articles in `index.html` (see Figure 7-19).

1. Open `index.html` in your text editor.

2. Find `Heading:2_Here` and replace the token with your heading text.

3. Find `Heading:3_Here` and replace the token with your heading text.

4. Find `Paragraph:1_Here` and replace the token with your paragraph text.

5. Find `LinkLabel:1_Here` and replace the token with the label text for this link.

6. Find `LinkURL:1_Here` and replace the token with the filename you have selected to be accessed from this link.

7. Find `Heading:4_Here` and replace the token with your heading text.

8. Find `Paragraph:2_Here` and replace the token with your paragraph text.

9. Find `Heading:5_Here` and replace the token with your heading text.

10. Find `Paragraph:3_Here` and replace the token with your paragraph text.

11. Save `index.html` in your text editor.

Placing Content in Subpages

Use the following operations to place content into all of your site subpages. Use the subpage token reference (see Figure 7-20) to see the position of the content and label tokens. Repeat this operation to enter content in all of your subpages.

---

9. Place subpage articles   Place article headings and text in your subpages.

  1. Open the selected subpage in your text editor.

  2. Find `Heading:2_Here` and replace the token with your heading text.

  3. Find `Heading:3_Here` and replace the token with your heading text.

  4. Find `Heading:4_Here` and replace the token with your heading text.

  5. Find `Paragraph:1_Here` and replace the token with your paragraph text.

  6. Find `LinkLabel:1_Here` and replace the token with the label text for this link.

  7. Find `LinkURL:1_Here` and replace the token with the filename you have selected to be accessed from this link.

  8. Save and close the file when you have finished editing.

Finalizing Your Site

10. Edit site logo and pictures   Turn to Chapter 3 for explanation and procedures to replace the default template logo and images with your own logo and images.

11. Display your Web site   Launch `index.html` from your computer by double-clicking the filename, or choose File ⇨ Open. Check your work in your browser window.

12. Edit and adjust   Make edits by opening up your home page or subpage page files in your text editor and making edits to the content. Be sure to edit only your content and not to disturb any of the surrounding code.

13. Publish   The basic parameters of what you should provide to your Web hosting company are outlined in Chapter 3. For the specifics on actually posting your live site to the Web, contact your service provider for details.

Variations

Variation 751 Overview   This variation uses different heading and text font treatments from the default design while retaining the essential background colors.

See the images in the CD-ROM's Gallery section.

Variation 752 Overview   In this version of the design the anchor photograph is presented on a solid black background and all text elements on the Home and subpage are reversed-out yellow or blue on black.

See the images in the CD-ROM's Gallery section.

✦   ✦   ✦

Entertainment Templates

The Web is a perfect medium to present entertainment because it engages the audience in ways that passive media like television cannot. An entertainment Web site allows the audience to discover the experience, whether it is a play, concert, television show, film, or game.

The essence of an effective site for a show, cultural product, or personality is to memorably convey the name, identity, and specifics. The goal is to get the audience involved by communicating the essence of the entertaining experience, and connecting the dots between that experience and the tastes and interests of the audience.

About Entertainment Templates

Entertainment templates are designed with an emphasis on visual style. Both the look and feel are important when you select the visual environment to carry your message. Some styles create dark environments, accented with bits of color. Others offer open and colorful presentations that convey brightness and light. Color on the Web plays a role that is analogous to music in movies: it telegraphs the emotional tone of the content to the audience. The style you select defines the mood for your content and invites the audience to continue exploring the site to discover more.

You can adapt the styles and variations shown in this template family to just about any entertainment purpose you might have. The example material shown with each site illustrates the potential uses for the design, but they certainly aren't limited to the examples presented. Some of the templates featured in other chapters might also be suitable for communicating your concept.

Engaging the audience

Cultural events and shows touch us both mentally and emotionally. A Web site can create a mood through its look and feel, and build on that emotional experience with information and discovery experiences that enable the individual to participate and get connected.

Once you have selected the template with the style you feel is appropriate, your next task is to clearly identify and brand your material. For entertainment offerings, branding is the process of naming your product clearly and distinctively. It's important to clearly establish the identity of the show, performer, or product. Use taglines and headings to focus on specifics of the entertainment experience or performer.

When introducing a new entertainment production or performer, it's helpful to establish associations with similar cultural experiences or worlds that the user may be familiar with. Entertainment products are often marketed to trigger associations — for example, reminding the audience of other movies that are similar to the one you are promoting, or creating a connection through a similar, well-known performer.

Style and experience

Visual appearance is only one dimension of the Web experience for entertainment content. Language is an equally important element of style. In the world of culture it's not just what you say but also the way you say it that adds to the experience.

Every movie, book, musical performance, or other cultural work tends to create its own language. Quotes from characters reflecting attitude, slang expressions, or witty and sharp turns of phrase are all ways that entertainment finds its way into your daily life. When you are developing this type of site, pay particular attention to the words you use and how they add to and develop the effectiveness of the presentation.

You may want to write the link labels to your subpages using stylized words or terms to build and expand your content, so it becomes part of the experience. Given that your purpose is to capture the audience's attention, try using verbs as links to your major content pages. Verbs like "discover," "see," "find," "explore," and "experience" can light up your page and motivate the audience to explore further.

Specifics

Beyond style, you must communicate the specifics. In entertainment sites, this usually takes the form of some kind of calendar, listing, or other direct notification of where the show is being offered (in a theater, on TV, or on the Web), and when it will take place. It is best to feature immediate details like these as an announcement or featured text on the home page and on subpages so they are always accessible.

Depending on the particular show or experience, you may also need to provide event details. These usually include bios of the artists, the production team, and significant others involved in the event or product. You can supplement background information with links to external sites that illustrate other work by the artists and establish clear associations between the current work and other works that are familiar to the audience.

Audience and community

Entertainment sites are a means to build awareness and an audience around your cultural venture. To make the most of this opportunity, you want to engage and motivate the audience to take action — for example, to send e-mail requests for free digital pictures about the production or product.

The audience can play a vital role in making your product legitimate to other readers. Featuring audience quotes and comments about an entertainment experience is a time-honored showbiz marketing technique. You can integrate comments like this into a dedicated audience page in your site, or can feature them in sidebar areas using text labels or subheadings that are available in the selected design.

Most important of all is to motivate the visitors to your site to share your URL with their friends. Make a point of including suggestions for them to e-mail your URL to others or to share it in instant messaging discussions or text messaging. This kind of electronic word of mouth can be one of the most valuable outcomes, helping you build your audience from the ground up.

Tip   Instead of navigating from the root of the CD to locate a template, you can click the Templates link in the CD browser application to directly access the chapters on the CD. For faster access, click the Gallery link in the CD browser application to view a listing of all templates. Then click any View Files link to view the files for that template.

Template 810 Studio Site

Studio site designed for use by entertainment companies, performers, producers, or any program or for media promotional purpose.

Figure 8-1: Template 810 home page

Figure 8-2: Template 810 subpage

Template Developer	Ken Milhous
Filename and Location	CD-ROM: \Templates\Chapter 8\81\810
Variations on this Design	811 812
Site Development Detail	Procedures and supporting information on placing content, links, and Web site images are presented in Chapter 3.

Design Summary

Recommended Use

Stylish entertainment destination site designed to showcase news items and information about an entertainment production. home page displays eight prominent links to interior pages, and interior pages create cross-links to all eight with additional headings and text for feature information covering the entertainment production and details.

Look and Feel

Textured black background is set off by vivid red and yellow blocks with stylized text to get maximum attention. This design allows you to emphasize key hot points of a production or performer or feature news items on a group of productions for an entertainment destination site.

The low-density, high-impact home page leads the site, and subpages offer greater text density to carry information about each of the major featured items.

Content Plan

Content Plan Overview

Before entering content in your site, make a list of the Web page labels and filenames you will use to build your Web site skeleton. Detailed coverage on building your content plan is presented in Chapter 3.

Home Page Link Layout

The home page for this site includes only links and no article areas or other paragraph content. Article links are presented in a stylized grid design against color backgrounds. All article or other content for this design must be placed in subpages.

Subpages

Design is a catalog layout that supports seven main and footer navigation links with a dedicated home page link.. The home page is set up as a display design, featuring the main navigation links in a large grid of colored boxes. Identify and write down the screen labels and the related filenames.

Article Areas

Home page carries no article or introduction space. The subpages feature three headings and supporting text to carry information and headlines for each of the major featured items and other content.

Sidebars

Design supports a sidebar area on the subpage to link to the eight featured areas in addition to the standard footer navigation area at the bottom of the screen.

Copy the Template

Follow these steps to copy the template to your hard drive:

1. Access the \Templates\Chapter 8\81\810 folder on your CD-ROM.

2. Drag the \810 folder to your desktop or copy and paste the \810 folder to your desktop.

Template Headings and Tags

Figure 8-3: Template 810 home page token reference

Figure 8-4: Template 810 subpage page token reference

Building Your Site Step-by-Step: 810 Studio Site

Building the Site Skeleton

Use the following set of operations to enter the central navigation. Perform the exact same operations within index.html and subpage.html. Web site navigation and building the site skeleton are presented in Chapter 3.

Note that when opening index.html or subpage.html in Internet Explorer from your hard drive, a security message may appear. Click for more options, and choose to display the full content so the template displays correctly.

---

1. Place navigation labels

Review the list of subpage labels and filenames from your content plan. Main navigation items (MNav) appear in boxed areas in the home page layout and in a sidebar on any the subpages. See Figures 8-3 for home and 8-4 for subpages.

1. Open index.html in your text editor.

2. Find MNavLabel:1_Here and replace the token with the label for subpage 1. Repeat this action for MNavLabel 2, 3, 4, 5, 6, and 7.

3. Find MNavURL:1_Here and replace the token with filename you selected for subpage 1. Repeat this action for MNavURL 2, 3, 4, 5, 6, and 7.

2. Place footer navigation	Review the list of subpage labels and filenames from your content plan. Footer navigation (FNav) appears at the bottom of home and subpages.

1. Find FNavLabel:1_Here and replace the token with the label for subpage 1. Repeat this action for FNavLabel 2, 3, 4, 5, 6, and 7.

2. Find FNavURL:1_Here and replace the token with the filename you selected for subpage 1. Repeat this action for FNavURL 2, 3, 4, 5, 6, and 7.

3. Place special features	Place the text of the Web site copyright in your pages.

1. Find WebsiteCopyright:1_Here and replace the token with your Web site copyright text.

2. Save and close index.html in your text editor.

4. Set up the subpage template	Perform the same set of edits that you completed for the index.html file on the subpage master template file, subpage.html.

1. Open subpage.html in your text editor.

2. Return to the beginning of this section ("Building the Site Skeleton"), and start with main Step 1, "Place navigation labels."

3. Complete main Steps 1, 2, and 3 using the subpage.html file instead of the index.html file.

4. Save subpage.html in your text editor. Do not rename the file.

Creating Subpage Files

5. Create subpage files	Use the Save As feature in your text editor to save the subpage.html template with the first of the subpage filenames you selected in your content plan. Repeat this to create all subpages listed in your content plan.
	Save all files to the \810 folder on your desktop.

1. Verify that subpage.html is open in your text editor.

2. Choose File ⇨ Save As or similar from your text editor. Enter the filename you selected for subpage 1, and click OK.

3. Repeat Step 2 for all subpages in your content plan.

4. Repeat Step 2 for any linked articles or catalog detail pages you identified in your content plan.

---

6. Display your site

Open your site to check that your labels and pages display correctly.

1. Launch `index.html` from your computer by double-clicking the filename, or choose File ⇨ Open (from most browsers) to open it in your browser. An empty home page should appear.

2. Click the navigation links at the top and bottom of the home page and you should see empty subpage pages.

3. Close the empty site skeleton.

Placing Content in Subpages

Use the following operations to place content into all of your site subpages. Use the subpage token reference (see Figure 8-4) to see the position of the content and label tokens. Repeat this operation to enter content in all of your subpages.

---

7. Place subpage headings

Use the following operations to place content into all of the named subpages you created from `subpage.html` (see Figure 8-4).

1. Select and open a named subpage for your site in your text editor.

2. Find `Heading:1_Here` and replace the token with your heading 1 text.

3. Find `Paragraph:1_Here` and replace the token with your paragraph text.

4. Find `Heading:2_Here` and replace the token with your heading 2 text.

5. Find `Paragraph:2_Here` and replace the token with your paragraph text.

6. Find `Heading:3_Here` and replace the token with your heading 3 text.

7. Find `Paragraph:3_Here` and replace the token with your paragraph text.

8. Save and close the file when you have finished editing.

Finalizing Your Site

8. Edit site logo and pictures Turn to Chapter 3 for explanation and procedures to replace the default template logo and images with your own logo and images.

9. Display your Web site Launch `index.html` from your computer by double-clicking the filename, or choose File ➪ Open. Check your work in your browser window.

10. Edit and adjust Make edits by opening up your home page or subpage page files in your text editor and making edits to the content. Be sure to edit only your content and not to disturb any of the surrounding code.

11. Publish The basic parameters of what you should provide to your Web hosting company are outlined in Chapter 3. For the specifics on actually posting your live site to the Web, contact your service provider for details.

Variations

Variation 811 Overview This variation of the design places navigation and content in blue, yellow, and pink accent areas over a knotty wood photographic background.

See the images in the CD-ROM's Gallery section.

Variation 812 Overview This version of the design uses black, white, and red for the content presentation area, and the background image is strong black and white with an array of palm trees in silhouette.

See the images in the CD-ROM's Gallery section.

Template 820 Sports Site

A sports information site designed to present sports contests, a sports team, or a sports organization; or a fan site dedicated to an athlete or a team.

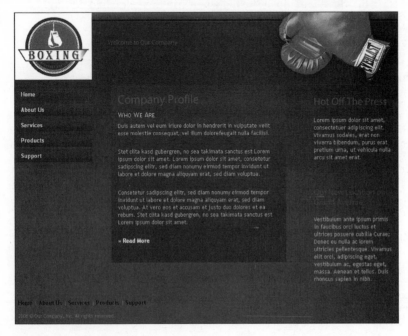

Figure 8-5: Template 820 home page

Figure 8-6: Template 820 subpage

Template Developer	Ken Milhous
Filename and Location	CD-ROM: \Templates\Chapter 8\82\820
Variations on this Design	821 822
Site Development Detail	Procedures and supporting information on placing content, links, and Web site images are presented in Chapter 3.

Design Summary

Recommended Use	Sports information site designed to present news and information about a sports organization. This layout is heavily headline driven with an emphasis on news items and featured information.
Look and Feel	Black background creates an edgy look and feel that is suitable for sports information or any entertainment content with a darker theme or more masculine interest.
	Medium-density layout offers feature links on the home pages and subpages, with information headings and text on both to carry lead stories or featured information.

Content Plan

Content Plan Overview

Before entering content in your site, make a list of the Web page labels and filenames you will use to build your Web site skeleton. Detailed coverage on building your content plan is presented in Chapter 3.

Subpages

Design is a catalog layout that supports four principal subpages through main and footer navigation links, plus a dedicated home link. Identify and write down the screen labels and the related filenames.

Article Areas

Home and subpages feature a main headline and supporting text and a "Read More" link to carry information and headlines for each of the major featured items and other content.

Sidebars

Design supports a sidebar area on the home and subpage to link to the four featured areas in addition to the standard footer navigation area at the bottom of the screen.

Copy the Template

Follow these steps to copy the template to your hard drive:

1. Access the `\Templates\Chapter 8\82\820` folder on your CD-ROM.

2. Drag the `\820` folder to your desktop or copy and paste the `\820` folder to your desktop.

Template Headings and Tags

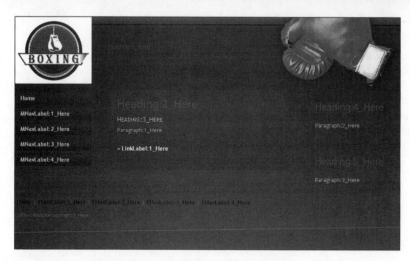

Figure 8-7: Template 820 home page token reference

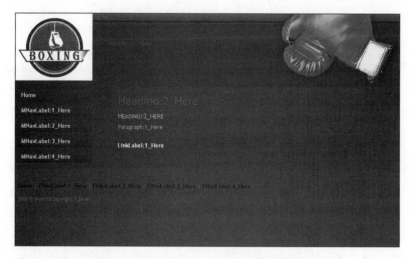

Figure 8-8: Template 820 subpage page token reference

Building Your Site Step-by-Step: 820 Sports Site

Building the Site Skeleton

Use the following set of operations to enter the central navigation. Perform the exact same operations within `index.html` and `subpage.html`. Web site navigation and building the site skeleton are presented in Chapter 3.

Note that when opening `index.html` or `subpage.html` in Internet Explorer from your hard drive, a security message may appear. Click for more options, and choose to display the full content so the template displays correctly.

1. Place navigation labels	Review the list of subpage labels and filenames from your content plan. Main navigation items (`MNav`) appear at the left of the home and subpages. See Figures 8-7 for home and 8-8 for subpages. 1. Open `index.html` in your text editor. 2. Find `MNavLabel:1_Here` and replace the token with the label for subpage 1. 3. Find `MNavURL:1_Here` and replace the token with filename you selected for subpage 1. 4. Repeat Steps 2 and 3 for `MNavLabel` and `MNavURL` 2, 3, and 4.
2. Place footer navigation	Review the list of subpage labels and filenames from your content plan. Footer navigation items (`FNav`) appear at the bottom of the home and subpages. 1. Find `FNavLabel:1_Here` and replace the token with the label for subpage 1. 2. Find `FNavURL:1_Here` and replace the token with the filename you selected for subpage 1. 3. Repeat Steps 1 and 2 for `FNavLabel` and `FNavURL` 2, 3, and 4.

3. Place special features	Place the text of the Web site copyright in your pages.

1. Find `WebsiteCopyright:1_Here` and replace the token with your Web site copyright text.

2. Save and close `index.html` in your text editor.

4. Set up the subpage template	Perform the same set of edits that you completed for the `index.html` file on the subpage master template file, `subpage.html`.

1. Open `subpage.html` in your text editor.

2. Return to the beginning of this section ("Building the Site Skeleton"), and start with main Step 1, "Place navigation labels."

3. Complete main Steps 1, 2, and 3 using the `subpage.html` file instead of the `index.html` file.

4. Save `subpage.html` in your text editor. Do not rename the file.

Creating Subpage Files

5. Create subpage files	Use the Save As feature in your text editor to save the `subpage.html` template with the first of the subpage filenames you selected in your content plan. Repeat this to create all subpages listed in your content plan.
	Save all files to the `\820` folder on your desktop.

1. Verify that `subpage.html` is open in your text editor.

2. Choose File ➪ Save As or similar from your text editor. Enter the filename you selected for subpage 1, and click OK.

3. Repeat Step 2 for all subpages in your content plan.

4. Repeat Step 2 for any linked articles or catalog detail pages you identified in your content plan.

6. Display your site

Open your site to check that your labels and pages display correctly.

1. Launch `index.html` from your computer by double-clicking the filename, or choose File ⇨ Open (from most browsers) to open it in your browser. An empty home page should appear.

2. Click the navigation links at the side and bottom of the home page and you should see empty subpage pages.

3. Close the empty site skeleton.

Placing Content in the Home Page

7. Place home feature article

Place the headings and paragraph text for the featured article in `index.html` (see Figure 8-7).

1. Open `index.html` in your text editor.

2. Find `Heading:1_Here` and replace the token with the heading text.

3. Find `Heading:2_Here` and replace the token with your heading text.

4. Find `Heading:3_Here` and replace the token with your heading text.

5. Find `Paragraph:1_Here` and replace the token with your paragraph text.

6. Find `LinkLabel:1_Here` and replace the token with the label text for this link. You can delete this token if you do not want to use this link.

7. Find `LinkURL:1_Here` and replace the token with the filename you have selected to be accessed from this link.

8. Place home sidebar articles

Place the headings and paragraph text for the two sidebar articles in `index.html` (see Figure 8-7).

1. Find `Heading:4_Here` and replace the token with your heading text.

2. Find `Paragraph:2_Here` and replace the token with your paragraph text.

3. Find `Heading:5_Here` and replace the token with your heading text.

4. Find `Paragraph:3_Here` and replace the token with your paragraph text.

5. Save `index.html` in your text editor.

Placing Content in Subpages

Use the following operations to place content into all of your site subpages. Use the subpage token reference (see Figure 8-8) to see the position of the content and label tokens. Repeat this operation to enter content in all of your subpages.

9. Place subpage articles	Place article headings and text into all of the named subpages you created from `subpage.html` (see Figure 8-8).

1. Select and open a named subpage for your site in your text editor.

2. Find `Heading:1_Here` and replace the token with the heading text.

3. Find `Heading:2_Here` and replace the token with your heading text.

4. Find `Heading:3_Here` and replace the token with your heading text.

5. Find `Paragraph:1_Here` and replace the token with your paragraph text.

6. Find `LinkLabel:1_Here` and replace the token with the label text for this link. You can delete this token if you do not want to use this link.

7. Find `LinkURL:1_Here` and replace the token with the filename you have selected to be accessed from this link.

8. Save and close the file when you have finished editing.

Finalizing Your Site

10. Edit site logo and pictures
Turn to Chapter 3 for explanation and procedures to replace the default template logo and images with your own logo and images.

11. Display your Web site
Launch `index.html` from your computer by double-clicking the filename, or choose File ➪ Open. Check your work in your browser window.

12. Edit and adjust
Make edits by opening up your home page or subpage page files in your text editor and making edits to the content. Be sure to edit only your content and not to disturb any of the surrounding code.

13. Publish
The basic parameters of what you should provide to your Web hosting company are outlined in Chapter 3. For the specifics on actually posting your live site to the Web, contact your service provider for details.

Variations

Variation 821 Overview
This variation uses a different logo to present the site for an astronomy club, with a photographic background of the moon in closeup and the surrounding stars.

See the images in the CD-ROM's Gallery section.

Variation 822 Overview
This version presents the default boxing themed design on a gray background for a lighter feel, with principal articles and navigation elements presented on boxed black backgrounds.

See the images in the CD-ROM's Gallery section.

Template 830 Entertainment News and Listing Site

News and information site designed to present entertainment calendar, entertainment or arts organization, or special-interest content.

Figure 8-9: Template 830 home page

Figure 8-10: Template 830 subpage

Template Developer	Ken Milhous
Filename and Location	CD-ROM: \Templates\Chapter 8\83\830
Variations on this Design	831 832
Site Development Detail	Procedures and supporting information on placing content, links, and Web site images are presented in Chapter 3.

Design Summary

Recommended Use	Simple layout is designed to present listings and article information for an arts organization. The design can be adapted to just about any information dissemination purpose.
Look and Feel	Gray background accented with site skeleton areas in orange and white blocks for displaying article information.
	Low- to medium-density layout is uncomplicated and provides single articles on the home page and subpages.

Content Plan

Content Plan Overview

Before entering content in your site, make a list of the Web page labels and filenames you will use to build your Web site skeleton. Detailed coverage on building your content plan is presented in Chapter 3.

Subpages

Design is a catalog layout that supports four subpages that can be linked at the top and bottom navigation bar on the site plus a dedicated home link. Identify and write down the screen labels and the related filenames.

Copy the Template

Follow these steps to copy the template to your hard drive:

1. Access the \Templates\Chapter 8\83\830 folder on your CD-ROM.

2. Drag the \830 folder to your desktop or copy and paste the \830 folder to your desktop.

Template Headings and Tags

Figure 8-11: Template 830 home page token reference

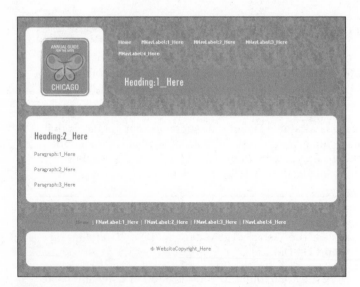

Figure 8-12: Template 830 subpage page token reference

Building Your Site Step-by-Step: 830 Entertainment News and Listing Site

Building the Site Skeleton

Use the following set of operations to enter the central navigation. Perform the exact same operations within index.html and subpage.html. Web site navigation and building the site skeleton are presented in Chapter 3.

Note that when opening index.html or subpage.html from your hard drive, a security message may appear. Click for more options, and choose to display the full content so the template displays correctly.

---

1. Place navigation labels

Review the list of subpage labels and filenames from your content plan. You place the labels for subpage 1 at the top (MNav) and bottom (FNav) of your page. See Figures 8-11 for home and 8-12 for subpages.

1. Open index.html in your text editor.

2. Find MNavLabel:1_Here and replace the token with the label for subpage 1.

3. Find `FNavLabel:1_Here` and replace the token with the label for subpage 1.

4. Repeat Steps 2 and 3 for `MNavLabel` and `FNavLabel` 2, 3, and 4.

---

2. Place navigation links

Review the list of subpage labels and filenames from your content plan. In the following operation, you place the links to the filename for subpage 1 at the top (MNav) and bottom (FNav) of your page. Enter all filenames in lowercase.

1. Find `MNavURL:1_Here` and replace the token with filename you selected for subpage 1.

2. Find `FNavURL:1_Here` and replace the token with the filename you selected for subpage 1.

3. Repeat Steps 1 and 2 for `MNavURL` and `FNavURL` 2, 3, and 4.

---

3. Place special features

Place the text of the Web site copyright in your pages.

1. Find `WebsiteCopyright:1_Here` and replace the token with your Web site copyright text.

2. Save and close `index.html` in your text editor.

---

4. Set up the subpage template

Perform the same set of edits that you completed for the `index.html` file on the subpage master template file, `subpage.html`.

1. Open `subpage.html` in your text editor.

2. Return to the beginning of this section ("Building the Site Skeleton"), and start with main Step 1, "Place navigation labels."

3. Complete main Steps 1, 2, and 3 using the `subpage.html` file instead of the `index.html` file.

4. Save `subpage.html` in your text editor. Do not rename the file.

Creating Subpage Files

5. Create subpage files

Use the Save As feature in your text editor to save the `subpage.html` template with the first of the subpage filenames you selected in your content plan. Repeat this to create all subpages listed in your content plan.

Save all files to the `\830` folder on your desktop.

1. Verify that `subpage.html` is open in your text editor.

2. Choose File ➪ Save As or similar from your text editor. Enter the filename you selected for subpage 1, and click OK.

3. Repeat Step 2 for all subpages in your content plan.

4. Repeat Step 2 for any linked articles or catalog detail pages you identified in your content plan.

---

6. Display your site

Open your site to check that your labels and pages display correctly.

1. Launch `index.html` from your computer by double-clicking the filename, or choose File ➪ Open (from most browsers) to open it in your browser. An empty home page should appear.

2. Click the navigation links at the top and bottom of the home page and you should see empty subpage pages.

3. Close the empty site skeleton.

Placing Content in the Home Page

7. Place home page main article

Place the headings and paragraph text for the featured article in `index.html` (see Figure 8-11).

1. Open `index.html` in your text editor.

2. Find `Heading:1_Here` and replace the token with the title of the page or the key message.

3. Find `Heading:2_Here` and replace the token with your article heading.

4. Find `Paragraph:1_Here` and replace the token with your paragraph text.

5. Find `LinkLabel:1_Here`. Replace the token with the label text for this link (such as "Read More" or "More Information"). You can delete this token if you do not want to use this link.

6. Find `LinkURL:1_Here`. Replace the token with the filename you have selected to be accessed from this link.

8. Place bottom article	Place the headings and paragraph text for the article at the bottom of the home page in `index.html` (see Figure 8-11).

1. Find `Heading:3_Here` and replace the token with your article heading.

2. Find `Paragraph:2_Here` and replace the token with your paragraph text.

3. Find `LinkLabel:2_Here`. Replace the token with the label text for this link (such as "Read More" or "More Information"). You can delete this token if you do not want to use this link.

4. Find `LinkURL:2_Here`. Replace the token with the filename you have selected to be accessed from this link.

5. Save `index.html` in your text editor.

Placing Content in Subpages

Use the following operations to place content into all of your site subpages. Use the subpage token reference (see Figure 8-12) to see the position of the content and label tokens. Repeat this operation to enter content in all of your subpages.

9. Place subpage articles	Place article headings and text into all of the named subpages you created from `subpage.html` (see Figure 8-12).

1. Open the selected subpage in your text editor.

2. Find `Heading:1_Here` and replace the token with the page title or key message.

3. Find `Heading:2_Here` and replace the token with your article heading.

4. Find `Paragraph:1_Here` and replace the token with your paragraph text. Repeat for `Paragraph` 2 and 3.

5. Save and close the file when you have finished editing.

Finalizing Your Site

10. Edit site logo and pictures

Turn to Chapter 3 for explanation and procedures to replace the default template logo and images with your own logo and images.

11. Display your Web site

Launch `index.html` from your computer by double-clicking the filename, or choose File ➪ Open. Check your work in your browser window.

12. Edit and adjust

Make edits by opening up your home page or subpage page files in your text editor and making edits to the content. Be sure to edit only your content and not to disturb any of the surrounding code.

13. Publish

The basic parameters of what you should provide to your Web hosting company are outlined in Chapter 3. For the specifics on actually posting your live site to the Web, contact your service provider for details.

Variations

Variation 831 Overview

This version is a dark version of the design, presented against a deep gray background, with brown accents for heading titles and footer navigation.

See the images in the CD-ROM's Gallery section.

Variation 832 Overview

In this variation the design is light and colorful with accent areas for headings and navigation in bright blue and green against a pastel background.

See the images in the CD-ROM's Gallery section.

✦   ✦   ✦

E-Commerce Templates

E-commerce has allowed us to conduct business in an entirely new way — virtually entirely via the Web. Technically, e-commerce encompasses many forms of online businesses, the transactions between these businesses themselves, creating and sharing of business information over the Web, developing partnerships and business affiliations, and outsourcing business services, just to name a few. The point of reference for this chapter is virtual businesses that have moved their stores (or part of them, at least) into a computer drive and conduct transactions over the Web.

Web business has reinvented industries such as the corner bookstore (Amazon.com) or the travel agency (Expedia.com and Travelocity.com) and provided entirely new relationships and services by taking these conventional businesses and moving them to the Web. Therein lies the essential communication challenge in building an e-commerce storefront or service offering — building on customers' expectations for a conventional business arrangement and educating them on how it changes for the better when it occurs online.

About E-Commerce Templates

E-commerce sites have many, if not most, of the same challenges that any business does. Like any business, the site must communicate credibility and value to customers and generate the sale of products or services. Because customers may have preconceptions based on conventional, non-Internet businesses, the particular challenge e-commerce offerings face is establishing credibility with the audience and teaching the audience how to use the system to their advantage.

This chapter includes Web site models for e-commerce businesses, including a tax preparation firm and a general business transaction Web site example. They illustrate the principle of e-commerce sites, but other sites in the 1 Hour

Web Site family, particularly in the general and retail business groups, might serve your purpose equally well.

This chapter includes three Web site models for e-commerce businesses: a commercial site offering products and services, a tax preparation firm, and a general business transaction site. They illustrate the principle of e-commerce sites, but others templates in this book, particularly in the general and retail business groups, might serve your purpose equally well.

Presenting an E-Commerce Site

The Internet is so flexible and adaptable that it's fair to say that in e-commerce, just about anything goes. New business models using the Internet are being invented all the time and the only limit is the imagination. This great freedom of invention imposes a constraint — the need to clearly communicate exactly what your e-commerce venture is about.

Your Internet business venture may be Internet-only, or just the Web presence of a brick-and-mortar operation, such as a store. You must explain your product array or service carefully on your Web site, because in some cases, people won't be ready to do business over the Web. This is particularly true in areas where extensive personal or financial information, such as credit card numbers, are exchanged. Potential customers need to be able to quickly recognize the value your business offers and the goods or services the business provides. Additionally, as they browse through your site, they should feel that any transaction they decide to make would be safe.

Establishing credibility

Establishing your credibility as an e-commerce provider is vital. Some of the information that you should provide in your e-commerce site includes

- ✦ Background information and the purpose of the business
- ✦ Value offered to the customer
- ✦ Product and service offerings
- ✦ Clear instructions on how to buy through the Web
- ✦ Customer service and guarantees
- ✦ Direct contact customer support and contact information
- ✦ Satisfied customer quotes
- ✦ Press notices

Most people are familiar with Web-based business in general. You should not assume, however, that every Web venture is, therefore, understood and accepted.

People are still adjusting to new ways of thinking about transactions on the Web, and it's your job to educate them on the value of your offering.

Building your value

The central question for any e-commerce site is "How does this business benefit from being on the Web?" For many people, the instant answer to that question is convenience—the ability to shop at home and have purchases arrive at their doorstep within a few days. Web shopping offers the widest possible selection of products and services without having to visit retail sites that may not have what you want in stock—or carry it at all. The Internet is also a powerful tool to manage costs, by comparing prices between different vendors and selecting the most desirable offering.

Convenience is important, but there are a number of risks associated with e-commerce. One of the most notorious negatives of e-commerce business is the perception or reality of poor customer service. A Web site is an image on a screen. The only connection the customer has is a URL and possibly a phone number. The Internet introduces a distance between you and the customers, no matter how close they are to their computer screens.

Your site content must address customer need for credibility. One of the best ways to build that value, particularly for a new e-commerce site, is to emphasize customer service and to clearly state contact information. Bringing the customer closer helps generate confidence and a willingness to try your offering.

Differentiating products and services

Web-based customers can't actually touch a product you're offering for sale; they have to settle for an image or some descriptive copy. Profiling products for sale is another primary challenge for any e-commerce enterprise. One of the trailblazers in this area is Amazon.com, which has developed detailed and navigable product profiles of book titles, and millions of customers have bought from the company. Its product descriptions convey enough valuable information about the books (and products) it sells that many people feel comfortable enough to buy the product—sight unseen.

It's a very good idea to keep the product profile principle in mind for anything you seek to sell on the Web. The product profile doesn't have to explain every detail about the product; it has to answer the key questions that enable the customer to buy it. Some of that information is user details and specs. Other information of value is discussing how the product is used and including the experiences and recommendations of others. Whatever your focus, remember that your job is to push your products through that computer screen so your audience can understand them, and be prompted to take action.

Secure and understandable transactions

The one essential for any e-commerce site is secure financial transactions. Now that the Web has matured as a business source, secure transaction services can be outsourced to Web service providers and you never have to touch a single credit card transaction. Even with that essential item checked off the list of important facets of your site, however, the delicate matter of escorting your customers into the transaction system and motivating them to buy remains.

Make sure your site fully explains your entire sales policy and approach, including customer satisfaction, guarantees, and how you handle the purchase process. Beyond security, you must create customer confidence. When customers have that assurance, they will be ready to try something new.

Tip   Instead of navigating from the root of the CD to locate a template, you can click the Templates link in the CD browser application to directly access the chapters on the CD. For faster access, click the Gallery link in the CD browser application to view a listing of all templates. Then click any View Files link to view the files for that template.

Template 910 Web Store

A Web store site designed for any commercial Web site selling products or services. The home page features areas for articles and the subpage features a photo display of products for sale.

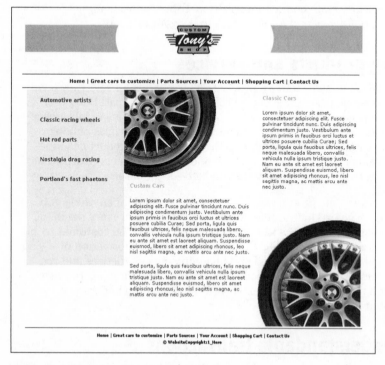

Figure 9-1: Template 910 home page

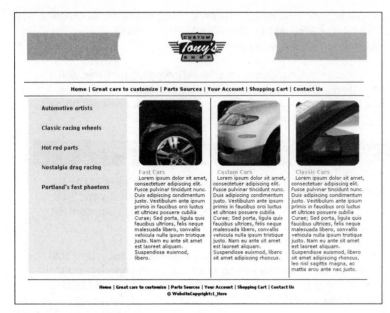

Figure 9-2: Template 910 subpage

Template Developer	Yana Beylinson
Filename and Location	CD-ROM: \Templates\Chapter 9\91\910
Variations on this Design	911 912
Site Development Detail	Procedures and supporting information on placing content, links, and Web site images are presented in Chapter 3.

Design Summary

Recommended Use	Simple, open design can be used to present a Web business offering of any kind. The home page provides areas to introduce the business and detail on products and services. The subpage design is built around galleries of captioned photographs and links. The design is simple and structured such that you can use it for any Web communication purpose where galleries of pictures are a key element in the content.

Look and Feel	Orange and yellow accents on a white background create a very readable layout that is suitable for many communication purposes.
	Low- to medium-density design showcases pictures and features a lead illustration on the home page. Use these illustrations to show galleries of products, or detail images of individual products.

Content Plan

Content Plan Overview	Before entering content in your site, make a list of the Web page labels and filenames you will use to build your Web site skeleton. Detailed coverage on building your content plan is presented in Chapter 3.
Subpages	Design is a catalog layout that supports six subpages that can be linked at the top and bottom navigation bar on the site. Identify and write down the screen labels and the related filenames.
Action Item Pages	Design supports a sidebar with eight action items on both the home page and subpages. You can use these to link to any pages within your site, such as articles or featured information not linked through the main and footer navigation.
Sidebars	Design supports a sidebar area on subpages, with action item titles and link labels.

Copy the Template	Follow these steps to copy the template to your hard drive:

1. Access the \Templates\Chapter 9\91\910 folder on your CD-ROM.

2. Drag the \910 folder to your desktop or copy and paste the \910 folder to your desktop.

Template Headings and Tags

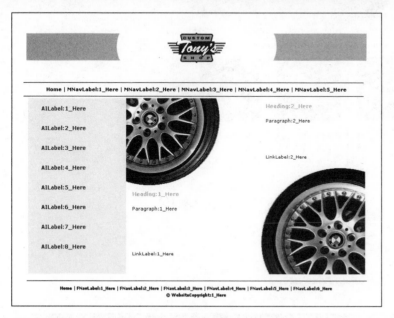

Figure 9-3: Template 910 home page token reference

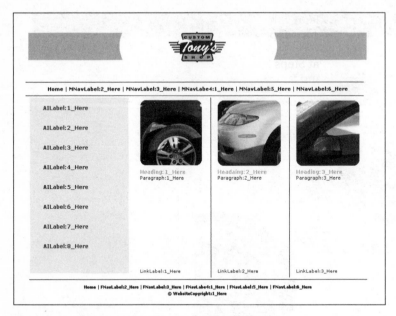

Figure 9-4: Template 910 subpage token reference

Building Your Site Step-by-Step: 910 Web Store

Building the Site Skeleton

Use the following set of operations to enter the central navigation. Perform the exact same operations within `index.html` and `subpage.html`. Web site navigation and building the site skeleton are presented in Chapter 3.

Note that when opening `index.html` or `subpage.html` in Internet Explorer from your hard drive, a security message may appear. Click for more options, and choose to display the full content so the template displays correctly.

---

1. Place navigation labels

Review the list of subpage labels and filenames from your content plan. You place the labels for subpage 1 at the top (`MNav`) and bottom (`FNav`) of your page. See Figures 9-3 for home and 9-4 for subpages.

1. Open `index.html` in your text editor.

2. Find `MNavLabel:1_Here` and replace the token with the label for subpage 1.

3. Find `FNavLabel:1_Here` and replace the token with the label for subpage 1.

4. Repeat Steps 2 and 3 for `MNavLabel` and `FNavLabel` 2, 3, 4, and 5.

---

2. Place navigation links

Review the list of subpage labels and filenames from your content plan. In the following operation you place the links to the filename for subpage 1 at the top (`MNav`) and bottom (`FNav`) of your page. Enter all filenames in lowercase.

1. Find `MNavURL:1_Here` and replace the token with the filename you selected for subpage 1.

2. Find `FNavURL:1_Here` and replace the token with the filename you selected for subpage 1.

3. Repeat Steps 1 and 2 for `MNavURL` and `FNavURL` 2, 3, 4, and 5.

---

3. Place action item sidebar

There is a sidebar featuring eight action item labels and related links on both the home and the subpages. You may elect to assign the same names and links to these elements in the home page, just like main and footer navigation elements. In that case, perform the following operations at this time.

You may choose to assign these labels and links to the home and subpages separately. In that case, perform these operations when you complete "Placing Content in the Home Page" and "Placing Content in Subpages" later in this operation.

1. Find `AILabel:1_Here` and replace the token with the text you selected for subpage 1. Repeat this operation for `AILabel` 2, 3, 4, 5, 6, 7, and 8.

2. Find `AIURL:1_Here` and replace the token with the filename you selected for subpage 1. Repeat this operation for `AIURL` 2, 3, 4, 5, 6, 7, and 8.

---

4. Place special features

Place the text of the Web site copyright in your pages.

1. Find `WebsiteCopyright:1_Here` and replace the token with your Web site copyright text.

2. Save and close `index.html` in your text editor.

5. Set up the subpage template	Perform the same set of edits that you completed for the `index.html` file on the subpage master template file, `subpage.html`.

1. Open `subpage.html` in your text editor.

2. Return to the beginning of this section ("Building the Site Skeleton"), and start with main Step 1, "Place navigation labels."

3. Complete main Steps 1, 2, 3, and 4 using the `subpage.html` file instead of the `index.html` file.

4. Save `subpage.html` in your text editor. Do not rename the file.

Creating Subpage Files

6. Create subpage files	Use the Save As feature in your text editor to save the `subpage.html` template with the first of the subpage filenames you selected in your content plan. Repeat this to create all subpages listed in your content plan. Save all files to the `\910` folder on your desktop.

1. Verify that `subpage.html` is open in your text editor.

2. Choose File ➪ Save As or similar from your text editor. Enter the filename you selected for subpage 1, and click OK.

3. Repeat Step 2 for all subpages in your content plan.

4. Repeat Step 2 for any linked articles or catalog detail pages you identified in your content plan.

7. Display your site	Open your site to check that your labels and pages display correctly.

1. Launch `index.html` from your computer by double-clicking the filename, or choose File ➪ Open (from most browsers) to open it in your Browser. An empty home page should appear.

2. Click the navigation links at the top and bottom of the home page and you should see empty subpage pages.

3. Close the empty site skeleton.

Placing Content in the Home Page

8. Place home feature article

Place the headings and paragraph text for the featured article in `index.html` (see Figure 9-3).

1. Open `index.html` in your text editor.

2. Find `Heading:1_Here` and replace the token with your heading text.

3. Find `Paragraph:1_Here` and replace the token with your paragraph text.

4. Find `LinkLabel:1_Here`. Replace the token with the chosen label text for this link (such as "Read More" or "More Information"). You can delete this token if you do not want to use this link.

5. Find `LinkURL:1_Here`. Replace the token with the filename you have selected to be accessed from this link.

6. Find `Heading:2_Here` and replace the token with your heading text.

7. Find `Paragraph:2_Here` and replace the token with your paragraph text.

8. Find `LinkLabel:2_Here`. Replace the token with the chosen label text for this link (such as "Read More" or "More Information"). You can delete this token if you do not want to use this link.

9. Find `LinkURL:2_Here`. Replace the token with the filename you have selected to be accessed from this link.

10. Save `index.html` in your text editor.

Placing Content in Subpages

Use the following operations to place content into all of your site subpages. Use the subpage token reference (see Figure 9-4) to see the position of the content and label tokens. Repeat this operation to enter content in all of your subpages.

---

9. Place subpage articles

Place article headings and text in your subpages.

1. Open the selected subpage in your text editor.

2. Find `Heading:1_Here` and replace the token with your heading text. Repeat for `Heading` 2 and 3.

3. Find `Paragraph:1_Here` and replace the token with your paragraph text. Repeat for `Paragraph` 2 and 3.

4. Find `LinkLabel:1_Here`. Replace the token with the chosen label text for this link (such as "Read More" or "More Information"). You can delete this token if you do not want to use this link. Repeat for `LinkLabel` 2 and 3.

5. Find `LinkURL:1_Here`. Replace the token with the filename you have selected to be accessed from this link. Repeat for `LinkURL` 2 and 3.

---

10. Place image label

The three images on the subpage each support a mouse over text label. When the mouse is placed over the image, this label appears. The image label should carry a description of the photograph or a message related to the photograph.

Note that if you do not replace this token, the text of the token appears when you mouse over the image.

1. To place the image label for the image above Heading 1, find `ImageLabel:1_Here` and replace with the desired content for the mouse over image label.

2. To place the image label for the image above Heading 2, find `ImageLabel:2_Here` and replace with the desired content for the mouse over image label.

3. To place the image label for the image above Heading 3, find `ImageLabel:3_Here` and replace with the desired content for the mouse over image label.

4. Save and close the file when you have finished editing.

Finalizing Your Site

11. Edit site logo and pictures

Turn to Chapter 3 for explanation and procedures to replace the default template logo and images with your own logo and images.

12. Display your Web site

Launch `index.html` from your computer by double-clicking the filename, or choose File ➪ Open. Check your work in your browser window.

13. Edit and adjust

Make edits by opening up your home page or subpage page files in your text editor and making edits to the content. Be sure to edit only your content and not to disturb any of the surrounding code.

14. Publish

The basic parameters of what you should provide to your Web hosting company are outlined in Chapter 3. For the specifics on actually posting your live site to the Web, contact your service provider for details.

Variations

Variation 911 Overview

This design replaces the yellow accent behind article areas on the home page and the sidebar on the subpages with a light blue. Otherwise the color mix and design layout are the same.

See the images in the CD-ROM's Gallery section.

Variation 912 Overview

This design replaces the yellow accent behind article areas on the home page and the sidebar on the subpages with the same dominant orange used at the top of both pages. Otherwise the color mix and design layout are the same.

See the images in the CD-ROM's Gallery section.

Template 920 Web-Based Services Site

Professional services site designed to present detailed information and content. The example shows an online tax preparation service, with strong business visuals and theme. The simplicity of the design lends itself to any business application.

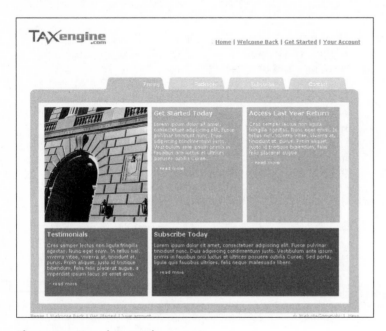

Figure 9-5: Template 920 home page

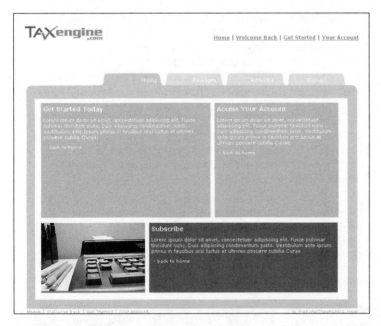

Figure 9-6: Template 920 subpage

Template Developer	Yana Beylinson
Filename and Location	CD-ROM: \Templates\Chapter 9\92\920
Variations on this Design	921 922
Site Development Detail	Procedures and supporting information on placing content, links, and Web site images are presented in Chapter 3.

Design Summary

Recommended Use	Design is built around headings and supporting paragraph text within a simple, colorful structure. Use the clearly framed areas of content to present background information, news, specific service offerings, or details on the background of people working for the company.

Look and Feel

Built around a tabbed-page structure, the layout is boxy with color content areas that are set off against a white background. A strong gray frame integrates the elements. Articles are set off in areas of orange, blue, and gray. The home page and subpages use the identical framing device, which enables the reader to click through the tab links and see similar page layouts throughout the site.

This design approach makes it easier to focus the audience's attention on key topics and themes, while breaking up the content into smaller and more readable chunks within the page.

Depending on the amount of content you place into this design, it can be a medium- or high-density presentation. The home page presents four heading and text areas to capture the audience's attention, and subpages support three content areas to break out and present topical material.

Content Plan

Content Plan Overview

Before entering content in your site, make a list of the Web page labels and filenames you will use to build your Web site skeleton. Detailed coverage on building your content plan is presented in Chapter 3.

Subpages Navigation Bar

Design is a catalog layout that supports three subpages in the main and footer navigation areas that can be linked at the top and bottom navigation bar on the site.

Tabbed Subpages

In addition to the main and footer navigation links, there are four tabbed subpages shown on both the home page and the subpage layout.

Article Areas

Design supports four article headings with paragraph text and links on the home page and three on the subpage layout.

Copy the Template

Follow these steps to copy the template to your hard drive:

1. Access the `\Templates\Chapter 9\92\920` folder on your CD-ROM.

2. Drag the `\920` folder to your desktop or copy and paste the `\920` folder to your desktop.

Template Headings and Tags

Figure 9-7: Template 920 home page token reference

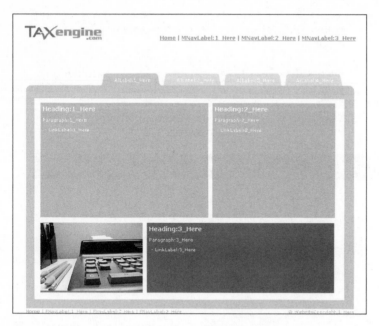

Figure 9-8: Template 920 subpage token reference

Building Your Site Step-by-Step: 920 Web-Based Services Site

Building the Site Skeleton

Use the following set of operations to enter the central navigation. Perform the exact same operations within `index.html` and `subpage.html`. Web site navigation and building the site skeleton are presented in Chapter 3.

Note that when opening `index.html` or `subpage.html` in Internet Explorer from your hard drive, a security message may appear. Click for more options, and choose to display the full content so the template displays correctly.

---

1. Place navigation labels

Review the list of subpage labels and filenames from your content plan. You place the labels for subpage 1 at the top (`MNav`) and bottom (`FNav`) of your page. See Figures 9-7 for home and 9-8 for subpages.

1. Open `index.html` in your text editor.

2. Find `MNavLabel:1_Here` and replace the token with the label for subpage 1.

3. Find `FNavLabel:1_Here` and replace the token with the label for subpage 1.

4. Repeat Steps 2 and 3 for `MNavLabel` and `FNavLabel` 2 and 3.

---

2. Place navigation links

Review the list of subpage labels and filenames from your content plan. In the following operation you place the links to the filename for subpage 1 at the top (`MNav`) and bottom (`FNav`) of your page. Enter all filenames in lowercase.

1. Find `MNavURL:1_Here` and replace the token with filename you selected for subpage 1.

2. Find `FNavURL:1_Here` and replace the token with the filename you selected for subpage 1.

3. Repeat Steps 1 and 2 for `MNavURL` and `FNavURL` 2 and 3.

---

3. Place action item tabs

There is a tabbed array of four action item labels and related links on both the home and the subpages. You can elect to assign the same names and links to these elements in the home page, just like main and footer navigation elements. In that case, perform the following operations at this time.

You may choose to assign these labels and links to the home and subpages separately. In that case, perform these operations when you complete the steps in the sections "Placing Content in the Home Page" and "Placing Content in Subpages."

1. Find `AILabel:1_Here` and replace the token with the text you selected for subpage 1. Repeat this operation for `AILabel` 2, 3, and 4.

2. Find `AIURL:1_Here` and replace the token with the text you selected for subpage 1. Repeat this operation for `AIURL` 2, 3, and 4.

---

4. Place special features

Place the text of the Web site copyright in your pages.

1. Find `WebsiteCopyright:1_Here` and replace the token with your Web site copyright text.

2. Save and close `index.html` in your text editor.

5. Set up the subpage template	Perform the same set of edits that you completed for the index.html file on the subpage master template file, subpage.html.

1. Open subpage.html in your text editor.

2. Return to the beginning of this section ("Building the Site Skeleton"), and start with main Step 1, "Place navigation labels."

3. Complete main Steps 1, 2, 3, and 4 using the subpage.html file instead of the index.html file.

4. Save subpage.html in your text editor. Do not rename the file.

Creating Subpage Files

6. Create subpage files	Use the Save As feature in your text editor to save the subpage.html template with the first of the subpage filenames you selected in your content plan. Repeat this to create all subpages listed in your content plan.

Save all files to the \920 folder on your desktop.

1. Verify that subpage.html is open in your text editor.

2. Choose File ➪ Save As or similar from your text editor. Enter the filename you selected for subpage 1, and click OK.

3. Repeat Step 2 for all subpages in your content plan.

4. Repeat Step 2 for any linked articles or catalog detail pages you identified in your content plan.

7. Display your site	Open your site to check that your labels and pages display correctly.

1. Launch index.html from your computer by double-clicking the filename, or choose File ➪ Open (from most browsers) to open it in your Browser. An empty home page should appear.

2. Click the navigation links at the top and bottom of the home page and you should see empty subpage pages.

3. Close the empty site skeleton.

Placing Content in the Home Page

8. Place home page articles

Place the headings and paragraph text for home page articles in `index.html` (see Figure 9-7).

1. Open `index.html` in your text editor.

2. Find `Heading:1_Here` and replace the token with your heading text.

3. Find `Paragraph:1_Here` and replace the token with your paragraph text.

4. Find `LinkLabel:1_Here`. Replace the token with the chosen label text for this link (such as "Read More" or "More Information"). You can delete this token if you do not want to use this link.

5. Find `LinkURL:1_Here`. Replace the token with the filename you have selected to be accessed from this link.

6. Repeat this operation for the three remaining article blocks on the home page. Each article area features the same number used for all applicable tokens. Complete series 2, 3, and 4.

7. Save `index.html` in your text editor.

Placing Content in Subpages

Use the following operations to place content into all of your site subpages. Use the subpage token reference (see Figure 9-8) to see the position of the content and label tokens. Repeat this operation to enter content in all of your subpages.

9. Place subpage articles

Place article headings and text in your subpages.

1. Open the selected subpage in your text editor.

2. Find `Heading:1_Here` and replace the token with your heading text. Repeat for `Heading` 2.

3. Find `Paragraph:1_Here` and replace the token with your paragraph text. Repeat for `Paragraph 2`.

4. Find `LinkLabel:1_Here`. Replace the token with the chosen label text for this link (such as "Read More" or "More Information"). You can delete this token if you do not want to use this link. Repeat for `LinkLabel 2`.

5. Find `LinkURL:1_Here`. Replace the token with the filename you have selected to be accessed from this link. Repeat for `LinkURL 2`.

6. Save and close the file when you have finished editing.

Finalizing Your Site

10. Edit site logo and pictures   Turn to Chapter 3 for explanation and procedures to replace the default template logo and images with your own logo and images.

11. Display your Web site   Launch `index.html` from your computer by double-clicking the filename, or choose File ➪ Open. Check your work in your browser window.

12. Edit and adjust   Make edits by opening up your home page or subpage page files in your text editor and making edits to the content. Be sure to edit only your content and not to disturb any of the surrounding code.

13. Publish   The basic parameters of what you should provide to your Web hosting company are outlined in Chapter 3. For the specifics on actually posting your live site to the Web, contact your service provider for details.

Variations

Variation 921 Overview   This version of the design uses a different color combination for article backgrounds, with a mix of orange, light gray, and green. Otherwise the layout and features are the same.

See the images in the CD-ROM's Gallery section.

Variation 922 Overview

This version of the design uses gray and shades of orange as the background colors for content areas. Otherwise the layout and features are the same.

See the images in the CD-ROM's Gallery section.

Template 930 Web Business Site

General business site for the Web or other business applications. Designed around a gaming theme, this layout makes strong use of color to display content with eye-catching link buttons and an engaging presentation.

Figure 9-9: Template 930 home page

Figure 9-10: Template 930 subpage

Template Developer	Yana Beylinson
Filename and Location	CD-ROM: \Templates\Chapter 9\93\930
Variations on this Design	931 932
Site Development Detail	Procedures and supporting information on placing content, links, and Web site images are presented in Chapter 3.

Design Summary

Recommended Use	With a strong feature photograph and a more complex array of articles and featured link buttons, this design engages the reader immediately with its color and complexity. This template is best used to present products or topic areas in the colorful link buttons.

Look and Feel

Background is white with soft blue article areas that are dramatically enhanced by control and navigation features in shades of bright red and orange. The home page supports three article areas, two with link-through options. The subpage is built around a primary article and two supporting article areas.

Depending on the amount of content you place into this design, it could be a medium- or a high-density presentation. The home page presents three heading and text areas to capture attention and subpages support three content areas to break out and present topical material.

Content Plan

Content Plan Overview

Before entering content in your site, make a list of the Web page labels and filenames you will use to build your Web site skeleton. Detailed coverage on building your content plan is presented in Chapter 3.

Subpages Navigation Bar

Design supports four subpages that can be linked at the top and bottom navigation bar on the site.

Subpages

Five of the principal subpages can be featured in dramatic link buttons that appear on the home page and subpages.

Action Items

There are ten action item links that appear at the side of both the home page and subpages. Given the size of the text and placement, you can use these for basic site information such as a company profile or contact information.

Article Areas

Design supports three article headings with paragraph text and links on the home page and subpage layouts.

Copy the Template

Follow these steps to copy the template to your hard drive:

1. Access the \Templates\Chapter 9\93\930 folder on your CD-ROM.

2. Drag the \930 folder to your desktop or copy and paste the \930 folder to your desktop.

Template Headings and Tags

Figure 9-11: Template 930 home page token reference

Figure 9-12: Template 930 subpage token reference

Building Your Site Step-by-Step: 930 Web Business Site

Building the Site Skeleton

Use the following set of operations to enter the central navigation. Perform the exact same operations within index.html and subpage.html. Web site navigation and building the site skeleton are presented in Chapter 3.

Note that when opening index.html or subpage.html in Internet Explorer from your hard drive, a security message may appear. Click for more options, and choose to display the full content so the template displays correctly.

---

1. Place navigation labels

Review the list of subpage labels and filenames from your content plan. You place the labels for subpage 1 at the top (MNav) and bottom (FNav) of your page. Action items are on the side. See Figures 9-11 for home and 9-12 for subpages.

1. Open `index.html` in your text editor.

2. Find `AILabel:1_Here` and replace the token with the action item label text you selected for subpage 1. Repeat this operation for `AILabel` 2 and 3. All `AILabels` are labels only and do not accept links.

3. Find `MNavLabel:1_Here` and replace the token with the label for subpage 1. Repeat this operation for `MNavLabel` 2, 3, and 4.

4. Find `FNavLabel:1_Here` and replace the token with the label for subpage 1. Repeat this operation for `FNavLabel` 2, 3, and 4.

---

2. Place navigation links

Review the list of subpage labels and filenames from your content plan. In the following operation you place the links to the filename for subpage 1 at the top (`MNav`) and bottom (`FNav`) of your page. Action items are on the side. Enter all filenames in lowercase.

1. Find `AIURL:2_Here` and replace the token with the filename you selected for subpage 1. Repeat this operation for `AIURL` 3.

2. Find `MNavURL:1_Here` and replace the token with the filename you selected for subpage 1. Repeat this operation for `MNavURL` 2, 3, and 4.

3. Find `FNavURL:1_Here` and replace the token with the filename you selected for subpage 1. Repeat this operation for `FNavURL` 2, 3, and 4.

---

3. Place action item sidebar

There is a sidebar featuring ten action item labels and related links on both the home and subpages. You can elect to assign the same names and links to these elements in the home page, just like main and footer navigation elements. In that case, perform the following operations at this time.

You can choose to assign these labels and links to the home and subpages separately. In that case, perform these operations when you complete the steps in the sections for "Placing Content in the Home Page" and "Placing Content in Subpages."

1. Find `AILabel:4_Here` and replace the token with the filename you selected for subpage 1. Repeat this operation for `AILabel` 5, 6, 7, 8, 9, 10, 11, 12, and 13.

2. Find `AIURL:4_Here` and replace the token with the filename you selected for subpage 1. Repeat this operation for `AIURL` 5, 6, 7, 8, 9, 10, 11, 12, and 13.

---

4. Place special features

Place the text of the Web site copyright in your pages.

1. Find `WebsiteCopyright:1_Here` and replace the token with your Web site copyright text.

2. Save and close `index.html` in your text editor.

---

5. Set up the subpage template

Perform the same set of edits that you completed for the `index.html` file on the subpage master template file, `subpage.html`.

1. Open `subpage.html` in your text editor.

2. Return to the beginning of this section ("Building the Site Skeleton"), and start with main Step 1, "Place navigation labels."

3. Complete main Steps 1, 2, 3, and 4 using the `subpage.html` file instead of the `index.html` file.

4. Save `subpage.html` in your text editor. Do not rename the file.

Creating Subpage Files

6. Create subpage files

Use the Save As feature in your text editor to save the `subpage.html` template with the first of the subpage filenames you selected in your content plan. Repeat this to create all subpages listed in your content plan.

Save all files to the `\930` folder on your desktop.

1. Verify that `subpage.html` is open in your text editor.

2. Choose File ➪ Save As or similar from your text editor. Enter the filename you selected for subpage 1, and click OK.

3. Repeat Step 2 for all subpages in your content plan.

4. Repeat Step 2 for any linked articles or catalog detail pages you identified in your content plan.

7. Display your site

Open your site to check that your labels and pages display correctly.

1. Launch `index.html` from your computer by double-clicking the filename, or choose File ➪ Open (from most browsers) to open it in your Browser. An empty home page should appear.

2. Click the navigation links at the top and bottom of the home page and you should see empty subpage pages.

3. Close the empty site skeleton.

Placing Content in the Home Page

8. Place home page articles

Place the headings and paragraph text for home page articles in `index.html` (see Figure 9-11).

1. Open `index.html` in your text editor.

2. Find `Heading:1_Here` and replace the token with your heading text.

3. Find `Paragraph:1_Here` and replace the token with your paragraph text.

4. Find `LinkLabel:1_Here`. Replace the token with the chosen label text for this link (such as "Read More" or "More Information"). You can delete this token if you do not want to use this link.

5. Find `LinkURL:1_Here`. Replace the token with the chosen filename you have selected to be accessed from this link.

6. Repeat this operation for the two remaining article blocks on the home page. Each article area features the same number used for all applicable tokens. Complete series 2 and 3.

7. Save `index.html` in your text editor.

Placing Content in Subpages

Use the following operations to place content into all of your site subpages. Use the subpage token reference (see Figure 9-12) to see the position of the content and label tokens. Repeat this operation to enter content in all of your subpages.

9. Place subpage articles

Place article headings and text in your subpages.

1. Open the selected subpage in your text editor.

2. Find `Heading:1_Here` and replace the token with your heading text. Repeat for `Heading` 2 and 3.

3. Find `Paragraph:1_Here` and replace the token with your paragraph text. Repeat for `Paragraph` 2 and 3.

4. Find `LinkLabel:1_Here`. Replace the token with the chosen label text for this link (such as "Read More" or "More Information"). You can delete this token if you do not want to use this link. Repeat for `LinkLabel` 2 and 3.

5. Find `LinkURL:1_Here`. Replace the token with the chosen filename you have selected to be accessed from this link. Repeat for `LinkURL` 2 and 3.

6. Save and close the file when you have finished editing.

Finalizing Your Site

10. Edit site logo and pictures   Turn to Chapter 3 for explanation and procedures to replace the default template logo and images with your own logo and images.

11. Display your Web site   Launch `index.html` from your computer by double-clicking the filename, or choose File ➪ Open. Check your work in your browser window.

12. Edit and adjust   Make edits by opening up your home page or subpage page files in your text editor and making edits to the content. Be sure to edit only your content and not to disturb any of the surrounding code.

13. Publish   The basic parameters of what you should provide to your Web hosting company are outlined in Chapter 3. For the specifics on actually posting your live site to the Web, contact your service provider for details.

Variations

Variation 931 Overview   This version of the design uses a light yellow for the article backgrounds. Otherwise the layout and features are the same.

See the images in the CD-ROM's Gallery section.

Variation 932 Overview   This version of the design uses orange as the background colors for article content areas. Otherwise the layout and features are the same.

See the images in the CD-ROM's Gallery section.

✦   ✦   ✦

Information and E-Publishing Templates

The Web began as a publishing medium long before anybody gave a thought to selling books, socks, and cars on a computer screen. The Internet is the largest library in the world with the proverbial billions and billions of pages. Some have even speculated how many lifetimes it would take to read all the material currently on the global Internet. Distributing information is the core capability of the Web. Getting information onto it and getting people to read that information amid those billions of pages is the core of this challenge. When you decide to build an information or e-publishing site, you should have a very good grip on who out there you want to be reading it, whether you have a list of these people in hand or just a good idea of how to capture their attention.

About Information and E-Publishing Templates

Information Web sites can be built to serve any purpose. They can be libraries with broad-based or specialized content, information sites designed to serve the needs of various communities, or articles and insights that people put up just because they care about the subject matter. Whatever your motivation is to create the site, you must have a direction on its purpose, the readers, and the kind of interaction that you want to gain by publishing over the Internet.

Every single Web site in the 1 Hour Web Site family is a potential publishing site. The designs in this chapter include templates for publishing lists and databases, information archives, article and resource banks, electronic magazines (or e-zines), and online newsletters. These forms provide a site skeleton; your challenge is to make that content compelling and interesting.

Publishing on the Internet

When you are looking at your search engine, the Internet can seem like a library struck by an earthquake. Random pages whiz by as you click and weave, tossing search terms in a quest for some elusive bit of wit or intelligence. It's not just you; everybody goes though this dizzying exercise using the Web. Unlike a book, which presents a whole topic that can be grasped neatly in hand, the Internet is a cacophony of visual impressions from global sources.

Any would-be Web publisher has this to overcome — making content available, comprehensible, and interesting to an audience. When you are working on your site's content, keep in mind that it is the *context* — the headlines, article names, navigation features, and home page summary of what's inside — that makes the *content* valuable.

Engaging the reader

A publisher has to know the reader. Like any business, it is incumbent on you to generate credibility for your Web offering and make the user stick and read along. Some points that can help establish the value of your information site include

+ Home page mission statement and an outline of the content

+ Links to subpages covering key topic areas

+ Use statement that helps the reader make the best use of what you have offered

+ Service specialties and expertise

+ Site introduction with the background of the site

+ Teaser items presenting some of the most interesting information in the site

+ Well-written links that direct the user through the site

+ Links to external sites with complementary information

+ Contact information (particularly e-mail) so your readers can provide feedback

Whatever your information publishing purpose, it's a good idea to write a Web site to sell and engage the user in every kind of content.

Audience networks

In a library, it is conventional to order volumes to the strict demands of the alphabet and the Dewey Decimal System. Computers can sort any list in a second, by name, date, type, author, or just about any parameter you bother to capture. But even the grand, flexible power of cyber technology has not resolved the essential problem of linking the reader to what he or she finds compelling.

When developing your information and publishing site, you must confront this organizational challenge to make your material useful. Many, if not most, sites resort to theme areas or topic organization to help the audience filter through the dross to find the particular jewel they seek. There is another approach, and that is to create pages in your site to organize information by audience appeal. The catchphrase that underlies this approach today is "social networks," and it means that it might be smarter to organize information around groups of people likely to use it, than it is to just surrender to the alphabet, the document filename, or a computer file explorer.

When developing your site, you might find it useful to identify distinct audiences or special-interest groups within your target group of readers. You can then create a subpage with links to content they might find particularly interesting. For example, it's a good bet that material that passionately engages computer engineers won't interest the people in the marketing department.

Use and action

Information on the Internet is interactive. In other words, what you present is a trigger and the audience has the ability to respond; before the age of e-mail, the only feedback was from the few who took the time to write letters. Now, with the Internet, talking back has become a national pastime.

When presenting information on the Web, always consider the use and response profile that you would like from your readers. If you want your readers to comment or respond to you, tell them to. If you want them to request additional information, or take action based on what you provide, tell them that, too. You should assume what you are presenting isn't static. Putting your content on the Web is a way to set the wheels of thought into action.

Tip Instead of navigating from the root of the CD to locate a template, you can click the Templates link in the CD browser application to directly access the chapters on the CD. For faster access, click the Gallery link in the CD browser application to view a listing of all templates. Then click any View Files link to view the files for that template.

Template 1010   Listings and Database

Information presentation site designed to present streamlined access to article content and links to Web resources. This site can be used for any Web publishing purpose, including archives of information, communities of interest, or networking communities.

Figure 10-1: Template 1010 home page

Figure 10-2: Template 1010 subpage

Template Developer	Yana Beylinson
Filename and Location	CD-ROM: \Templates\Chapter 10\101\1010
Variations on this Design	1011 1012
Site Development Detail	Procedures and supporting information on placing content, links, and Web site images are presented in Chapter 3.

Design Summary

Recommended Use

Strong, simple design based on framed areas that accents content of interest and links to site pages as well as external Web sites. This design is best used as an information access or a portal site.

Look and Feel

Style is aggressive simplicity. The home page has a bold green framing area to hold neatly aligned white article and content display areas. The effect is to create an information grid that is easy for the eye to track and identify information.

Design can accept large blocks of information, so it can be a low-, medium-, or high-density layout depending on the content you enter. A cluster of links on the subpages is ideally positioned for placing links to external Web sites.

Content Plan

Content Plan Overview

Before entering content in your site, make a list of the Web page labels and filenames you will use to build your Web site skeleton. Detailed coverage on building your content plan is presented in Chapter 3.

Subpages

Design supports a dedicated home link with three main navigation items highlighted in green font display, mirrored in the footer navigation bar, presented in gray. There three additional top of page action items. These can be used to identify six principal subpages. Identify and write down the screen labels and the related filenames.

Articles

Home page includes three article areas, each supporting follow-on links. Subpages offer a single feature article with a supporting link block beneath.

Link Blocks

Design includes a framed area of dedicated links beneath subpage article areas. You can use these links to cross link articles within the site or to link to external Web sites that relate to the article content.

Copy the Template

Follow these steps to copy the template to your hard drive:

1. Access the `\Templates\Chapter 10\101\1010` folder on your CD-ROM.

2. Drag the `\1010` folder to your desktop or copy and paste the `\1010` folder to your desktop.

Template Headings and Tags

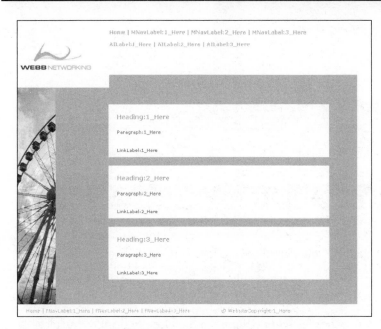

Figure 10-3: Template 1010 home page token reference

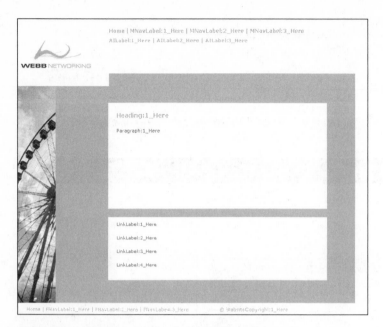

Figure 10-4: Template 1010 subpage token reference

Building Your Site Step-by-Step: 1010 Listings and Database

Building the Site Skeleton

Use the following set of operations to enter the central navigation. Perform the exact same operations within `index.html` and `subpage.html`. Web site navigation and building the site skeleton are presented in Chapter 3.

Note that when opening `index.html` or `subpage.html` in Internet Explorer from your hard drive, a security message may appear. Click for more options, and choose to display the full content so the template displays correctly.

---

1. Place navigation labels

Review the list of subpage labels and filenames from your content plan. You place the labels for subpage 1 at the top (`MNav`) and bottom (`FNav`) of your page. See Figures 10-3 for home and 10-4 for subpages.

1. Open `index.html` in your text editor.

2. Find `MNavLabel:1_Here` and replace the token with the label for subpage 1. Repeat this operation for `MNavLabel` 2 and 3.

3. Find `AILabel:1_Here` and replace the token with the label for the first action item at the top of the page. Repeat this operation for `AILabel` 2 and 3.

4. Find `FNavLabel:1_Here` and replace the token with the label for subpage 1. Repeat this operation for `FNavLabel` 2 and 3.

---

2. Place navigation links

Review the list of subpage labels and filenames from your content plan. In the following operation you place the links to the filename for subpage 1 at the top (`MNav`) and bottom (`FNav`) of your page. Enter all filenames in lowercase.

1. Find `MNavURL:1_Here` and replace the token with the filename you selected for subpage 1. Repeat this operation for `MNavURL` 2 and 3.

2. Find `AIURL:1_Here` and replace the token with the destination for the first action item link at the top of the page. Repeat this operation for `AIURL` 2 and 3.

3. Find `FNavURL:1_Here` and replace the token with the filename you selected for subpage 1. Repeat this operation for `FNavURL` 2 and 3.

---

3. Place special features

Place Web site copyright in your pages.

1. Find `WebsiteCopyright:1_Here` and replace the token with your Web site copyright text.

2. Save and close `index.html` in your text editor.

---

4. Set up the subpage template

Perform the same set of edits that you completed for the `index.html` file on the subpage master template file, `subpage.html`.

1. Open `subpage.html` in your text editor.

2. Return to the beginning of this section ("Building the Site Skeleton"), and start with main Step 1, "Place navigation labels."

3. Complete main Steps 1, 2, and 3 using the `subpage.html` file instead of the `index.html` file.

4. Save `subpage.html` in your text editor. Do not rename the file.

Creating Subpage Files

5. Create subpage files

Use the Save As feature in your text editor to save the `subpage.html` template with the first of the subpage filenames you selected in your content plan. Repeat this to create all subpages listed in your content plan.

Save all files to the `\1010` folder on your desktop.

1. Verify that `subpage.html` is open in your text editor.

2. Choose File ➪ Save As or similar from your text editor. Enter the filename you selected for subpage 1, and click OK.

3. Repeat Step 2 for all subpages in your content plan.

4. Repeat Step 2 for any linked articles or catalog detail pages you identified in your content plan.

6. Display your site

Open your site to check that your labels and pages display correctly.

1. Launch `index.html` from your computer by double-clicking the filename, or choose File ➪ Open (from most browsers) to open it in your browser. An empty home page should appear.

2. Click the navigation links at the top and bottom of the home page and you should see empty subpage pages.

3. Close the empty site skeleton.

Placing Content in the Home Page

7. Place home articles

Place the headings and paragraph text for the articles in `index.html` (see Figure 10-4).

1. Open `index.html` in your text editor.

2. Find `Heading:1_Here` and replace the token with your heading text. Repeat for `Heading 2` and `3`.

3. Find `Paragraph:1_Here` and replace the token with your paragraph text. Repeat for `Paragraph` 2 and 3.

4. Find `LinkLabel:1_Here` and replace the token with the label text for this link. Repeat for `LinkLabel` 2 and 3.

5. Find `LinkURL:1_Here`. Replace the token with the filename you have selected to be accessed from this link. Repeat for `LinkURL` 2 and 3.

6. Save `index.html` in your text editor.

Placing Content in Subpages

Use the following operations to place content into all of your site subpages. Use the subpage token reference (see Figure 10-4) to see the position of the content and label tokens. Repeat this operation to enter content in all of your subpages.

---

8. Place subpage articles   Place article headings and text in your subpages.

1. Open the selected subpage in your text editor.

2. Find `Heading:1_Here` and replace the token with your heading text.

3. Find `Paragraph:1_Here` and replace the token with your paragraph text.

---

9. Place link blocks   Assign the labels and links to other pages within the site or to external Web sites using the block of links provided (see Figure 10-4).

1. Find `LinkLabel:1_Here` and replace the token with the label text for this link.

2. Find `LinkURL:1_Here` and replace the token with the filename you have selected to be accessed from this link.

3. Repeat Steps 1 and 2 for the three remaining `LinkLabel` and `LinkURL` items 2, 3, and 4.

4. Save and close the file when you have finished editing.

Finalizing Your Site

10. Edit site logo and pictures   Turn to Chapter 3 for explanation and procedures to replace the default template logo and images with your own logo and images.

11. Display your Web site   Launch `index.html` from your computer by double-clicking the filename, or choose File ➪ Open. Check your work in your browser window.

12. Edit and adjust   Make edits by opening up your home page or subpage page files in your text editor and making edits to the content. Be sure to edit only your content and not to disturb any of the surrounding code.

13. Publish   The basic parameters of what you should provide to your Web hosting company are outlined in Chapter 3. For the specifics on actually posting your live site to the Web, contact your service provider for details.

Variations

Variation 1011 Overview   This version of the design replaces the bright green framing area with a soft gray. Otherwise the design and layout are the same. Main navigation items are presented in gray, top-of-page action items are presented in green bold, and footer navigation items are presented in green regular font display.

See the images in the CD-ROM's Gallery section.

Variation 1012 Overview   This version of the design replaces the bright green framing area with a strong orange. Otherwise the design and layout are the same. Main navigation items are presented in orange bold, top-of-page action items are presented in black bold, and footer navigation are presented in orange regular font display.

See the images in the CD-ROM's Gallery section.

Template 1020 Archives of Information

Information archive site offers a single article per page supported by multiple headlines. You can use it to present a variety of content with clear headlines, and subheadings and focus elements introduce content visually and dramatically.

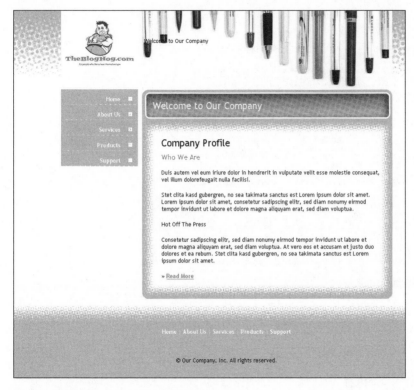

Figure 10-5: Template 1020 home page

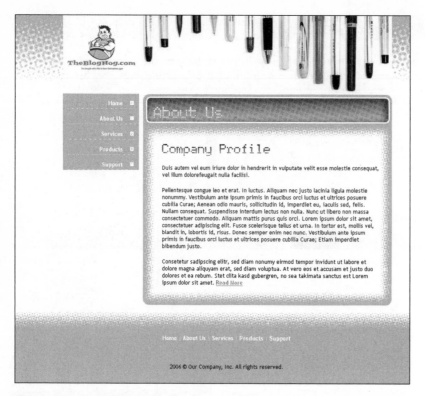

Figure 10-6: Template 1020 subpage

Template Developer   Ken Milhous

Filename and Location   CD-ROM: `\Templates\Chapter 10\102\1020`

Variations on this Design   1021
                                  1022

Site Development Detail   Procedures and supporting information on placing content,
                                  links, and Web site images are presented in Chapter 3.

Design Summary

Recommended Use

Enhanced article presentation to create online information repositories, portals, and other reference pages.

Look and Feel

Style is based on a white background with blue framing elements and colorful anchor artwork. The home page and subpages are identical in layout and format.

This design presents one article per page with multiple lead headings. This supports multiple layers of titles and subheadings to help readers get a sense of the content before reading it.

Content Plan

Content Plan Overview

Before entering content in your site, make a list of the Web page labels and filenames you will use to build your Web site skeleton. Detailed coverage on building your content plan is presented in Chapter 3.

Subpages

Design supports a dedicated home link and four principal subpages. Identify and write down the screen labels and the related filenames.

Articles

Home page and subpages are identical with multiple headlines for the single feature article on the page.

Copy the Template

Follow these steps to copy the template to your hard drive:

1. Access the `\Templates\Chapter 10\102\1020` folder on your CD-ROM.

2. Drag the `\1020` folder to your desktop or copy and paste the `\1020` folder to your desktop.

Template Headings and Tags

Figure 10-7: Template 1020 home page token reference

Figure 10-8: Template 1020 subpage token reference

Building Your Site Step-by-Step: 1020 Archives of Information

Building the Site Skeleton

Use the following set of operations to enter the central navigation. Perform the exact same operations within index.html and subpage.html. Web site navigation and building the site skeleton are presented in Chapter 3.

Note that when opening index.html or subpage.html in Internet Explorer from your hard drive, a security message may appear. Click for more options, and choose to display the full content so the template displays correctly.

1. Place navigation labels

Review the list of subpage labels and filenames from your content plan. You place the labels for subpage 1 at the top (MNav) and bottom (FNav) of your page. See Figures 10-7 for home and 10-8 for subpages.

1. Open `index.html` in your text editor.

2. Find `MNavLabel:1_Here` and replace the token with the label for subpage 1.

3. Find `FNavLabel:1_Here` and replace the token with the label for subpage 1.

4. Repeat Steps 2 and 3 for `MNavLabel` and `FNavLabel` 2, 3, and 4.

2. Place navigation links

Review the list of subpage labels and filenames from your content plan. In the following operation you place the links to the filename for subpage 1 at the top (MNav) and bottom (FNav) of your page. Enter all filenames in lowercase.

1. Find `MNavURL:1_Here` and replace the token with the filename you selected for subpage 1.

2. Find `FNavURL:1_Here` and replace the token with the filename you selected for subpage 1.

3. Repeat Steps 1 and 2 for `MNavURL` and `FNavURL` 2, 3, and 4.

3. Place special features

Place Web site copyright in your pages.

1. Find `WebsiteCopyright:1_Here` and replace the token with your Web site copyright text.

2. Save and close `index.html` in your text editor.

4. Set up the subpage template

Perform the same set of edits that you completed for the `index.html` file on the subpage master template file, `subpage.html`.

1. Open `subpage.html` in your text editor.

2. Return to the beginning of this section ("Building the Site Skeleton"), and start with main Step 1, "Place navigation labels."

3. Complete main Steps 1, 2, and 3 using the `subpage.html` file instead of the `index.html` file.

4. Save `subpage.html` in your text editor. Do not rename the file.

Creating Subpage Files

5. Create subpage files

Use the Save As feature in your text editor to save the `subpage.html` template with the first of the subpage filenames you selected in your content plan. Repeat this to create all subpages listed in your content plan.

Save all files to the `\1020` folder on your desktop.

1. Verify that `subpage.html` is open in your text editor.

2. Choose File ➪ Save As or similar from your text editor. Enter the filename you selected for subpage 1, and click OK.

3. Repeat Step 2 for all subpages in your content plan.

4. Repeat Step 2 for any linked articles or catalog detail pages you identified in your content plan.

6. Display your site

Open your site to check that your labels and pages display correctly.

1. Launch `index.html` from your computer by double-clicking the filename, or choose File ➪ Open (from most browsers) to open it in your browser. An empty home page should appear.

2. Click the navigation links at the top and bottom of the home page and you should see empty subpage pages.

3. Close the empty site skeleton.

Placing Content in the Home Page

7. Place home articles   Place the headings and paragraph text for the articles in `index.html` (see Figure 10-7).

1. Open `index.html` in your text editor.

2. Find `Heading:1_Here` and replace the token with your heading text. Repeat this operation for `Heading` 2, 3, and 4.

3. Find `Paragraph:1_Here` and replace the token with your paragraph text.

4. Find `LinkLabel:1_Here` and replace the token with the label text for this link.

5. Find `LinkURL:1_Here` and replace the token with the filename you have selected to be accessed from this link.

6. Save `index.html` in your text editor.

Placing Content in Subpages

Use the following operations to place content into all of your site subpages. Use the subpage token reference (see Figure 10-8) to see the position of the content and label tokens. Repeat this operation to enter content in all of your subpages.

8. Place subpage articles   Place article headings and text in your subpages.

1. Open the selected subpage in your text editor

2. Find `Heading:1_Here` and replace the token with your heading text. Repeat this operation for `Heading` 2, 3, and 4.

3. Find `Paragraph:1_Here` and replace the token with your paragraph text.

4. Find `LinkLabel:1_Here` and replace the token with the label text for this link.

5. Find `LinkURL:1_Here` and replace the token with the filename you have selected to be accessed from this link.

6. Save and close the file when you have finished editing.

Finalizing Your Site

9. Edit site logo and pictures

Turn to Chapter 3 for explanation and procedures to replace the default template logo and images with your own logo and images.

10. Display your Web site

Launch `index.html` from your computer by double-clicking the filename, or choose File ➪ Open. Check your work in your browser window.

11. Edit and adjust

Make edits by opening up your home page or subpage page files in your text editor and making edits to the content. Be sure to edit only your content and not to disturb any of the surrounding code.

12. Publish

The basic parameters of what you should provide to your Web hosting company are outlined in Chapter 3. For the specifics on actually posting your live site to the Web, contact your service provider for details.

Variations

Variation 1021 Overview

This variation presents a dark version of the design, with backgrounds in shades of gray and black. The anchor image is a black-and-white abstract.

See the images in the CD-ROM's Gallery section.

Variation 1022 Overview

In this version, the page is presented with a gray background and black framing areas. The main navigation area is presented in bright green, enhanced by an anchor image of bright green grass.

See the images in the CD-ROM's Gallery section.

Template 1030   Articles and Resources

Resource information site that you can use for any information presentation purpose, including presenting articles, research, and information resources.

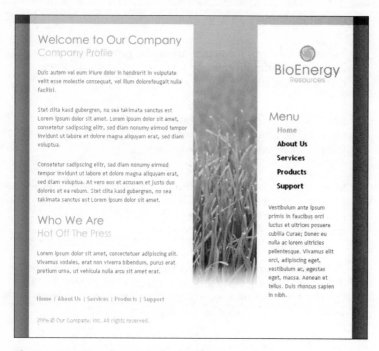

Figure 10-9: Template 1030 home page

Figure 10-10: Template 1030 subpage

Template Developer	Ken Milhous
Filename and Location	CD-ROM: \Templates\Chapter 10\103\1030
Variations on this Design	1031 1032
Site Development Detail	Procedures and supporting information on placing content, links, and Web site images are presented in Chapter 3.

Design Summary

Recommended Use   Enhanced article presentation to create online information repositories, portals, and other reference pages.

Look and Feel   White background with accents and anchor photograph in shades of green create a simple uncluttered presentation, with content left aligned and an unconventional positioning of main navigation elements to the right of the design.

Design presents two articles on the home page and one on the subpages, with main and subheading elements presenting lead information about the content.

Content Plan

Content Plan Overview   Before entering content in your site, make a list of the Web page labels and filenames you will use to build your Web site skeleton. Detailed coverage on building your content plan is presented in Chapter 3.

Subpages   Design supports a dedicated home link and four principal subpages. Identify and write down the screen labels and the related filenames.

Articles   Home page and subpages are identical, with multiple headlines for the single feature article on the page.

Copy the Template   Follow these steps to copy the template to your hard drive:

1. Access the `\Templates\Chapter 10\103\1030` folder on your CD-ROM.

2. Drag the `\1030` folder to your desktop or copy and paste the `\1030` folder to your desktop.

Template Headings and Tags

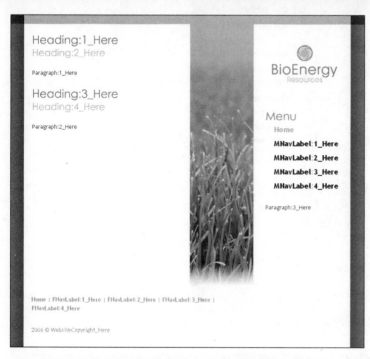

Figure 10-11: Template 1030 home page token reference

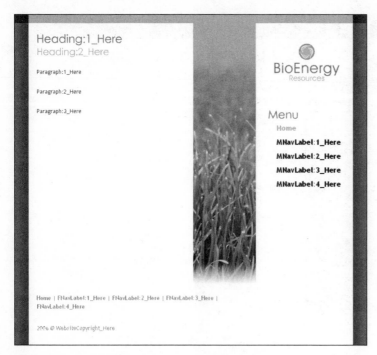

Figure 10-12: Template 1030 subpage token reference

Building Your Site Step-by-Step: 1030 Articles and Resources

Building the Site Skeleton

Use the following set of operations to enter the central navigation. Perform the exact same operations within `index.html` and `subpage.html`. Web site navigation and building the site skeleton are presented in Chapter 3.

Note that when opening `index.html` or `subpage.html` in Internet Explorer from your hard drive, a security message may appear. Click for more options, and choose to display the full content so the template displays correctly.

1. Place navigation labels	Review the list of subpage labels and filenames from your content plan. You place the labels for subpage 1 on the side (MNav) and bottom (FNav) of your page. See Figures 10-11 for home and 10-12 for subpages.

1. Open `index.html` in your text editor.

2. Find `MNavLabel:1_Here` and replace the token with the label for subpage 1.

3. Find `FNavLabel:1_Here` and replace the token with the label for subpage 1.

4. Repeat Steps 2 and 3 for `MNavLabel` and `FNavLabel` 2, 3, and 4.

2. Place navigation links	Review the list of subpage labels and filenames from your content plan. In the following operation you place the links to the filename for subpage 1 at the top (MNav) and bottom (FNav) of your page. Enter all filenames in lowercase.

1. Find `MNavURL:1_Here` and replace the token with the filename you selected for subpage 1.

2. Find `FNavURL:1_Here` and replace the token with the filename you selected for subpage 1.

3. Repeat Steps 1 and 2 for `MNavURL` and `FNavURL` 2, 3, and 4.

3. Place special features	Place Web site copyright in your pages.

1. Find `WebsiteCopyright:1_Here` and replace the token with your Web site copyright text.

2. Save and close `index.html` in your text editor.

4. Set up the subpage template	Perform the same set of edits that you completed for the `index.html` file on the subpage master template file, `subpage.html`.

1. Open `subpage.html` in your text editor.

2. Return to the beginning of this section ("Building the Site Skeleton"), and start with main Step 1, "Place navigation labels."

3. Complete main Steps 1, 2, and 3 using the `subpage.html` file instead of the `index.html` file.

4. Save `subpage.html` in your text editor. Do not rename the file.

Creating Subpage Files

5. Create subpage files

Use the Save As feature in your text editor to save the `subpage.html` template with the first of the subpage filenames you selected in your content plan. Repeat this to create all subpages listed in your content plan.

Save all files to the `\1030` folder on your desktop.

1. Verify that `subpage.html` is open in your text editor.

2. Choose File ➪ Save As or similar from your text editor. Enter the filename you selected for subpage 1, and click OK.

3. Repeat Step 2 for all subpages in your content plan.

4. Repeat Step 2 for any linked articles or catalog detail pages you identified in your content plan.

6. Display your site

Open your site to check that your labels and pages display correctly.

1. Launch `index.html` from your computer by double-clicking the filename, or choose File ➪ Open (from most browsers) to open it in your browser. An empty home page should appear.

2. Click the navigation links at the top and bottom of the home page and you should see empty subpage pages.

3. Close the empty site skeleton.

Placing Content in the Home Page

7. Place home articles

Place the headings and paragraph text for the articles in `index.html` (see Figure 10-11).

1. Open `index.html` in your text editor.

2. Find `Heading:1_Here` and replace the token with your heading text. Repeat this operation for `Heading` 2, 3, and 4.

3. Find `Paragraph:1_Here` and replace the token with your paragraph text.

4. Find `Paragraph:2_Here` and replace the token with your paragraph text.

8. Place sidebar paragraph

Place a descriptive paragraph in the sidebar at the right, beneath the Main Navigation links.

1. Find `Paragraph:3_Here` and replace the token with a descriptive paragraph. You can delete this token if you do not want to use it.

2. Save `index.html` in your text editor.

Placing Content in Subpages

Use the following operations to place content into all of your site subpages. Use the subpage token reference (see Figure 10-12) to see the position of the content and label tokens. Repeat this operation to enter content in all of your subpages.

9. Place subpage articles

Place article headings and text in your subpages.

1. Open the selected subpage in your text editor.

2. Find `Heading:1_Here` and replace the token with your heading text. Repeat this operation for `Heading` 2.

3. Find `Paragraph:1_Here` and replace the token with your paragraph text. Repeat this operation for `Paragraph` 2 and 3.

4. Save and close the file when you have finished editing.

Finalizing Your Site

10. Edit site logo and pictures Turn to Chapter 3 for explanation and procedures to replace the default template logo and images with your own logo and images.

11. Display your Web site Launch `index.html` from your computer by double-clicking the filename, or choose File ⇨ Open. Check your work in your browser window.

12. Edit and adjust Make edits by opening up your home page or subpage page files in your text editor and making edits to the content. Be sure to edit only your content and not to disturb any of the surrounding code.

13. Publish The basic parameters of what you should provide to your Web hosting company are outlined in Chapter 3. For the specifics on actually posting your live site to the Web, contact your service provider for details.

Variations

Variation 1031 Overview The design is presented with a blue background and related coloring in some of the principal heading text. The anchor image is a silhouette view of a Ferris wheel.

See the images in the CD-ROM's Gallery section.

Variation 1032 Overview A rainbow treatment of the Ferris wheel anchor image is reflected in a rainbow color bar at the top of the design. Fonts for headings are in shades of blue and green.

See the images in the CD-ROM's Gallery section.

Template 1040 E-Zines

Electronic magazine or e-zine layout for publishing specialty news, features, and content over the Web. You can adapt this design to serve as an electronic newsletter or to present information archives and resources on any topic.

Figure 10-13: Template 1040 home page

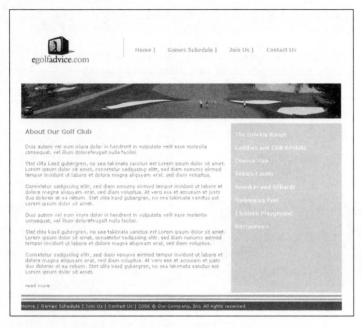

Figure 10-14: Template 1040 subpage

Template Developer	Yana Beylinson
Filename and Location	CD-ROM: \Templates\Chapter 10\104\1040
Variations on this Design	1041 1042
Site Development Detail	Procedures and supporting information on placing content, links, and Web site images are presented in Chapter 3.

Design Summary

Recommended Use	An e-zine is an electronic newsletter that readers can access like a Web site. Often these sites are supported with regular e-mail blasts to members of a community of interest that contain links to the sites with notes on any updates. This site is an information array like others in this chapter, and you can use it for an e-zine or any other information presentation, archive, or resource application.

Look and Feel

Style is based on a white background with gray accent areas. The anchor image carries a golf theme but you can adapt the site with a different image to carry themed content.

Design presents a home page with three side-by-side newspaper style column article areas. Subpages carry a single article and contain a sidebar with links to eight separate main navigation pages.

Content Plan

Content Plan Overview

Before entering content in your site, make a list of the Web page labels and filenames you will use to build your Web site skeleton. Detailed coverage on building your content plan is presented in Chapter 3.

Subpages

Design supports three main navigation links plus a dedicated home link. Identify and write down the screen labels and the related filenames.

Articles

The home page supports three article leads, and the subpage presents a single article and eight action item links to other pages or external URLs.

Copy the Template

Follow these steps to copy the template to your hard drive:

1. Access the `\Templates\Chapter 10\104\1040` folder on your CD-ROM.

2. Drag the `\1040` folder to your desktop or copy and paste the `\1040` folder to your desktop.

Template Headings and Tags

Figure 10-15: Template 1040 home page token reference

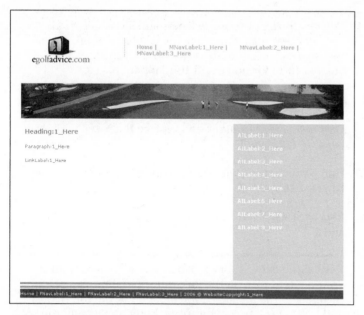

Figure 10-16: Template 1040 subpage token reference

Building Your Site Step-by-Step: 1040 E-Zines

Building the Site Skeleton

Use the following set of operations to enter the central navigation. Perform the exact same operations within `index.html` and `subpage.html`. Web site navigation and building the site skeleton are presented in Chapter 3.

Note that when opening `index.html` or `subpage.html` in Internet Explorer from your hard drive, a security message may appear. Click for more options, and choose to display the full content so the template displays correctly.

1. Place navigation labels

Review the list of subpage labels and filenames from your content plan. You place the labels for subpage 1 at the top (`MNav`) and bottom (`FNav`) of your page. See Figures 10-15 for home and 10-16 for subpages.

1. Open `index.html` in your text editor.

2. Find `MNavLabel:1_Here` and replace the token with the label for subpage 1.

3. Find `FNavLabel:1_Here` and replace the token with the label for subpage 1.

4. Repeat Steps 2 and 3 for `MNavLabel` and `FNavLabel` 2 and 3.

2. Place navigation links

Review the list of subpage labels and filenames from your content plan. In the following operation you place the links to the filename for subpage 1 at the top (`MNav`) and bottom (`FNav`) of your page. Enter all filenames in lowercase.

1. Find `MNavURL:1_Here` and replace the token with the filename you selected for subpage 1.

2. Find `FNavURL:1_Here` and replace the token with the filename you selected for subpage 1.

3. Repeat Steps 1 and 2 for `MNavURL` and `FNavURL` 2 and 3.

3. Place special features

Place Web site copyright in your pages.

1. Find `WebsiteCopyright:1_Here` and replace the token with your Web site copyright text.

2. Save and close `index.html` in your text editor.

4. Set up the subpage template

Perform the same set of edits that you completed for the `index.html` file on the subpage master template file, `subpage.html`.

1. Open `subpage.html` in your text editor.

2. Return to the beginning of this section ("Building the Site Skeleton"), and start with main Step 1, "Place navigation labels."

3. Complete main Steps 1, 2, and 3 using the `subpage.html` file instead of the `index.html` file.

4. Save `subpage.html` in your text editor. Do not rename the file.

Creating Subpage Files

5. Create subpage files

Use the Save As feature in your text editor to save the `subpage.html` template with the first of the subpage filenames you selected in your content plan. Repeat this to create all subpages listed in your content plan.

Save all files to the `\1040` folder on your desktop.

1. Verify that `subpage.html` is open in your text editor.

2. Choose File ⇨ Save As or similar from your text editor. Enter the filename you selected for subpage 1, and click OK.

3. Repeat Step 2 for all subpages in your content plan.

4. Repeat Step 2 for any linked articles or catalog detail pages you identified in your content plan.

6. Display your site

Open your site to check that your labels and pages display correctly.

1. Launch `index.html` from your computer by double-clicking the filename, or choose File ⇨ Open (from most browsers) to open it in your browser. An empty home page should appear.

2. Click the navigation links at the top and bottom of the home page and you should see empty subpage pages.

3. Close the empty site skeleton.

Placing Content in the Home Page

7. Place home articles

Place the headings and paragraph text for the articles in `index.html` (see Figure 10-15).

1. Open `index.html` in your text editor.

2. Find `Heading:1_Here` and replace the token with your heading text. Repeat for `Heading` 2 and 3.

3. Find `Paragraph:1_Here` and replace the token with your paragraph text. Repeat for `Paragraph` 2 and 3.

4. Find `LinkLabel:1_Here` and replace the token with the label text for this link. Repeat for `LinkLabel` 2 and 3.

5. Find `LinkURL:1_Here` and replace the token with the filename you have selected to be accessed from this link. Repeat for `LinkURL` 2 and 3.

6. Save `index.html` in your text editor.

Placing Content in Subpages

Use the following operations to place content into all of your site subpages. Use the subpage token reference (see Figure 10-16) to see the position of the content and label tokens. Repeat this operation to enter content in all of your subpages.

---

8. Place subpage articles

Place article headings and text in your subpages.

1. Open the selected subpage in your text editor.

2. Find `Heading:1_Here` and replace the token with your heading text.

3. Find `Paragraph:1_Here` and replace the token with your paragraph text.

4. Find `LinkLabel:1_Here` and replace the token with the label text for this link.

5. Find `LinkURL:1_Here` and replace the token with the filename you have selected to be accessed from this link.

6. Save and close the file when you have finished editing.

9. Place action item sidebar

Place the headings and paragraph text for the featured article in the selected subpage.

1. Find `AILabel:1_Here` and replace the token with your action item heading text.

2. Find `AIURL:1_Here` and replace the token with the filename for the action itemlink.

3. Repeat Steps 1 and 2 for `AILabel` and `AIURL` 2, 3, 4, 5, 6, 7, and 8.

Finalizing Your Site

9. Edit site logo and pictures
Turn to Chapter 3 for explanation and procedures to replace the default template logo and images with your own logo and images.

10. Display your Web site
Launch `index.html` from your computer by double-clicking the filename, or choose File ⇨ Open. Check your work in your browser window.

11. Edit and adjust
Make edits by opening up your home page or subpage page files in your text editor and making edits to the content. Be sure to edit only your content and not to disturb any of the surrounding code.

12. Publish
The basic parameters of what you should provide to your Web hosting company are outlined in Chapter 3. For the specifics on actually posting your live site to the Web, contact your service provider for details.

Variations

Variation 1041 Overview
This version of the design uses different color accents in the footer line on the home page and a pink background for the sidebar on the subpages. Otherwise the design and layout are the same as the default form.

See the images in the CD-ROM's Gallery section.

Variation 1042 Overview
This version of the design uses different color accents in the footer line on the home page and a dark gray background for the sidebar on the subpages. Otherwise the design and layout are the same as the default form.

See the images in the CD-ROM's Gallery section.

Template 1050 Newsletter

Electronic newsletter site offering a simple presentation for any kind of informational content. The presented example is a church newsletter, but you can adapt this site for any organization, for any application.

Figure 10-17: Template 1050 home page

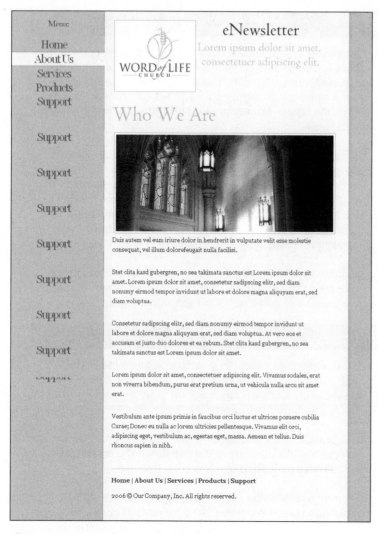

Figure 10-18: Template 1050 subpage

Template Developer	Ken Milhous
Filename and Location	**CD-ROM:** \Templates\Chapter 10\105\1050
Variations on this Design	1051 1052
Site Development Detail	Procedures and supporting information on placing content, links, and Web site images are presented in Chapter 3.

Design Summary

Recommended Use

Newsletter layout emphasizes headings presented in white space for emphasis. It is ideal to convey topics of interest with maximum attention. The open style of the pages makes good use of empty space to set off content. You can adapt the layout for any general information or community application.

Look and Feel

Using soft earth tones offset by white content areas, this site creates a simple and elegant presentation for content. Particular emphasis is placed on large format headings that are grouped to support main and subtitle introductions to article content. You can also set up the heading array as theme headings at the top that carry an organizational message on every page of the site.

Medium- to low-density design presents a home page with large format headings and paragraph elements integrated into a series of sectional photographic images.

Content Plan

Content Plan Overview

Before entering content in your site, make a list of the Web page labels and filenames you will use to build your Web site skeleton. Detailed coverage on building your content plan is presented in Chapter 3.

Subpages

Design supports a dedicated home page plus four main navigation links. Identify and write down the screen labels and the related filenames.

Theme Headings

You may use Heading 1 and Heading 2 elements with paragraph text as recurring theme elements across all pages (the default operation) or enter text for them differently on each page with key messages or inspirational content.

Articles

Home page and subpages both carry multiple headlines for the single feature article on the page.

Copy the Template

Follow these steps to copy the template to your hard drive:

1. Access the `\Templates\Chapter 10\105\1050` folder on your CD-ROM.

2. Drag the `\1050` folder to your desktop or copy and paste the `\1050` folder to your desktop.

Template Headings and Tags

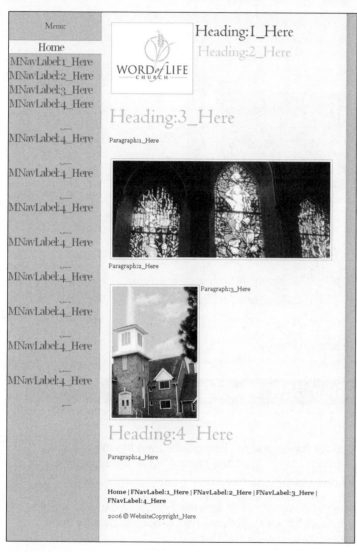

Figure 10-19: Template 1050 home page token reference

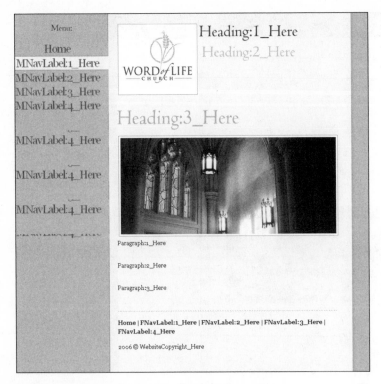

Figure 10-20: Template 1050 subpage token reference

Building Your Site Step-by-Step: 1050 Newsletter

Building the Site Skeleton

Use the following set of operations to enter the central navigation. Perform the exact same operations within index.html and subpage.html. Web site navigation and building the site skeleton are presented in Chapter 3.

Note that when opening index.html or subpage.html in Internet Explorer from your hard drive, a security message may appear. Click for more options, and choose to display the full content so the template displays correctly.

1. Place navigation labels	Review the list of subpage labels and filenames from your content plan. You place the labels for subpage 1 at the top (MNav) and bottom (FNav) of your page. See Figures 10-19 for home and 10-20 for subpages.

1. Open `index.html` in your text editor.

2. Find `MNavLabel:1_Here` and replace the token with the label for subpage 1.

3. Find `FNavLabel:1_Here` and replace the token with the label for subpage 1.

4. Repeat Steps 2 and 3 for `MNavLabel` and `FNavLabel` 2, 3, and 4.

2. Place navigation links	Review the list of subpage labels and filenames from your content plan. In the following operation you place the links to the filename for subpage 1 at the top (MNav) and bottom (FNav) of your page. Enter all filenames in lowercase.

1. Find `MNavURL:1_Here` and replace the token with the filename you selected for subpage 1.

2. Find `FNavURL:1_Here` and replace the token with the filename you selected for subpage 1.

3. Repeat Steps 1 and 2 for `MNavURL` and `FNavURL` 2, 3, and 4.

3. Place theme headings	Place the same theme message and supporting text across every page of your site. You can apply these steps individually to the home page and individual subpages if you want to present different themes at the top of the page design.

1. Find `Heading:1_Here` and replace the token with your page tagline text.

2. Find `Heading:2_Here` and replace the token with your page tagline text.

4. Place special features	Place Web site copyright in your pages.

1. Find `WebsiteCopyright:1_Here` and replace the token with your Web site copyright text.

2. Save and close `index.html` in your text editor.

5. Set up the subpage template	Perform the same set of edits that you completed for the `index.html` file on the subpage master template file, `subpage.html`.

1. Open `subpage.html` in your text editor.

2. Return to the beginning of this section ("Building the Site Skeleton"), and start with main Step 1, "Place navigation labels."

3. Complete main Steps 1, 2, 3, and 4 using the `subpage.html` file instead of the `index.html` file.

4. Save `subpage.html` in your text editor. Do not rename the file.

Creating Subpage Files

6. Create subpage files	Use the Save As feature in your text editor to save the `subpage.html` template with the first of the subpage filenames you selected in your content plan. Repeat this to create all subpages listed in your content plan.

Save all files to the `\1050` folder on your desktop.

1. Verify that `subpage.html` is open in your text editor.

2. Choose File ➪ Save As or similar from your text editor. Enter the filename you selected for subpage 1, and click OK.

3. Repeat Step 2 for all subpages in your content plan.

4. Repeat Step 2 for any linked articles or catalog detail pages you identified in your content plan.

| **7. Display your site** | Open your site to check that your labels and pages display correctly. |

1. Launch `index.html` from your computer by double-clicking the filename, or choose File ⇨ Open (from most browsers) to open it in your browser. An empty home page should appear.

2. Click the navigation links at the top and bottom of the home page and you should see empty subpage pages.

3. Close the empty site skeleton.

Placing Content in the Home Page

| **8. Place home articles** | Place the headings and paragraph text for the articles in `index.html` (see Figure 10-19). |

1. Open `index.html` in your text editor.

2. Find `Heading:3_Here` and replace the token with your heading text. Repeat this operation for `Heading` 4.

3. Find `Paragraph:1_Here` and replace the token with your paragraph text. Repeat this operation for `Paragraph` 2, 3, and 4.

4. Save `index.html` in your text editor.

Placing Content in Subpages

Use the following operations to place content into all of your site subpages. Use the subpage token reference (see Figure 10-20) to see the position of the content and label tokens. Repeat this operation to enter content in all of your subpages.

| **9. Place subpage articles** | Place article headings and text in your subpages. |

1. Open the selected subpage in your text editor.

2. Find `Heading:3_Here` and replace the token with your heading text.

3. Find `Paragraph:1_Here` and replace the token with your paragraph text. Repeat this operation for `Paragraph` 2 and 3.

4. Save and close the file when you have finished editing.

Finalizing Your Site

10. Edit site logo and pictures   Turn to Chapter 3 for explanation and procedures to replace the default template logo and images with your own logo and images.

11. Display your Web site   Launch index.html from your computer by double-clicking the filename, or choose File ➪ Open. Check your work in your browser window.

12. Edit and adjust   Make edits by opening up your home page or subpage page files in your text editor and making edits to the content. Be sure to edit only your content and not to disturb any of the surrounding code.

13. Publish   The basic parameters of what you should provide to your Web hosting company are outlined in Chapter 3. For the specifics on actually posting your live site to the Web, contact your service provider for details.

Variations

Variation 1051 Overview   The design is presented in a vibrant array of color: brown for the left-aligned navigation areas, shades of orange for the content area, and bright red for the right accent area.

See the images in the CD-ROM's Gallery section.

Variation 1052 Overview   A simple version of the design based on a background of light green for the left-aligned navigation area and framing areas and white background for the content area.

See the images in the CD-ROM's Gallery section.

✦   ✦   ✦

Community Templates

Community Web sites are a means to building networks of people interested in a common idea or an objective. The Web is a medium of participation, and it hasn't taken people long to realize that the old-fashioned handbill or flyer pales next to the power of a Web site for drawing people together and encouraging them to take action.

Given the universal assumption of inexpensive Web access, community templates are not a luxury or a tool for the privileged few. Your community can be as simple as a neighborhood watch group or as great as a global alliance to protect the environment.

About Community Templates

Serving the community is one of the prime functions of the Web. Some of the earliest Web experimental sites were communities of interest that allowed people to exchange ideas using a primitive form of what is now called a blog.

Given the many facets of community formation, many of the sites in this book could function as the seed of a workable community site. In this chapter, Web models for community sites have been designed for a cultural community page, a religious outreach, a partisan political club, an environmental organization, and a school. The purpose of each of these organizations is different, but their need to organize people around ideas and action is a common thread.

Building Communities

Community Web sites can be created as a destination for, or as the focus of, action. Destination sites are simply a patch of cyber real estate where an organization or ad hoc group can stake out a spot and stay there, so that those who are interested in their mission can find them. Typically destination sites are driven by calendars that provide information on meetings, programs, and dates of interest, and they serve as the source for simple organizational activities.

Action communities, on the other hand, arise around a shared objective. It's commonplace to hear in the news how local groups have organized to resist new projects by developers or to keep a freeway from being built through the school playground. Communities of action are driven primarily by a long-term agenda expressed as a series of short-term goals.

Other communities can arise from simple shared interests — the need to connect with others who share an interest in a topic. Typically communities such as this are driven by an anchor person or group of contributors who do the work to keep the site going and motivate others to join in and take part.

Community information

A viable community needs to establish credibility and an identity to attract members and participation. Some of the information elements that define a community include

- ✦ Statement of purpose and the mission of the group
- ✦ Group history and founders
- ✦ Prominent members of the group
- ✦ Community calendar activities
- ✦ Accomplishments
- ✦ Goals and objectives for action
- ✦ Member list
- ✦ Activities for member participation

Defining the community is a key function of the Web site. Once the site is created, this information can sit on the Web as a destination and can make others aware of the function of the group. Active communities may need to update their calendars frequently, or to supplement Web site content with event e-mails to a member list.

Calendar and actions

The definitive community document is an events and activities calendar. To remain cohesive, communities generally keep some kind of activities or meetings going, and the Web is an ideal place to post the calendar of actions. In the pre-Internet days, this task was usually accomplished via mailing a newsletter or providing handouts at a meeting. However, with the Web at your disposal, you can post newsletters and information directly on your community site.

When putting together calendars on a community Web site, keep in mind that the Web can be a very effective tool in selling participation. For example, if your group is holding a fund-raising event, of course you want as many people as possible to come. You could just post the announcement on the site, but you can also send out e-mails and ask for RSVPs. Posting the confirmed number of attendees on the site can then project the momentum of the event, encouraging others to attend.

Calendars can also serve as a map for community action. By posting all the events for a given month or an even longer period of time, the community appears larger and organized. The Web can create that impression and help generate interest. Because community time is almost always volunteer time, interest and continuing involvement is a big concern.

Recognition and reward

Everybody likes to see their name in the paper. The principle of recognition extends to the Web as well and can be a great impetus for developing involvement in your community project. In addition to the community information and calendar presented on your Web site, keep in mind that nothing motivates people to read a Web site more than seeing their names in print. Make a point of posting recognition for people who have been involved.

Unlike the local newspaper, the Web travels fast. Recognition is one good motivator for sharing your Web site with others and potentially bringing others into the group. The logic of community action is people acting for a common goal, and the Web is one of the best tools to get people to get up out of their chairs and come forward.

Recognition begins by allowing members to see each other and their contributions to the group. You may want to include member profiles that focus on individual contributions as well as collective activities of the group in fundraising, events, and community projects. Giving awards is a very effective way for a group to confer recognition on its members or involved community leaders. Finally, a simple rule of thumb: A community is made up of individuals, so use every means possible to name and identify your members throughout your site.

Tip   Instead of navigating from the root of the CD to locate a template, you can click the Templates link in the CD browser application to directly access the chapters on the CD. For faster access, click the Gallery link in the CD browser application to view a listing of all templates. Then click any View Files link to view the files for that template.

Template 1110 Cultural Communities

A cultural community site can be used for a local organization, a Web group, or a commercial cultural venture. The design makes dramatic use of color and fonts and offers a vivid and eye-catching site skeleton for any content.

Figure 11-1: Template 1110 home page

Figure 11-2: Template 1110 subpage

Template Developer	Ken Milhous
Filename and Location	CD-ROM: `\Templates\Chapter 11\111\1110`
Variations on this Design	1111 1112
Site Development Detail	Procedures and supporting information on placing content, links, and Web site images are presented in Chapter 3.

Design Summary

Recommended Use

Bright and colorful design that gives dramatic flair to any content. This design is best used by organizations or businesses that want to present a strong and contemporary image. It is particularly well suited for art, entertainment, or youth-oriented sites.

Look and Feel

Deep blue sets the tone for this rich layout. The banner area is offset with a stylized yellow-orange background area, complete with a heading token that you can use either as a tagline or as an individual heading for the home page and subpages.

Design can accept large blocks of information, so it can be a low-, medium-, or high-density layout depending on the content you enter.

Content Plan

Content Plan Overview

Before entering content in your site, make a list of the Web page labels and filenames you will use to build your Web site skeleton. Detailed coverage on building your content plan is presented in Chapter 3.

Subpages

Design supports a dedicated home link and three principal subpages. Identify and write down the screen labels and the related filenames.

Articles

Home page includes three article areas, each supporting follow-on links. Subpages offer two feature articles with a supporting link block beneath.

Link Blocks

Design includes a framed area of dedicated links beneath subpage article areas. You can use these links to cross-link articles within the site or to link to external Web sites that relate to the article content.

Copy the Template

Follow these steps to copy the template to your hard drive:

1. Access the `\Templates\Chapter 11\111\1110` folder on your CD-ROM.

2. Drag the `\1110` folder to your desktop or copy and paste the `\1110` folder to your desktop.

Template Headings and Tags

Figure 11-3: Template 1110 home page token reference

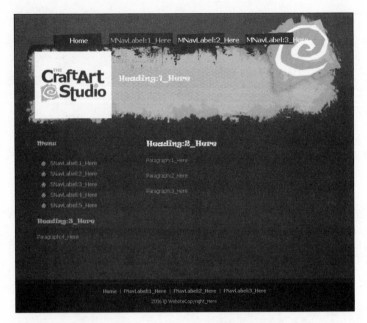

Figure 11-4: Template 1110 subpage token reference

Building Your Site Step-by-Step: 1110 Cultural Communities

Building the Site Skeleton

Use the following set of operations to enter the central navigation. Perform the exact same operations within `index.html` and `subpage.html`. Web site navigation and building the site skeleton are presented in Chapter 3.

Note that when opening `index.html` or `subpage.html` in Internet Explorer from your hard drive, a security message may appear. Click for more options, and choose to display the full content so the template displays correctly.

1. Place navigation labels

Review the list of subpage labels and filenames from your content plan. You place the labels for subpage 1 at the top (MNav) and bottom (FNav) of your page. See Figures 11-3 for home and 11-4 for subpages.

Note that this design includes a sidebar of subnavigation tags that allow you to identify five additional principal pages. Subnavigation (SNav) tokens operate just like the other Nav tokens; they allow you to create and link to additional subpages. These principal pages can be accessed from both the home page and subpages. These pages are in addition to the main navigation pages that appear at the top of the design and the footer navigation pages at the bottom.

1. Open index.html in your text editor.

2. Find MNavLabel:1_Here and replace the token with the label for subpage 1. Repeat this operation for MNavLabel 2 and 3.

3. Find SNavLabel:1_Here and replace the token with the label for featured page 1. Repeat this operation for SNavLabel 2, 3, 4, and 5.

4. Find FNavLabel:1_Here and replace the token with the label for subpage 1. Repeat this operation for FNavLabel 2 and 3.

2. Place navigation links

Review the list of subpage labels and filenames from your content plan. In the following operation you place the links to the filename for subpage 1 at the top (MNav) and bottom (FNav) of your page. Enter all filenames in lowercase.

1. Find MNavURL:1_Here and replace the token with the filename you selected for subpage 1. Repeat this operation for MNavURL 2 and 3.

2. Find SNavURL:1_Here and replace the token with the label for featured page 1. Repeat this operation for SNavLabel 2, 3, 4, and 5.

3. Find FNavURL:1_Here and replace the token with the filename you selected for subpage 1. Repeat this operation for FNavURL 2 and 3.

3. Place special features

Place the text of the Web site copyright in your pages.

1. Find `WebsiteCopyright:1_Here` and replace the token with your Web site copyright text.

2. Find `Heading:1_Here`. Use this to place a prominent tagline on the home page and subpages throughout the site. You can elect to use this token to place individual headlines on the home page and subpages. In that case, change it individually for each page desired.

3. Save and close `index.html` in your text editor.

4. Set up the subpage template

Perform the same set of edits that you completed for the `index.html` file on the subpage master template file, `subpage.html`.

1. Open `subpage.html` in your text editor.

2. Return to the beginning of this section ("Building the Site Skeleton"), and start with main Step 1, "Place navigation labels."

3. Complete main Steps 1, 2, and 3 using the `subpage.html` file instead of the `index.html` file.

4. Save `subpage.html` in your text editor. Do not rename the file.

Creating Subpage Files

5. Create subpage files

Use the Save As feature in your text editor to save the `subpage.html` template with the first of the subpage filenames you selected in your content plan. Repeat this to create all subpages listed in your content plan.

Save all files to the `\1110` folder on your desktop.

1. Verify that `subpage.html` is open in your text editor.

2. Choose File ➪ Save As or similar from your text editor. Enter the filename you selected for subpage 1, and click OK.

3. Repeat Step 2 for all subpages in your content plan.

4. Repeat Step 2 for any linked articles or catalog detail pages you identified in your content plan.

---

6. Display your site

Open your site to check that your labels and pages display correctly.

1. Launch `index.html` from your computer by double-clicking the filename, or choose File ➪ Open (from most browsers) to open it in your browser. An empty home page should appear.

2. Click the navigation links at the top and bottom of the home page and you should see empty subpage pages.

3. Close the empty site skeleton.

Placing Content in the Home Page

7. Place home articles

Place the headings and paragraph text for the articles in `index.html` (see Figure 11-3).

1. Open `index.html` in your text editor.

2. Find `Heading:2_Here` and replace the token with your heading text.

3. Find `Paragraph:1_Here` and replace the token with your paragraph text.

4. Find `Heading:3_Here` and replace the token with your heading text.

5. Find `Paragraph:2_Here` and replace the token with your paragraph text.

6. Find `Paragraph:3_Here` and replace the token with your paragraph text.

8. Place sidebar articles	Place the heading and text to appear directly below the sidebar containing the five subnavigation links.

1. Find `Heading:4_Here` and replace the token with your heading text.

2. Find `Paragraph:4_Here` and replace the token with your paragraph text.

3. Save `index.html` in your text editor.

Placing Content in Subpages

Use the following operations to place content into all of your site subpages. Use the subpage token reference (see Figure 11-4) to see the position of the content and label tokens. Repeat this operation to enter content in all of your subpages.

9. Place subpage articles	Place article headings and text in your subpages.

1. Open the selected subpage in your text editor.

2. Find `Heading:2_Here` and replace the token with your heading text.

3. Find `Paragraph:1_Here` and replace the token with your paragraph text. Repeat this operation for `Paragraph` 2 and 3.

10. Place sidebar articles	Place article headings and text in your subpages.

1. Find `Heading:3_Here` and replace the token with your heading text.

2. Find `Paragraph:4_Here` and replace the token with your paragraph text.

3. Save and close the subpage file when you have finished editing.

Finalizing Your Site

11. Edit site logo and pictures

Turn to Chapter 3 for explanation and procedures to replace the default template logo and images with your own logo and images.

12. Display your Web site

Launch `index.html` from your computer by double-clicking the filename, or choose File ➪ Open. Check your work in your browser window.

13. Edit and adjust

Make edits by opening up your home page or subpage page files in your text editor and making edits to the content. Be sure to edit only your content and not to disturb any of the surrounding code.

14. Publish

The basic parameters of what you should provide to your Web hosting company are outlined in Chapter 3. For the specifics on actually posting your live site to the Web, contact your service provider for details.

Variations

Variation 1111 Overview

The design is presented with background and content area in a green gradient, accented with a complementary green anchor image. Navigation highlights and accent artwork are in orange.

See the images in the CD-ROM's Gallery section.

Variation 1112 Overview

A dark version of the design built on a black-gray background. The anchor image is a creative graffiti pattern on brightly colored brick. Heading fonts are presented in a dramatic and stylized script form in bright red.

See the images in the CD-ROM's Gallery section.

Template 1120 Inspirational / Religious

This inspirational or religious community site is a colorful and dynamic layout that communicates excitement. This design can be adapted to any information presentation or community action purpose.

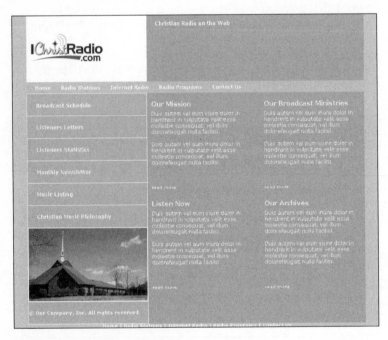

Figure 11-5: Template 1120 home

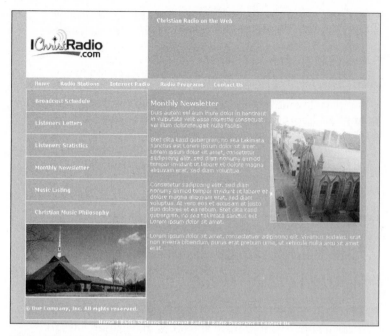

Figure 11-6: Template 1120 subpage

Template Developer	Yana Beylinson
Filename and Location	CD-ROM: \Templates\Chapter 11\112\1120
Variations on this Design	1121 1122
Site Development Detail	Procedures and supporting information on placing content, links, and Web site images are presented in Chapter 3.

Design Summary

Recommended Use	With a mix of bright orange, yellow, and earth tones in the text area and an anchor photograph providing contrast, this site is an upbeat presentation of content for any purpose. The home page offers four equally balanced article areas and a site tagline to set the message.

Look and Feel

An orange background makes this a warm and engaging site, with text primarily presented in white over shades of orange. The home page and subpages carry the same essential layout with different article presentations.

Design offers a high-density home page with a low-density subpage layout. The four article areas on the home page support information and news items that can each take their own following subpage. This layout supports 11 main navigation items, with some arrayed in framed sidebar areas and the remainder in a conventional navigation bar near the top of the design. The single subpage article supports a photo accent.

Content Plan

Content Plan Overview

Before entering content in your site, make a list of the Web page labels and filenames you will use to build your Web site skeleton. Detailed coverage on building your content plan is presented in Chapter 3.

Subpages

Design supports four main and footer navigation links to subpages. Identify and write down the screen labels and the related filenames.

Action Items

A left-aligned sidebar on home and subpage layouts contains six action items that can also be used to identify principal subpages.

Articles

Home page includes four article areas, each supporting follow-on links. Subpages offer a single feature article.

Copy the Template

Follow these steps to copy the template to your hard drive:

1. Access the `\Templates\Chapter 11\112\1120` folder on your CD-ROM.

2. Drag the `\1120` folder to your desktop or copy and paste the `\1120` folder to your desktop.

Template Headings and Tags

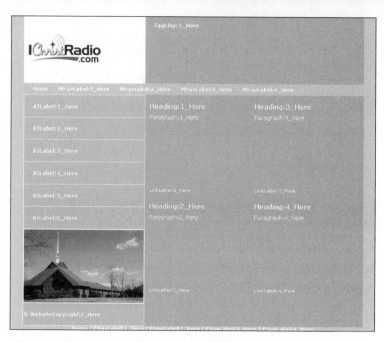

Figure 11-7: Template 1120 home page token reference

Figure 11-8: Template 1120 subpage token reference

Building Your Site Step-by-Step: 1120 Inspirational / Religious

Building the Site Skeleton

Use the following set of operations to enter the central navigation. Perform the exact same operations within `index.html` and `subpage.html`. Web site navigation and building the site skeleton are presented in Chapter 3.

Note that when opening `index.html` or `subpage.html` in Internet Explorer from your hard drive, a security message may appear. Click for more options, and choose to display the full content so the template displays correctly.

1. Place navigation labels	Review the list of subpage labels and filenames from your content plan. You place the labels for subpage 1 at the top (`MNav`) and bottom (`FNav`) of your page. See Figures 11-7 for home and 11-8 for subpages.

1. Open `index.html` in your text editor.

2. Find `MNavLabel:1_Here` and replace the token with the label for subpage 1.

3. Find `FNavLabel:1_Here` and replace the token with the label for subpage 1.

4. Repeat Steps 2 and 3 for `MNavLabel` and `FNavLabel` 2, 3, and 4.

2. Place navigation links	Review the list of subpage labels and filenames from your content plan. In the following operation you place the links to the filename for subpage 1 at the top (`MNav`) and bottom (`FNav`) of your page. Enter all filenames in lowercase.

1. Find `MNavURL:1_Here` and replace the token with the filename you selected for subpage 1.

2. Find `FNavURL:1_Here` and replace the token with the filename you selected for subpage 1.

3. Repeat Steps 1 and 2 for `MNavURL` and `FNavURL` 2, 3, and 4.

3. Place action items	You can enter action items separately for home and individual subpages if you want. In that case, perform these steps when you place content in home and subpages, later in this operation.

1. Find `AILabel:1_Here` and replace the token with the label you selected for action item 1. Repeat this operation for `AILabel` 2, 3, 4, 5, and 6.

2. Find `AIURL:1_Here` and replace the token with the filename you selected for action item 1. Repeat this operation for `AIURL` 2, 3, 4, 5, and 6.

4. Place special features   Place the text of the Web site copyright in your pages.

1. Find `WebsiteCopyright:1_Here` and replace the token with your Web site copyright text.

2. Find `Tagline:1_Here`. Use this to place a prominent tagline on the home page and subpages throughout the site. Enter the text of your desired tagline.

3. Save and close `index.html` in your text editor.

5. Set up the subpage template   Perform the same set of edits that you completed for the `index.html` file on the subpage master template file, `subpage.html`.

1. Open `subpage.html` in your text editor.

2. Return to the beginning of this section ("Building the Site Skeleton"), and start with main Step 1, "Place navigation labels."

3. Complete main Steps 1, 2, 3, and 4 using the `subpage.html` file instead of the `index.html` file.

4. Save `subpage.html` in your text editor. Do not rename the file.

Creating Subpage Files

6. Create subpage files   Use the Save As feature in your text editor to save the `subpage.html` template with the first of the subpage filenames you selected in your content plan. Repeat this to create all subpages listed in your content plan.

Save all files to the `\1120` folder on your desktop.

1. Verify that `subpage.html` is open in your text editor.

2. Choose File ⇨ Save As or similar from your text editor. Enter the filename you selected for subpage 1, and click OK.

3. Repeat Step 2 for all subpages in your content plan.

4. Repeat Step 2 for any linked articles or catalog detail pages you identified in your content plan.

7. Display your site
    Open your site to check that your labels and pages display correctly.

1. Launch `index.html` from your computer by double-clicking the filename, or choose File ➪ Open (from most browsers) to open it in your browser. An empty home page should appear.

2. Click the navigation links at the top and bottom of the home page and you should see empty subpage pages.

3. Close the empty site skeleton.

Placing Content in the Home Page

8. Place home articles
    Place the headings and paragraph text for the articles in `index.html` (see Figure 11-7).

1. Open `index.html` in your text editor.

2. Find `Heading:1_Here` and replace the token with your heading text. Repeat for `Heading` 2, 3, and 4.

3. Find `Paragraph:1_Here` and replace the token with your paragraph text. Repeat for `Paragraph` 2, 3, and 4.

4. Find `LinkLabel:1_Here`. Replace the token with the chosen label text for this link (such as "Read More" or "More Information"). You can delete this token if you do not want to use this link. Repeat for `LinkLabel` 2, 3, and 4.

5. Find `LinkURL:1_Here`. Replace the token with the filename you have selected to be accessed from this link. Repeat for `LinkLabel` 2, 3, and 4.

6. Save `index.html` in your text editor.

Placing Content in Subpages

Use the following operations to place content into all of your site subpages. Use the subpage token reference (see Figure 11-8) to see the position of the content and label tokens. Repeat this operation to enter content in all of your subpages.

9. Place subpage articles	Place article headings and text in your subpages.
	1. Open the selected subpage in your text editor.
	2. Find `Heading:1_Here` and replace the token with your heading text.
	3. Find `Paragraph:1_Here` and replace the token with your paragraph text.
	4. Save and close the file when you have finished editing.

Finalizing Your Site

10. Edit site logo and pictures	Turn to Chapter 3 for explanation and procedures to replace the default template logo and images with your own logo and images.
11. Display your Web site	Launch `index.html` from your computer by double-clicking the filename, or choose File ⇨ Open. Check your work in your browser window.
12. Edit and adjust	Make edits by opening up your home page or subpage page files in your text editor and making edits to the content. Be sure to edit only your content and not to disturb any of the surrounding code.
13. Publish	The basic parameters of what you should provide to your Web hosting company are outlined in Chapter 3. For the specifics on actually posting your live site to the Web, contact your service provider for details.

Variations

Variation 1121 Overview	This version presents the site design with a dominant background of blue with sidebar accents in yellow.
	See the images in the CD-ROM's Gallery section.

Variation 1122 Overview   This version presents the site design with a dominant background in brown and sidebar accents in blue.

See the images in the CD-ROM's Gallery section.

Template 1130 Political Organizations

A political site designed for a great number of topical items and news. The design integrates many standard subpages and link items to offer a highly effective news dissemination layout. You can adapt this design for any information presentation purpose centering on news or galleries of topics.

Figure 11-9: Template 1130 home page

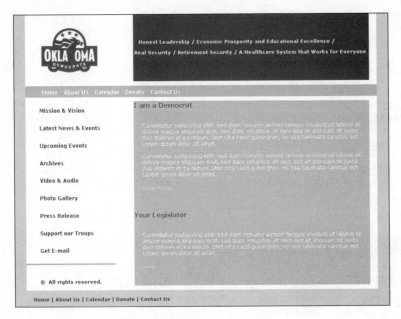

Figure 11-10: Template 1130 subpage

Template Developer	Yana Beylinson
Filename and Location	CD-ROM: \Templates\Chapter 11\113\1130
Variations on this Design	1131 1132
Site Development Detail	Procedures and supporting information on placing content, links, and Web site images are presented in Chapter 3.

Design Summary

Recommended Use

Red, white, and blue are the signature of this site, which offers both a high number of linked pages and a sidebar of links that you can use to create more internal pages or link to external sites.

Look and Feel

With a white background supporting layout elements in red and blue, this is an all-American look and feel that is well-suited to politics, government, or other community or patriotic applications.

The home page features a single lead article with a multi-part anchor image, framed by 13 programmable links to subpages. The design is ideal to engage the reader with articles and items of interest from the home with the content delivered in subpages.

Content Plan

Content Plan Overview

Before entering content in your site, make a list of the Web page labels and filenames you will use to build your Web site skeleton. Detailed coverage on building your content plan is presented in Chapter 3.

Subpages

Design supports four main and footer navigation links for principal subpages. Identify and write down the screen labels and the related filenames.

Action Items

A left-aligned sidebar on home and subpage layouts contains nine action items that can also be used to identify principal subpages.

Articles

Home page includes four article areas, each supporting follow-on links. Subpages offer a single feature article and a photo illustration accent.

Copy the Template

Follow these steps to copy the template to your hard drive:

1. Access the \Templates\Chapter 11\113\1130 folder on your CD-ROM.

2. Drag the \1130 folder to your desktop or copy and paste the \1130 folder to your desktop.

Template Headings and Tags

Figure 11-11: Template 1130 home page token reference

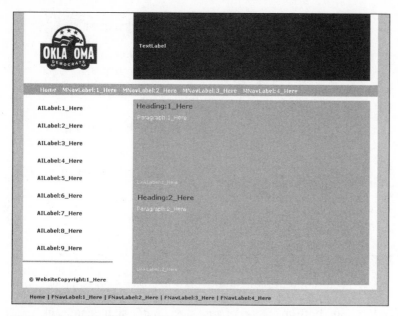

Figure 11-12: Template 1130 subpage token reference

Building Your Site Step-by-Step: 1130 Political Organizations

Building the Site Skeleton

Use the following set of operations to enter the central navigation. Perform the exact same operations within `index.html` and `subpage.html`. Web site navigation and building the site skeleton are presented in Chapter 3.

Note that when opening `index.html` or `subpage.html` in Internet Explorer from your hard drive, a security message may appear. Click for more options, and choose to display the full content so the template displays correctly.

1. Place navigation labels	Review the list of subpage labels and filenames from your content plan. You place the labels for subpage 1 at the top (`MNav`) and bottom (`FNav`) of your page. See Figures 11-11 for home and 11-12 for subpages.

1. Open `index.html` in your text editor.

2. Find `MNavLabel:1_Here` and replace the token with the label for subpage 1.

3. Find `FNavLabel:1_Here` and replace the token with the label for subpage 1.

4. Repeat Steps 2 and 3 for `MNavLabel` and `FNavLabel` 2, 3, and 4.

2. Place navigation links	Review the list of subpage labels and filenames from your content plan. In the following operation you place the links to the filename for subpage 1 at the top (`MNav`) and bottom (`FNav`) of your page. Enter all filenames in lowercase.

1. Find `MNavURL:1_Here` and replace the token with the filename you selected for subpage 1.

2. Find `FNavURL:1_Here` and replace the token with the filename you selected for subpage 1 or a Web site URL.

3. Repeat Steps 1 and 2 for `MNavURL` and `FNavURL` 2, 3, and 4.

3. Place action items	You can enter action items separately for home and individual subpages if you want. In that case, perform these steps when you place content in home and subpages, later in this operation.

1. Find `AILabel:1_Here` and replace the token with the label you selected for action item 1. Repeat this operation for `AILabel` 2, 3, 4, 5, 6, 7, 8, and 9.

2. Find `AIURL:1_Here` and replace the token with the filename you selected for action item 1. Repeat this operation for `AIURL` 2, 3, 4, 5, 6, 7, 8, and 9.

4. Place special features	Place the text of the Web site copyright in your pages.
	1. Find `WebsiteCopyright:1_Here` and replace the token with your Web site copyright text.
	2. Find `Tagline:1_Here`. Use this to place a prominent tagline on the home page and subpages throughout the site. Enter the text of your desired tagline.
	3. Save and close `index.html` in your text editor.
5. Set up the subpage template	Perform the same set of edits that you completed for the `index.html` file on the subpage master template file, `subpage.html`.
	1. Open `subpage.html` in your text editor.
	2. Return to the beginning of this section ("Building the Site Skeleton"), and start with main Step 1, "Place navigation labels."
	3. Complete main Steps 1, 2, 3, and 4 using the `subpage.html` file instead of the `index.html` file.
	4. Save `subpage.html` in your text editor. Do not rename the file.

Creating Subpage Files

6. Create subpage files	Use the Save As feature in your text editor to save the `subpage.html` template with the first of the subpage filenames you selected in your content plan. Repeat this to create all subpages listed in your content plan.
	Save all files to the \1130 folder on your desktop.
	1. Verify that `subpage.html` is open in your text editor.
	2. Choose File ⇨ Save As or similar from your text editor. Enter the filename you selected for subpage 1, and click OK.
	3. Repeat Step 2 for all subpages in your content plan.
	4. Repeat Step 2 for any linked articles or catalog detail pages you identified in your content plan.

7. Display your site	Open your site to check that your labels and pages display correctly.

1. Launch `index.html` from your computer by double-clicking the filename, or choose File ➪ Open (from most browsers) to open it in your browser. An empty home page should appear.

2. Click the navigation links at the top and bottom of the home page and you should see empty subpage pages.

3. Close the empty site skeleton.

Placing Content in the Home Page

8. Place home articles	Place the headings and paragraph text for the articles in `index.html` (see Figure 11-11).

1. Open `index.html` in your text editor.

2. Find `Heading:1_Here` and replace the token with your heading text.

3. Find `Paragraph:1_Here` and replace the token with your paragraph text.

4. Find `LinkLabel:1_Here`. Replace the token with the chosen label text for this link (such as "Read More" or "More Information"). You can delete this token if you do not want to use this link.

5. Find `LinkURL:1_Here`. Replace the token with the filename you have selected to be accessed from this link.

Placing Content in Subpages

Use the following operations to place content into all of your site subpages. Use the subpage token reference (see Figure 11-12) to see the position of the content and label tokens. Repeat this operation to enter content in all of your subpages.

9. Place subpage articles	Place article headings and text in your subpages.

1. Open the selected subpage in your text editor.

2. Find `Heading:1_Here` and replace the token with your heading text.

3. Find `Paragraph:1_Here` and replace the token with your paragraph text.

4. Find `LinkLabel:1_Here` and replace the token with the label text for this link.

5. Find `LinkURL:1_Here` and replace the token with the filename you have selected to be accessed from this link.

6. Find `Heading:2_Here` and replace the token with your heading text.

7. Find `Paragraph:2_Here` and replace the token with your paragraph text.

8. Find `LinkLabel:2_Here` and replace the token with the label text for this link.

9. Find `LinkURL:2_Here` and replace the token with the filename you have selected to be accessed from this link.

10. Save and close the file when you have finished editing.

Finalizing Your Site

10. Edit site logo and pictures

Turn to Chapter 3 for explanation and procedures to replace the default template logo and images with your own logo and images.

11. Display your Web site

Launch `index.html` from your computer by double-clicking the filename, or choose File ➪ Open. Check your work in your browser window.

12. Edit and adjust

Make edits by opening up your home page or subpage page files in your text editor and making edits to the content. Be sure to edit only your content and not to disturb any of the surrounding code.

13. Publish

The basic parameters of what you should provide to your Web hosting company are outlined in Chapter 3. For the specifics on actually posting your live site to the Web, contact your service provider for details.

Variations

Variation 1131 Overview

This version presents the site design with a shade of blue in the banner area. Main navigation elements are presented on a deep blue banner, and footer navigation elements are presented in blue text beneath a red-tinted banner.

See the images in the CD-ROM's Gallery section.

Variation 1132 Overview

This version presents the site design with a white background. Main navigation elements are presented on a red banner, and footer navigation elements are presented in red text beneath a red-tinted banner.

See the images in the CD-ROM's Gallery section.

Template 1140 Environmental Organizations

Environmental action site themed to present conservation and environmental preservation content.

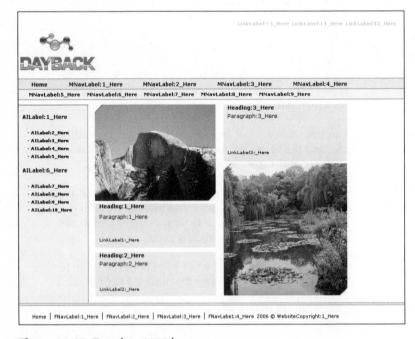

Figure 11-13: Template 1140 home page

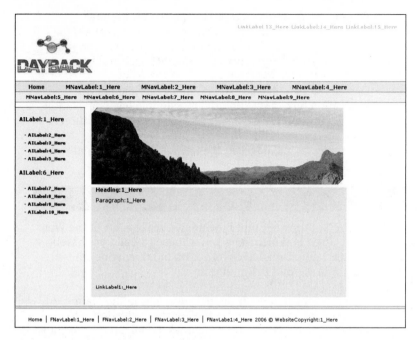

Figure 11-14: Template 1140 subpage

Template Developer	Yana Beylinson
Filename and Location	CD-ROM: \Templates\Chapter 11\114\1140
Variations on This Design	1141 1142
Site Development Detail	Procedures and supporting information on how to place content, links, and Web site images are presented in Chapter 3.

Design Summary

Recommended Use	Site is designed to present both information in articles and offers labeled groups of links that you can use to set up a large number of internal pages or link to external sites of interest. The natural imagery makes this site ideal for any environmentally aware organization or business offering products and services that are nature friendly. You can also use this design to feature outdoor sports, hiking, and similar activities.

Look and Feel

Site design is simple and unobtrusive with a white background with accents in pastel yellow and other light tones. The visual force of the design comes through the embedded photographs that present the natural theme.

Design offers a high-density home page. Nine main navigation links are presented in a double-level navigation bar. In addition twelve link labels are presented in three headlined groups. These can be used to carry news items, link to additional pages in the site, or link to external Web sites.

Content Plan

Content Plan Overview

Before entering content in your site, make a list of the Web page labels and filenames you will use to build your Web site skeleton. Detailed coverage on building your content plan is presented in Chapter 3.

Subpages

Design supports nine principal subpages in the Main navigation area, and four in the Footer navigation. The footer navigation area only includes a dedicated Home link. Identify and write down the screen labels and the related filenames.

Link Sidebar

Both Home and subpage include a linked sidebar that includes 12 Links, broken out in to three groups of four, each with a lead heading. This can be used to link to subpages or to place links to external sites of interest.

Articles

Home page includes three article areas, each supporting follow-on links. Subpages offer a single feature article.

Copy the template

Follow these steps to copy the template to your hard drive:

1. Access the \Templates\Chapter 11\114\1140 folder on your CD-ROM.

2. Drag the \1140 folder to your desktop or copy and paste the \1140 folder to your desktop.

Template Headings and Tags

Figure 11-15: Template 1140 home page token reference

Figure 11-16: Template 1140 subpage token reference

Building Your Site Step-by-Step: 1140 Environmental Organizations

Building The Site Skeleton

Use the following set of operations to enter the central navigation. Perform the exact same operations within `index.html` and `subpage.html`. Web site navigation and building the site skeleton are presented in Chapter 3.

Note that when opening `index.html` or `subpage.html` in Internet Explorer from your hard drive, a security message may appear. Click for more options, and choose to display the full content so the template displays correctly.

1. Place navigation labels

Review the list of subpage labels and filenames from your content plan. You place the labels for subpage 1 at the top (`MNav`) and bottom (`FNav`) of your page. See Figure 11-15 for Home and Figure 11-16 for subpage.

1. Open `index.html` in your text editor.

2. Find `MNavLabel:1_Here` and replace the token with the label for subpage 1. Repeat this operation for `MNavLabel` 2, 3, 4, 5, 6, 7, 8, and 9.

3. Find `FNavLabel:1_Here` and replace the token with the label for subpage 1. Repeat this operation for `FNavLabel` 2, 3, and 4.

4. Find `LinkLabel:13_Here` and replace the token with the label for the subpage associated with this top of page link. Repeat this operation for `LinkLabel` 14 and 15.

---

2. Place navigation links

Review the list of subpage labels and filenames from your content plan. In the following operation you place the links to the filename for subpage 1 at the top (`MNav`) and bottom (`FNav`) of your page. Enter all filenames in lowercase.

1. Find `MNavURL:1_Here` and replace the token with the filename you selected for subpage 1. Repeat this operation for `MNavURL` 2, 3, 4, 5, 6, 7, 8, and 9.

2. Find `FNavURL:1_Here` and replace the token with the filename you selected for subpage 1. Repeat this operation for `FNavURL` 2, 3, and 4.

3. Find `LinkURL:13_Here` and replace the token with the destination filename for the subpage associated with this top of page link. Repeat this operation for `LinkURL` 14 through 15.

---

3. Place Link Sidebar

Place the headings, link labels, and link destinations for the sidebar that appears on the home and subpages. Note that action items 1 and 6 are used as headings in this sidebar and do not accept links (`AIURL` token).

You can delete these tokens if you do not want to use these headings.

1. Find `AILabel:1_Here` and replace the token with the heading for the first group of links in the home page sidebar. Repeat this operation with `AILabel:6_Here`.

2. Find `AILabel:2_Here` and replace the token with the label for subpage 1. Repeat this operation for `AILabel` 2, 3, 4, 5, 7, 8, 9, and 10.

3. Find `AIURL:1_Here` and replace the token with the filename for the link destination. Repeat this operation for `AIURL` 6.

4. Find `AIURL:2_Here` and replace the token with the filename for the link destination you selected for subpage 1 or a Web site URL. Repeat this operation for `AIURL` 3, 4, 5, 7, 8, 9, and 10.

---

4. Place special features

Place the text of the Web site copyright in your pages.

1. Find `WebsiteCopyright:1_Here` and replace the token with your Web site copyright text.

2. Save and close `index.html` in your text editor.

---

5. Set up the subpage template

Perform the same set of edits that you completed for the `index.html` file on the subpage master template file, `subpage.html`.

1. Open `subpage.html` in your text editor.

2. Return to the beginning of this section ("Building the Site Skeleton"), and start with main Step 1, "Place navigation labels."

3. Complete main Steps 1 through 4 using the `subpage.html` file instead of the `index.html` file.

4. Save `subpage.html` in your text editor. Do not rename the file.

Creating Subpage Files

6. Create subpage files

Use the Save As feature in your text editor to save the `subpage.html` template with the first of the subpage filenames you selected in your content plan. Repeat this to create all subpages listed in your content plan.

Save all files to the \1140 folder on your desktop.

1. Verify that `subpage.html` is open in your text editor.

2. Choose File ➪ Save As or similar from your text editor. Enter the filename you selected for subpage 1, and click OK.

3. Repeat Step 2 for all subpages in your content plan.

7. Display your site   Open your site to check that your labels and pages display correctly.

1. Launch `index.html` from your computer by double-clicking the filename, or choose File ➪ Open (from most browsers) to open it in your browser. An empty home page should appear.

2. Click the navigation links at the top and bottom of the home page and you should see empty subpage pages.

3. Close the empty site skeleton.

Placing Content in the Home Page

8. Place home articles   Place the headings and paragraph text for the articles in `index.html` (see Figure 11-15).

1. Open `index.html` in your text editor.

2. Find `Heading:1_Here` and replace the token with your heading text. Repeat for `Heading` 2 and 3.

3. Find `Paragraph:1_Here` and replace the token with your paragraph text. Repeat for `Paragraph` 2 and 3.

4. Find `LinkLabel:1_Here`. Replace the token with the chosen label text for this link (such as "Read More" or "More Information"). You can delete this token if you do not want to use this link. Repeat for `LinkLabel` 2 and 3.

5. Find `LinkURL:1_Here`. Replace the token with the filename you have selected to be accessed from this link. Repeat for `LinkURL` 2 and 3.

6. Save `index.html` in your text editor.

Placing Content in Subpages

Use the following operations to place content into all of your site subpages. Use the subpage token reference (see Figure 11-16) to see the position of the content and label tokens. Repeat this operation to enter content in all of your subpages.

---

9. Place subpage article

Place the headings and paragraph text for the articles in the selected subpage.

1. Open the selected subpage in your text editor.

2. Find `Heading:1_Here` and replace the token with your heading text.

3. Find `Paragraph:1_Here` and replace the token with your paragraph text.

4. Find `LinkLabel:1_Here.` Replace the token with the label text for this link.

5. Find `LinkURL:1_Here`. Replace the token with the filename you have selected to be accessed from this link.

6. Save and close the file when you have finished editing.

Finalizing Your Site

11. Edit site logo and pictures

Turn to Chapter 3 for explanation and procedures to replace the default template logo and images with your own logo and images.

12. Display your Web site

Launch `index.html` from your computer by double-clicking the filename, or choose File ➪ Open. Check your work in your browser window.

13. Edit and adjust

Make edits by opening up your home page or subpage page files in your text editor and making edits to the content. Be sure to edit only your content and not to disturb any of the surrounding code.

14. Publish

The basic parameters of what you should provide to your Web hosting company are outlined in Chapter 3. For the specifics on actually posting your live site to the Web, contact your service provider for details.

Variations

Variation 1141 Overview	This version presents the site design with a light shade of blue in the sidebar area containing three groups of links, and this blue accent in the navigation bar. Top of page link labels are presented in matching light blue font.
	See the images in the CD-ROM's Gallery section.
Variation 1142 Overview	This version presents the site design with a darker gray in the sidebar area containing three groups of links, and a strong green background for one of the navigation bars and article area background. Top of page link labels are presented in gray font.
	See the images in the CD-ROM's Gallery section.

Template 1150 Schools

Educational site designed to present a school or online Web learning program. The site includes features that enable it to serve as a course catalog and provide detailed background on a range of educational offerings.

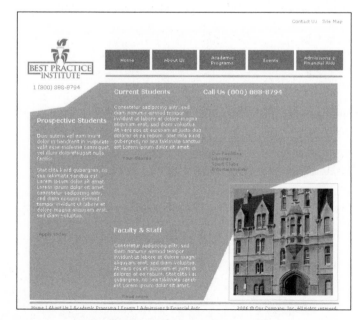

Figure 11-17: Template 1150 home page

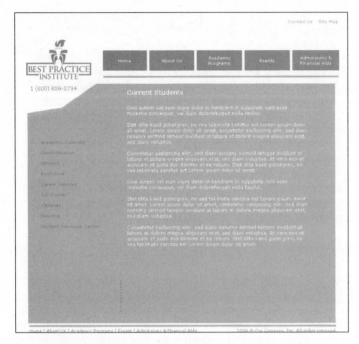

Figure 11-18: Template 1150 subpage

Template Developer	Yana Beylinson
Filename and Location	CD-ROM: \Templates\Chapter 11\115\1150
Variations on this Design	1151 1152
Site Development Detail	Procedures and supporting information on placing content, links, and Web site images are presented in Chapter 3.

Design Summary

Recommended Use	Education is an information-intensive business. This site has been designed as a presentation of the institution and, potentially, a course catalog listing. This design is recommended for any educational organization or business. You can also adapt it easily to serve as a community or information site.

Look and Feel

White background sets off a freeform geometric overlay that presents four home page articles, and a single feature article in subpages.

Design offers a high-density home page. Five main navigation links are presented prominently as buttons, and the four articles each carry at least one extending link. Subpages contain a single feature article framed with a sidebar containing eight links. You can use links as a live list of course offerings related to the feature article. The link availability in this site enables you to add essentially as many pages as you want.

Content Plan

Content Plan Overview

Before entering content in your site, make a list of the Web page labels and filenames you will use to build your Web site skeleton. Detailed coverage on building your content plan is presented in Chapter 3.

Subpages

Design supports five principal subpages. Subpages include a sidebar of eight links. You can enter these individually for each subpage. Identify and write down the screen labels and the related filenames.

Articles

Home page includes four article areas, each supporting follow-on links. Subpages offer a single feature article.

Copy the Template

Follow these steps to copy the template to your hard drive:

1. Access the \Templates\Chapter 11\115\1150 folder on your CD-ROM.

2. Drag the \1150 folder to your desktop or copy and paste the \1150 folder to your desktop.

Template Headings and Tags

Figure 11-19: Template 1150 home page token reference

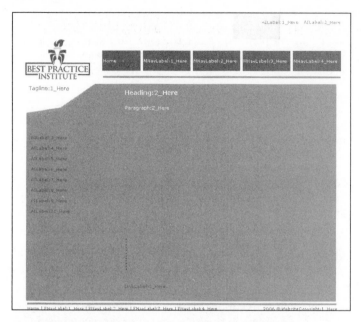

Figure 11-20: Template 1150 subpage token reference

Building Your Site Step by Step: 1150 Schools

Building the Site Skeleton

Use the following set of operations to enter the central navigation. Perform the exact same operations within `index.html` and `subpage.html`. Web site navigation and building the site skeleton are presented in Chapter 3.

Note that when opening `index.html` or `subpage.html` in Internet Explorer from your hard drive, a security message may appear. Click for more options, and choose to display the full content so the template displays correctly.

1. Place navigation labels	Review the list of subpage labels and filenames from your content plan. You place the labels for subpage 1 at the top (MNav) and bottom (FNav) of your page. See Figures 11-19 for home and 11-20 for subpages.

1. Open `index.html` in your text editor.

2. Find `MNavLabel:1_Here` and replace the token with the label for subpage 1. Repeat this operation for `MNavLabel` 2, 3, and 4.

3. Find `FNavLabel:1_Here` and replace the token with the label for subpage 1. Repeat this operation for `FNavLabel` 2, 3, and 4.

4. Find `AILabel:1_Here` and replace the token with the filename for the destination of this top of page link. Repeat this operation for `AILabel` 2.

2. Place navigation links	Review the list of subpage labels and filenames from your content plan. In the following operation you place the links to the filename for subpage 1 at the top (MNav) and bottom (FNav) of your page. Enter all filenames in lowercase.

1. Find `MNavURL:1_Here` and replace the token with filename you selected for subpage 1. Repeat this operation for `MNavURL` 2, 3, and 4.

2. Find `FNavURL:1_Here` and replace the token with filename you selected for subpage 1. Repeat this operation for `FNavURL` 2, 3, and 4.

3. Find `AIURL:1_Here` and replace the token with the filename for the destination of this top of page link. Repeat this operation for `AIURL` 2.

3. Place special features	Place the text of the Web site copyright in your pages.

1. Find `WebsiteCopyright:1_Here` and replace the token with your Web site copyright text.

2. Find `Tagline:1_Here` and replace the token with the text for the tagline that appears directly beneath the logo area on the home page and subpages.

3. Save and close `index.html` in your text editor.

4. Set up the subpage template

Perform the same set of edits that you completed for the `index.html` file on the subpage master template file, `subpage.html`.

1. Open `subpage.html` in your text editor.

2. Return to the beginning of this section ("Building the Site Skeleton"), and start with main Step 1, "Place navigation labels."

3. Complete main Steps 1, 2, and 3 using the `subpage.html` file instead of the `index.html` file.

4. Save `subpage.html` in your text editor. Do not rename the file.

Creating Subpage Files

5. Create subpage files

Use the Save As feature in your text editor to save the `subpage.html` template with the first of the subpage filenames you selected in your content plan. Repeat this to create all subpages listed in your content plan.

Save all files to the \1150 folder on your desktop.

1. Verify that `subpage.html` is open in your text editor.

2. Choose File ➪ Save As or similar from your text editor. Enter the filename you selected for subpage 1, and click OK.

3. Repeat Step 2 for all subpages in your content plan.

4. Repeat Step 2 for any linked articles or catalog detail pages you identified in your content plan.

6. Display your site

Open your site to check that your labels and pages display correctly.

1. Launch `index.html` from your computer by double-clicking the filename, or choose File ➪ Open (from most browsers) to open it in your browser. An empty home page should appear.

2. Click the navigation links at the top and bottom of the home page and you should see empty subpage pages.

3. Close the empty site skeleton.

Placing Content in the Home Page

7. Place home articles

Place the headings and paragraph text for the articles in index.html (see Figure 11-19).

1. Open index.html in your text editor.

2. Find Heading:1_Here and replace the token with your heading text. Repeat for Heading 2 and 3.

3. Find Paragraph:1_Here and replace the token with your paragraph text. Repeat for Paragraph 2 and 3.

4. Find LinkLabel:1_Here. Replace the token with the chosen label text for this link (such as "Read More" or "More Information"). You can delete this token if you do not want to use this link. Repeat for LinkLabel 2 and 3.

5. Find LinkURL:1_Here. Replace the token with the filename you have selected to be accessed from this link. Repeat for LinkURL 2 and 3.

8. Place home specialty article

Use the Heading 4 group — specialty articles that support five follow-on links — as links to subpages containing details on specific programs, courses, or other educational offerings.

1. Find Heading:4_Here and replace the token with your heading text.

2. Find Paragraph:4_Here and replace the token with your paragraph text.

3. Find LinkLabel:4_Here. Replace the token with the label text for this link.

4. Find LinkURL:4_Here. Replace the token with the filename you have selected to be accessed from this link.

5. Repeat Steps 3 and 4 for LinkLabel and LinkURL 5, 6, 7, and 8.

6. Save index.html in your text editor.

Placing Content in Subpages

Use the following operations to place content into all of your site subpages. Use the subpage token reference (see Figure 11-20) to see the position of the content and label tokens. Repeat this operation to enter content in all of your subpages.

---

9. Place subpage articles	Place article headings and text in your subpages.

1. Open the selected subpage in your text editor.

2. Find `Heading:2_Here` and replace the token with your heading text.

3. Find `Paragraph:2_Here` and replace the token with your paragraph text.

4. Find `LinkLabel:2_Here` and replace the token with the label text for this link.

5. Find `LinkURL:2_Here` and replace the token with the filename you have selected to be accessed from this link.

---

10. Place subpage sidebar	There are eight link labels in the sidebar. You can use all eight or only as many as you want. You can delete link tokens you do not want to use, beginning with the link at the bottom of the list. Place links at the top of the list, starting with `LinkLabel` 1, and keep any blank links at the end of the list so they can be deleted to keep the sidebar layout looking clean.

1. Find `AILabel:3_Here` and replace the token with the label text for this link.

2. Find `AIURL:3_Here` and replace the token with the filename you have selected to be accessed from this link.

3. Repeat Steps 1 and 2 with `AILabel` and `AIURL` 4, 5, 6, 7, 8, 9, and 10.

4. Save and close the file when you have finished editing.

Finalizing Your Site

11. Edit site logo and pictures   Turn to Chapter 3 for explanation and procedures to replace the default template logo and images with your own logo and images.

12. Display your Web site   Launch `index.html` from your computer by double-clicking the filename, or choose File ➪ Open. Check your work in your browser window.

13. Edit and adjust   Make edits by opening up your home page or subpage page files in your text editor and making edits to the content. Be sure to edit only your content and not to disturb any of the surrounding code.

14. Publish   The basic parameters of what you should provide to your Web hosting company are outlined in Chapter 3. For the specifics on actually posting your live site to the Web, contact your service provider for details.

Variations

Variation 1151 Overview   This version presents the site design with headline fonts in yellow and paragraph text in gray. Otherwise the layout and features of the design are the same.

See the images in the CD-ROM's Gallery section.

Variation 1152 Overview   This version presents the site design with headline fonts in black and link labels in yellow. Main navigation items appear on a dark brown background. Otherwise the layout and features of the design are the same.

See the images in the CD-ROM's Gallery section.

✦   ✦   ✦

Personal Templates

Personal Web pages are the ultimate advertisement for yourself. There is really no pre-Internet equivalent to the phenomenon of the personal Web page. There were certainly those who attempted kitchen table autobiographies or dedicated themselves to garnering attention in the media, but it would never have occurred to most people to mine their lives and personal preferences to tell their story to the world.

Today, personal Web pages have become commonplace. Big service providers such as AOL started giving out free Web pages, an idea that became more refined through the technology of MySpace.com, and the rest is history. People love to tell their stories, share their tastes, and meet others out in the cyber world.

About Personal Templates

Personal Web sites can range from serious and purposeful to whimsical and just-for-fun. Posting personal information can be useful for an individual's business life, or a personal site can be a destination for friends and family. It's important to be clear on what your purpose is and for whom you are writing the site.

The styles in the 1 Hour Web Site family of templates offer you many models to choose from for personal expression. You can adapt many of the sites here to your purpose depending on the style you are looking for. The sites in this chapter are Web models for specific personal communication tasks such as posting business résumés, designing family information sharing portal sites, and creating sites for personal interests and hobbies. There are two more designs here that focus on personal community activities — a wedding site and a design for you to create your own personal blog.

Presenting . . . You!

When you assemble a personal Web site, the most important considerations are to know your purpose and know who you intend to view the site. Each of us has many groups of people in our lives and most of us have some conscious or subconscious barriers between them. For example, you don't necessarily want the people at the office to know about that spirited college reunion party the other night at the Old Fireside Inn. You create cultures around yourself, and even thought you're not always aware of it, you might speak very differently to family than to your best friends and might talk about very different things.

When you build a personal Web site, you have to be very clear which of these groups in your life you are speaking to. For example, MySpace.com has made a thriving business around young people sharing their life experiences with their friends, but it's a good bet many of the kids don't intend for their parents or relatives to be surfing their pages.

The pivotal consideration in writing personal pages is using language to create your personal voice. Unlike business or community pages, which are written to express the voice and identity of a group of people, personal pages represent your individual voice. To develop your personal voice, begin with an assessment of your audience — who you want to speak to and for what purpose. Anticipate those who are likely to visit your site, either from your direct invitation or through shared links from others.

Clearly state your site's purpose right at the top of the home page. Personal pages may be placed for any number of reasons, and it is very important to set audience expectations for what you are communicating there. Equally important is to signal what, if any, response or interaction you want from the audience. For example, in a family site, you may want readers to contribute stories and news; in a personal hobby site, you may want readers to share information and experiences; and in a political, religious, or blog site, you may want to ask your readers to engage in dialog and share their thoughts and input.

You can say a lot about yourself in personal pages. Some of the information you might include

- ✦ Personal history
- ✦ Cultural interests and music, movie, and theater tastes
- ✦ Photographs
- ✦ Business background and résumé
- ✦ Family information and news
- ✦ Special interests and hobbies

Whatever you want to say about yourself, do your best to make it consistent, interesting, and edit it tightly. Leave your audience wanting more; they'll get bored if there's too much information to wade through.

Tip Instead of navigating from the root of the CD to locate a template, you can click the Templates link in the CD browser application to directly access the chapters on the CD. For faster access, click the Gallery link in the CD browser application to view a listing of all templates. Then click any View Files link to view the files for that template.

Template 1210 Résumé

A résumé layout is designed to present a person's work experience over the Web. You can adapt this layout to many personal and professional information applications.

Figure 12-1: Template 1210 home page

Figure 12-2: Template 1210 subpage

Template Developer	Ken Milhous
Filename and Location	CD-ROM: \Templates\Chapter 12\121\1210
Variations on this Design	1211 1212
Site Development Detail	Procedures and supporting information on placing content, links, and Web site images are presented in Chapter 3.

Design Summary

Recommended Use	Simple and direct résumé site offers standard navigation and heading features to present your experience in detail. You can adapt this design to present personal and professional forms, including a standard résumé format, project lists for consultants and independent contractors, and a professional biography.
Look and Feel	Design is electronically simulated white paper with no design features save the text on the page. Main navigation features are presented as a sidebar for easy reading alongside the headings and paragraph text in the content area.

Content Plan

Content Plan Overview   Before entering content in your site, make a list of the Web page labels and filenames you will use to build your Web site skeleton. Detailed coverage on building your content plan is presented in Chapter 3.

Subpages   Design supports a home page and four principal subpages.

Résumé Lead   At the top of both the home page and subpages there are two large format headings and an area for contact info and date available. These collectively make up the résumé lead.

Articles   Home page includes three article areas, each supporting follow-on links. Subpages offer a single feature article.

Copy the Template   Follow these steps to copy the template to your hard drive:

1. Access the \Templates\Chapter 12\121\1210 folder on your CD-ROM.

2. Drag the \1210 folder to your desktop or copy and paste the \1210 folder to your desktop.

Template Headings and Tags

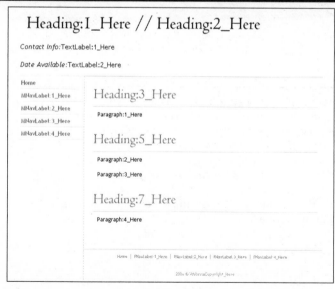

Figure 12-3: Template 1210 home page token reference

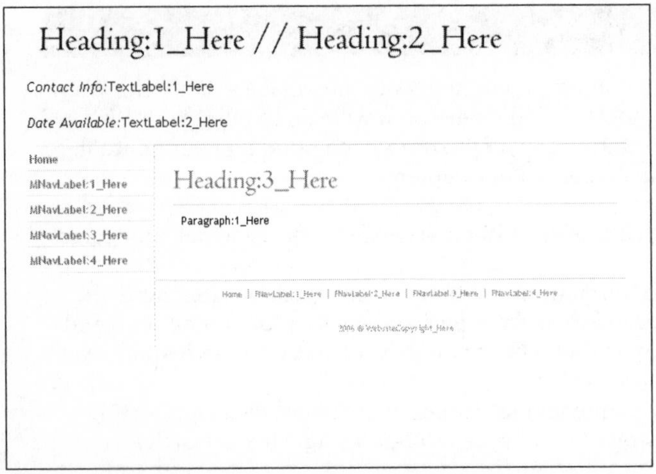

Heading:1_Here // Heading:2_Here

*Contact Info:*TextLabel:1_Here

*Date Available:*TextLabel:2_Here

Home

MNavLabel:1_Here

MNavLabel:2_Here   Heading:3_Here

MNavLabel:3_Here   Paragraph:1_Here

MNavLabel:4_Here

Home | FNavLabel:1_Here | FNavLabel:2_Here | FNavLabel:3_Here | FNavLabel:4_Here

2006 © WebsiteCopyright_Here

Figure 12-4: Template 1210 subpage token reference

Building Your Site Step-by-Step: 1210 Résumé

Building the Site Skeleton

Use the following set of operations to enter the central navigation. Perform the exact same operations within `index.html` and `subpage.html`. Web site navigation and building the site skeleton are presented in Chapter 3.

Note that when opening `index.html` or `subpage.html` in Internet Explorer from your hard drive, a security message may appear. Click for more options, and choose to display the full content so the template displays correctly.

1. Place navigation labels

Review the list of subpage labels and filenames from your content plan. You place the labels for subpage 1 at the top (`MNav`) and bottom (`FNav`) of your page. See Figures 12-3 for home and 12-4 for subpages.

1. Open `index.html` in your text editor.

2. Find `MNavLabel:1_Here` and replace the token with the label for subpage 1.

3. Find `FNavLabel:1_Here` and replace the token with the label for subpage 1.

4. Repeat Steps 2 and 3 for `MNavLabel` and `FNavLabel` 2, 3, and 4.

---

2. Place navigation links

Review the list of subpage labels and filenames from your content plan. In the following operation you place the links to the filename for subpage 1 on the side (`MNav`) and bottom (`FNav`) of your page. Enter all filenames in lowercase.

1. Find `MNavURL:1_Here` and replace the token with the filename you selected for subpage 1.

2. Find `FNavURL:1_Here` and replace the token with the filename you selected for subpage 1.

3. Repeat Steps 1 and 2 for `MNavURL` and `FNavURL` 2, 3, and 4.

---

3. Place résumé lead

Fill in all this material to be standard across all pages, or selectively edit the headings to present different information on different pages. For example, you might use Heading 1 to present your name and Heading 2 to carry the page title.

1. Find `Heading:1_Here` and replace the token with your name or other desired heading.

2. Find `TextLabel:1_Here` and replace the token with your contact information — this appears next to the embedded label Contact Info.

3. Find `TextLabel:2_Here` and replace the token with date available — this appears next to the embedded label Date Available.

---

4. Place special features

Place the text of the Web site copyright in your pages.

1. Find `WebsiteCopyright:1_Here` and replace the token with your Web site copyright text.

2. Save and close `index.html` in your text editor.

5. Set up the subpage template

Perform the same set of edits that you completed for the `index.html` file on the subpage master template file, `subpage.html`.

1. Open `subpage.html` in your text editor.

2. Return to the beginning of this section ("Building the Site Skeleton"), and start with main Step 1, "Place navigation labels."

3. Complete main Steps 1, 2, 3, and 4 using the `subpage.html` file instead of the `index.html` file.

4. Save `subpage.html` in your text editor. Do not rename the file.

Creating Subpage Files

6. Create subpage files

Use the Save As feature in your text editor to save the `subpage.html` template with the first of the subpage filenames you selected in your content plan. Repeat this to create all subpages listed in your content plan.

Save all files to the `\1210` folder on your desktop.

1. Verify that `subpage.html` is open in your text editor.

2. Choose File ➪ Save As or similar from your text editor. Enter the filename you selected for subpage 1, and click OK.

3. Repeat Step 2 for all subpages in your content plan.

4. Repeat Step 2 for any linked articles or catalog detail pages you identified in your content plan.

7. Display your site

Open your site to check that your labels and pages display correctly.

1. Launch `index.html` from your computer by double-clicking the filename, or choose File ➪ Open (from most browsers) to open it in your browser. An empty home page should appear.

2. Click the navigation links at the top and bottom of the home page and you should see empty subpage pages.

3. Close the empty site skeleton.

Placing Content in the Home Page

8. Place home articles

Place the headings and paragraph text for the articles in `index.html` (see Figure 12-3).

1. Open `index.html` in your text editor.

2. Find `Heading:2_Here` and replace the token with your desired heading for your home page. You can extend the heading and wrap it to multiple lines by inserting the code for line break, `<br />`, between words in your heading text.

3. Find `Heading:3_Here` and replace the token with your heading text.

4. Find `Paragraph:1_Here` and replace the token with your paragraph text.

5. Find `Heading:4_Here` and replace the token with your heading text.

6. Find `Paragraph:2_Here` and replace the token with your paragraph text. Repeat for `Paragraph` 3.

7. Find `Heading:5_Here` and replace the token with your heading text.

8. Find `Paragraph:4_Here` and replace the token with your paragraph text.

9. Save `index.html` in your text editor.

Placing Content in Subpages

Use the following operations to place content into all of your site subpages. Use the subpage token reference (see Figure 12-4) to see the position of the content and label tokens. Repeat this operation to enter content in all of your subpages.

9. Place subpage title	Place the heading in the résumé lead carrying the name of the current subpage. If you have used Heading 1 to carry your name on every page, this text appears next to it in the layout.
	1. Open the selected subpage in your text editor.
	2. Find `Heading:2_Here` and replace the token with the name of the subpage. Keep content to one or two words. You can extend the heading and wrap it to multiple lines by inserting the code for line break, ` `, between words in your heading text.
10. Place subpage articles	Place article headings and text in your subpages.
	1. Find `Heading:3_Here` and replace the token with your heading text.
	2. Find `Paragraph:1_Here` and replace the token with your paragraph text.
	3. Save and close the file when you have finished editing.

Finalizing Your Site

11. Edit site logo and pictures	Turn to Chapter 3 for explanation and procedures to replace the default template logo and images with your own logo and images.

12. Display your Web site

Launch `index.html` from your computer by double-clicking the filename, or choose File ➪ Open. Check your work in your browser window.

13. Edit and adjust

Make edits by opening up your home page or subpage page files in your text editor and making edits to the content. Be sure to edit only your content and not to disturb any of the surrounding code.

14. Publish

The basic parameters of what you should provide to your Web hosting company are outlined in Chapter 3. For the specifics on actually posting your live site to the Web, contact your service provider for details.

Variations

Variation 1211 Overview

This version presents the site design with headline fonts in yellow and paragraph text in gray. Otherwise the layout and features of the design are the same.

See the images in the CD-ROM's Gallery section.

Variation 1212 Overview

This version presents the site design with headline fonts in black and link labels in yellow. Otherwise the layout and features of the design are the same.

See the images in the CD-ROM's Gallery section.

Template 1220 Family Information

Family news site features articles, headlines, and announcements. This design includes announcement headlines, article areas, and links to other family member Web sites.

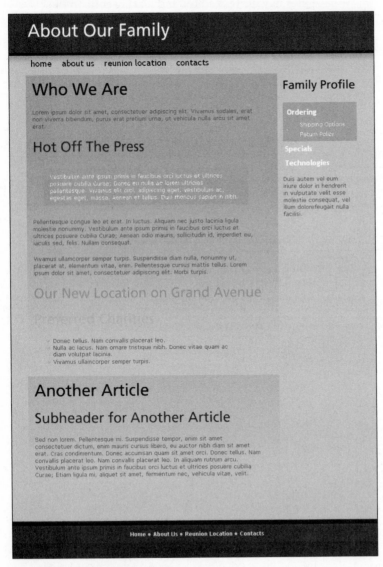

Figure 12-5: Template 1220 home page

Figure 12-6: Template 1220 subpage

Template Developer	Ken Milhous
Filename and Location	CD-ROM: \Templates\Chapter 12\122\1220
Variations on this Design	1221 1222
Site Development Detail	Procedures and supporting information on placing content, links, and Web site images are presented in Chapter 3.

Design Summary

Recommended Use	Design is essentially a newspaper or newsletter for family information. The home page is dense with headlines and paragraph text links for articles, and includes a special link sidebar. Site is best used for personal or family information or any information presentation application involving high levels of detail.

Look and Feel	Design uses a light background with gradient areas framing headlines and article areas. The whole page is highlighted by red banner areas on the top to carry the site name and the bottom to carry the navigation bar.
	Site can be developed as medium to high density depending on the amount of content you place into the page. Design makes extensive use of headlines. It also contains a link sidebar that can be used to place links to related family or personal interest sites on the home page and all subpages.

Content Plan

Content Plan Overview	Before entering content in your site, make a list of the Web page labels and filenames you will use to build your Web site skeleton. Detailed coverage on building your content plan is presented in Chapter 3.
Subpages	Design supports a home page and three principal subpages.
Link Sidebar	Sidebar at the right on the home page and subpages is built around subnavigation links (SNav tokens) that are, in effect, a second level of navigation links. You can use them to link to a dedicated subpage or to link to external Web sites, such as those of family members.
Articles	Home page includes three article areas, each with at least one subheading supporting the lead heading. This allows you to create newspaper-style headings, subheads, and taglines for family stories of interest. Subpages offer a single feature article, also with double headings.

Copy the Template	Follow these steps to copy the template to your hard drive:

1. Access the \Templates\Chapter 12\122\1220 folder on your CD-ROM.

2. Drag the \1220 folder to your desktop or copy and paste the \1220 folder to your desktop.

Template Headings and Tags

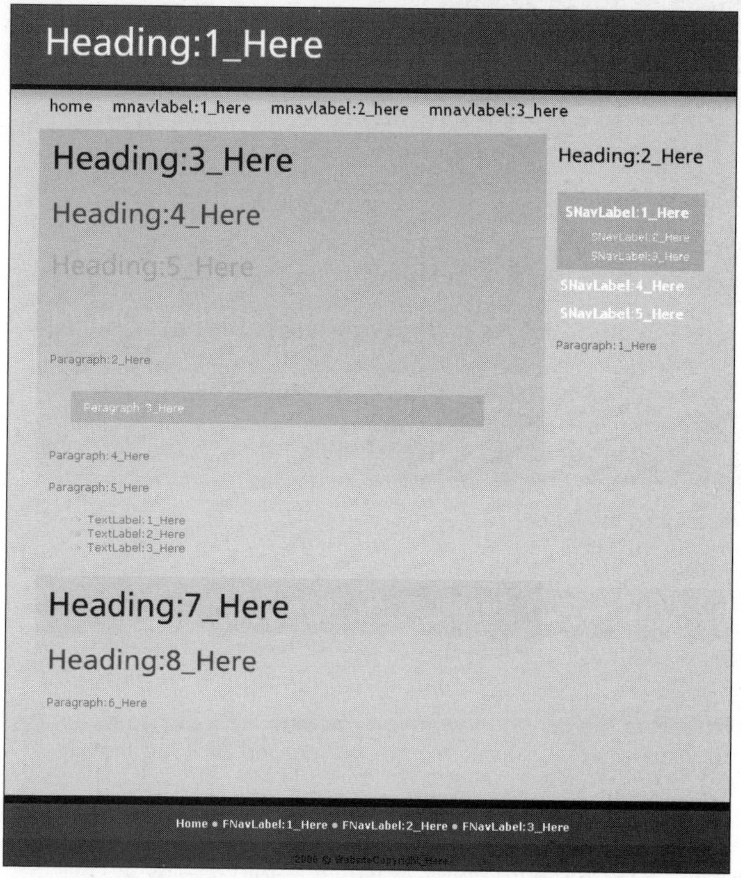

Heading:1_Here

home   mnavlabel:1_here   mnavlabel:2_here   mnavlabel:3_here

Heading:3_Here

Heading:4_Here

Heading:5_Here

Heading:2_Here

SNavLabel:1_Here

SNavLabel:2_Here
SNavLabel:3_Here

SNavLabel:4_Here

SNavLabel:5_Here

Paragraph:1_Here

Paragraph:2_Here

Paragraph:3_Here

Paragraph:4_Here

Paragraph:5_Here

TextLabel:1_Here
TextLabel:2_Here
TextLabel:3_Here

Heading:7_Here

Heading:8_Here

Paragraph:6_Here

Home • FNavLabel:1_Here • FNavLabel:2_Here • FNavLabel:3_Here

2006 © WebsiteCopyright_Here

Figure 12-7: Template 1220 home page token reference

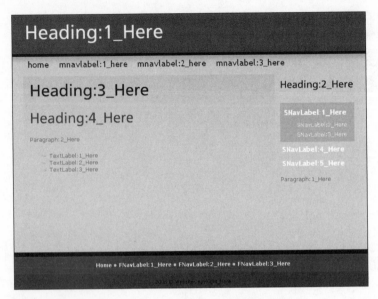

Figure 12-8: Template 1220 subpage token reference

Building Your Site Step-by-Step: 1220 Family Information

Building the Site Skeleton

Use the following set of operations to enter the central navigation. Perform the exact same operations within index.html and subpage.html. Web site navigation and building the site skeleton are presented in Chapter 3.

Note that when opening index.html or subpage.html in Internet Explorer from your hard drive, a security message may appear. Click for more options, and choose to display the full content so the template displays correctly.

---

1. Place navigation labels

Review the list of subpage labels and filenames from your content plan. You place the labels for subpage 1 at the top (MNav) and bottom (FNav) of your page. See Figures 12-7 for home and 12-8 for subpages.

1. Open index.html in your text editor.

2. Find `MNavLabel:1_Here` and replace the token with the label for subpage 1. Repeat this operation for `MNavLabel` 2 and 3. Note that main navigation labels in this design appear in lowercase when the page is displayed in the browser.

3. Find `FNavLabel:1_Here` and replace the token with the label for subpage 1. Repeat this operation for `FNavLabel` 2 and 3.

---

2. Place navigation links

Review the list of subpage labels and filenames from your content plan. In the following operation you place the links to the filename for subpage 1 at the top (`MNav`) and bottom (`FNav`) of your page. Enter all filenames in lowercase.

1. Find `MNavURL:1_Here` and replace the token with filename you selected for subpage 1. Repeat this operation for `MNavURL` 2 and 3.

2. Find `FNavURL:1_Here` and replace the token with filename you selected for subpage 1. Repeat this operation for `FNavURL` 2 and 3.

---

3. Place site title and sidebar

Use Heading 1 to present the title of the site on the home page and subpages. This can be your name, your family name, or the name of your family newsletter.

Place links to family Web sites or other pages in this site. This area functions as a second navigation area within the home page and subpages to present links of interest (see Figures 12-7 and 12-8).

1. Find `Heading:1_Here` and replace the token with your site title.

2. Find `Heading:2_Here` and replace the token with the title for the sidebar area.

3. Find `SNavLabel:1_Here` and replace the token with the label for the page or Web site name you are linking to. Repeat this operation for `SNavLabel` 2, 3, 4, and 5.

4. Find `SNavURL:1_Here` and replace the token with the filename for the linked subpage or the URL for the Web site you want to link to. Repeat this operation for `SNavURL` 2, 3, 4, and 5.

5. Find `Paragraph:1_Here` and replace the token with a paragraph or short article item describing the content of the sidebar or of the site in general.

---

4. Place special features   Place the text of the Web site copyright in your pages.

1. Find `WebsiteCopyright:1_Here` and replace the token with your Web site copyright text.

2. Save and close `index.html` in your text editor.

---

5. Set up the subpage template   Perform the same set of edits that you completed for the `index.html` file on the subpage master template file, `subpage.html`.

1. Open `subpage.html` in your text editor.

2. Return to the beginning of this section ("Building the Site Skeleton"), and start with main Step 1, "Place navigation labels."

3. Complete main Steps 1, 2, 3, and 4 using the `subpage.html` file instead of the `index.html` file.

4. Save `subpage.html` in your text editor. Do not rename the file.

Creating Subpage Files

6. Create subpage files   Use the Save As feature in your text editor to save the `subpage.html` template with the first of the subpage filenames you selected in your content plan. Repeat this to create all subpages listed in your content plan.

Save all files to the `\1220` folder on your desktop.

1. Verify that `subpage.html` is open in your text editor.

2. Choose File ⇨ Save As or similar from your text editor. Enter the filename you selected for subpage 1, and click OK.

3. Repeat Step 2 for all subpages in your content plan.

4. Repeat Step 2 for any linked articles or catalog detail pages you identified in your content plan.

7. Display your site   Open your site to check that your labels and pages display correctly.

1. Launch `index.html` from your computer by double-clicking the filename, or choose File ⇨ Open (from most browsers) to open it in your browser. An empty home page should appear.

2. Click the navigation links at the top and bottom of the home page and you should see empty subpage pages.

3. Close the empty site skeleton.

Placing Content in the Home Page

8. Place home article block 1   Place the headings and paragraph text for the articles in `index.html`. Note that the text label tokens included in this operation are not linked and allow you to display simple text for such things as contact telephone numbers, names, and announcements (see Figure 12-7).

1. Open `index.html` in your text editor.

2. Find `Heading:3_Here` and replace the token with your heading text. Repeat the operation for `Heading` 4, 5, and 6.

3. Find `Paragraph:2_Here` and replace the token with your paragraph text. Repeat the operation for `Paragraph` 3, 4, and 5.

4. Find `TextLabel:1_Here` and replace the token with announcement text. Repeat the operation for `TextLabel` 2 and 3.

9. Place home article block 2   Place the headings and paragraph text for the articles in `index.html`.

1. Find `Heading:7_Here` and replace the token with your heading text. Repeat the operation for Heading 8.

2. Find `Paragraph:6_Here` and replace the token with your paragraph text.

3. Save `index.html` in your text editor.

Placing Content in Subpages

Use the following operations to place content into all of your site subpages. Use the subpage token reference (see Figure 12-8) to see the position of the content and label tokens. Repeat this operation to enter content in all of your subpages.

10. Place subpage articles	Place article headings and text in your subpages.
	1. Open the selected subpage in your text editor.
	2. Find `Heading:3_Here` and replace the token with your heading text. Repeat the operation for `Heading` 4.
	3. Find `Paragraph:2_Here` and replace the token with your paragraph text.
	4. Find `TextLabel:1_Here` and replace the token with announcement text. Repeat the operation for `TextLabel` 2 and 3.
	5. Save and close the file when you have finished editing.

Finalizing Your Site

11. Edit site logo and pictures	Turn to Chapter 3 for explanation and procedures to replace the default template logo and images with your own logo and images.
12. Display your Web site	Launch `index.html` from your computer by double-clicking the filename, or choose File ⇨ Open. Check your work in your browser window.
13. Edit and adjust	Make edits by opening up your home page or subpage page files in your text editor and making edits to the content. Be sure to edit only your content and not to disturb any of the surrounding code.
14. Publish	The basic parameters of what you should provide to your Web hosting company are outlined in Chapter 3. For the specifics on actually posting your live site to the Web, contact your service provider for details.

Variations

Variation 1221 Overview   This version presents the site design with headline fonts in yellow and paragraph text in gray. Otherwise the layout and features of the design are the same.

See the images in the CD-ROM's Gallery section.

Variation 1222 Overview   This version presents the site design with headline fonts in black and link labels in yellow. Otherwise the layout and features of the design are the same.

See the images in the CD-ROM's Gallery section.

Template 1230 Personal Interest / Hobby

A stylish site designed to share a personal biography, cultural interests, hobbies, or information and links on an individual's interests.

Figure 12-9: Template 1230 home page

Figure 12-10: Template 1230 subpage

Template Developer	Ken Milhous
Filename and Location	CD-ROM: `\Templates\Chapter 12\123\1230`
Variations on this Design	1231 1232
Site Development Detail	Procedures and supporting information on placing content, links, and Web site images are presented in Chapter 3.

Design Summary

Recommended Use	Stylish design to share personal information that includes article and information presentation areas over a colorful artistic background. Individuals can use this design to post biographical or personal background information, including cultural interests and hobbies. Businesses that want a simple, stylish presentation of their offerings can adapt this site for their use.

Look and Feel	Colorful, impressionistic background sets the emotional tone for an alternative Web experience. The design incorporates elaborate display fonts for headings and a sidebar to post announcements and personal information.
	Design works best as a low- to medium-density content layout. To make the most of the design features, use subpages as theme areas for personal information.

Content Plan

Content Plan Overview	Before entering content in your site, make a list of the Web page labels and filenames you will use to build your Web site skeleton. Detailed coverage on building your content plan is presented in Chapter 3.
Subpages	Design supports a home page and four principal subpages.
Articles	Home and subpage include a main article that is the focal point of the page, and supported by the sidebar to the right.
Text Label Sidebar	This design supports sidebar areas to the right of the layout, which are formatted slightly differently on the home page and subpages. They contain a heading and text labels that you can use to post short bits of personal information. These tokens do not accept links. The sidebar on the home page can also accept a brief article following the heading.

Copy the Template	Follow these steps to copy the template to your hard drive:

1. Access the \Templates\Chapter 12\123\1230 folder on your CD-ROM.

2. Drag the \1230 folder to your desktop or copy and paste the \1230 folder to your desktop.

Template Headings and Tags

Figure 12-11: Template 1230 home page token reference

Figure 12-12: Template 1230 subpage token reference

Building Your Site Step-by-Step: 1230 Personal Interest / Hobby

Building the Site Skeleton

Use the following set of operations to enter the central navigation. Perform the exact same operations within `index.html` and `subpage.html`. Web site navigation and building the site skeleton are presented in Chapter 3.

Note that when opening `index.html` or `subpage.html` in Internet Explorer from your hard drive, a security message may appear. Click for more options, and choose to display the full content so the template displays correctly.

---

1. Place navigation labels

Review the list of subpage labels and filenames from your content plan. You place the labels for subpage 1 at the top (`MNav`) and bottom (`FNav`) of your page. See Figures 12-11 for home and 12-12 for subpages.

1. Open `index.html` in your text editor.

2. Find `MNavLabel:1_Here` and replace the token with the label for subpage 1.

3. Find `FNavLabel:1_Here` and replace the token with the label for subpage 1.

4. Repeat Steps 2 and 3 for `MNavLabel` and `FNavLabel` 2, 3, and 4.

---

2. Place navigation links

Review the list of subpage labels and filenames from your content plan. In the following operation you place the links to the filename for subpage 1 on the side (`MNav`) and bottom (`FNav`) of your page. Enter all filenames in lowercase.

1. Find `MNavURL:1_Here` and replace the token with filename you selected for subpage 1.

2. Find `FNavURL:1_Here` and replace the token with filename you selected for subpage 1.

3. Repeat Steps 1 and 2 for `MNavURL` and `FNavURL` 2, 3, and 4.

3. Place special features	Place the text of the Web site copyright in your pages.

Use Heading 1 to present the title of the site on the home page and subpages. This can be your name, your family name, or the name of your family newsletter.

1. Find `WebsiteCopyright:1_Here` and replace the token with your Web site copyright text.

2. Find `Heading:1_Here` and replace the token with your site title.

3. Save and close `index.html` in your text editor.

4. Set up the subpage template	Perform the same set of edits that you completed for the `index.html` file on the subpage master template file, `subpage.html`.

1. Open `subpage.html` in your text editor.

2. Return to the beginning of this section ("Building the Site Skeleton"), and start with main Step 1, "Place navigation labels."

3. Complete main Steps 1, 2, and 3 using the `subpage.html` file instead of the `index.html` file.

4. Save `subpage.html` in your text editor. Do not rename the file.

Creating Subpage Files

5. Create subpage files	Use the Save As feature in your text editor to save the `subpage.html` template with the first of the subpage filenames you selected in your content plan. Repeat this to create all subpages listed in your content plan.

Save all files to the `\1230` folder on your desktop.

1. Verify that `subpage.html` is open in your text editor.

2. Choose File ⇨ Save As or similar from your text editor. Enter the filename you selected for subpage 1, and click OK.

3. Repeat Step 2 for all subpages in your content plan.

4. Repeat Step 2 for any linked articles or catalog detail pages you identified in your content plan.

---

6. Display your site

Open your site to check that your labels and pages display correctly.

1. Launch index.html from your computer by double-clicking the filename, or choose File ⇨ Open (from most browsers) to open it in your browser. An empty home page should appear.

2. Click the navigation links at the top and bottom of the home page and you should see empty subpage pages.

3. Close the empty site skeleton.

Placing Content in the Home Page

7. Place text sidebar

Place notes and comments in this sidebar area. Heading allows you to title the area and put article content in the following paragraph, leading into text label tokens (see Figures 12-11 and 12-12).

1. Open index.html in your text editor.

2. Find Heading:3_Here and replace the token with the title for the sidebar area.

3. Find Paragraph:4_Here and replace the token with your text.

4. Find TextLabel:1_Here and replace the token with desired text. Repeat this operation for TextLabel 2 and 3.

8. Place home article block

Place the headings and paragraph text for the articles in `index.html` (see Figure 12-11).

1. Find `Heading:2_Here` and replace the token with your heading text.

2. Find `Paragraph:1_Here` and replace the token with your paragraph text. Repeat the operation for `Paragraph` 2 and 3.

3. Save `index.html` in your text editor.

Place Content in Subpages

Use the following operations to place content into all of your site subpages. Use the subpage token reference (sed Figure 12-12) to see the position of the content and label tokens. Repeat this operation to enter content in all of your subpages.

9. Place subpage articles

Place article headings and text in your subpages.

1. Open the selected subpage in your text editor.

2. Find `Heading:1_Here` and replace the token with your heading text. Repeat the operation for `Heading` 2.

3. Find `Paragraph:1_Here` and replace the token with your paragraph text.

10. Place text sidebar

Place notes and comments in this sidebar area (see Figures 12-11 and 12-12).

1. Find `TextLabel:1_Here` and replace the token with the text to appear on the page. Repeat this operation for `TextLabel` 2 and 3.

2. Save and close the file when you have finished editing.

Finalizing Your Site

11. Edit site logo and pictures

Turn to Chapter 3 for explanation and procedures to replace the default template logo and images with your own logo and images.

12. Display your Web site

Launch `index.html` from your computer by double-clicking the filename, or choose File ⇨ Open. Check your work in your browser window.

13. Edit and adjust

Make edits by opening up your home page or subpage page files in your text editor and making edits to the content. Be sure to edit only your content and not to disturb any of the surrounding code.

14. Publish

The basic parameters of what you should provide to your Web hosting company are outlined in Chapter 3. For the specifics on actually posting your live site to the Web, contact your service provider for details.

Variations

Variation 1231 Overview

This version presents the site design with headline fonts in yellow and paragraph text in gray. Otherwise the layout and features of the design are the same.

See the images in the CD-ROM's Gallery section.

Variation 1232 Overview

This version presents the site design with headline fonts in black and link labels in yellow. Otherwise the layout and features of the design are the same.

See the images in the CD-ROM's Gallery section.

Template 1240 Wedding

A wedding information site to inform friends and family on the background and details of wedding event and activities.

Figure 12-13: Template 1240 home page

Figure 12-14: Template 1240 subpage

Template Developer	Ken Milhous
Filename and Location	CD-ROM: `\Templates\Chapter 12\124\1240`
Variations on this Design	1241 1242
Site Development Detail	Procedures and supporting information on placing content, links, and Web site images are presented in Chapter 3.

Design Summary

Recommended Use	Specialized wedding site creates a festive and romantic mood to set up the event, involve family members, and present details of the ceremony and associated parties. Companies or individuals active in the wedding services business can also adapt this site for their use.
Look and Feel	Look and feel suggests a wedding invitation, with elaborate script headings. The mood is enhanced with related photographs and a signature ring image at the top of the home page and subpages.
	Site design has a simple layout for posting news and information in article areas and sidebars. Main navigation items are positioned to the right of article areas to serve as an index to key areas of information and events.

Content Plan

Content Plan Overview	Before entering content in your site, make a list of the Web page labels and filenames you will use to build your Web site skeleton. Detailed coverage on building your content plan is presented in Chapter 3.
Subpages	Design supports a home page and four principal subpages.
Sidebar	Sidebars at the right of the home and subpage layouts include an embedded title "Explore" leading in to the main navigation links. Home and subpage have an article area beneath the navigation links to carry information and notices about the event.
Articles	Home page includes three article areas. Subpages offer a single feature article.

Copy the Template	Follow these steps to copy the template to your hard drive:

1. Access the \Templates\Chapter 12\124\1240 folder on your CD-ROM.

2. Drag the \1240 folder to your desktop or copy and paste the \1240 folder to your desktop.

Template Headings and Tags

Figure 12-15: Template 1240 home page token reference

Figure 12-16: Template 1240 subpage token reference

Building Your Site Step-by-Step: 1240 Wedding

Building the Site Skeleton

Use the following set of operations to enter the central navigation. Perform the exact same operations within `index.html` and `subpage.html`. Web site navigation and building the site skeleton are presented in Chapter 3.

Note that when opening `index.html` or `subpage.html` in Internet Explorer from your hard drive, a security message may appear. Click for more options, and choose to display the full content so the template displays correctly.

---

1. Place navigation labels   Review the list of subpage labels and filenames from your content plan. You place the labels for subpage 1 at the top (`MNav`) and bottom (`FNav`) of your page. See Figures 12-15 for home and 12-16 for subpages.

1. Open `index.html` in your text editor.

    2. Find `MNavLabel:1_Here` and replace the token with the label for subpage 1.

    3. Find `FNavLabel:1_Here` and replace the token with the label for subpage 1.

    4. Repeat Steps 2 and 3 for `MNavLabel` and `FNavLabel` 2, 3, and 4.

---

2. Place navigation links

Review the list of subpage labels and filenames from your content plan. In the following operation you place the links to the filename for subpage 1 on the side (`MNav`) and bottom (`FNav`) of your page. Enter all filenames in lowercase.

    1. Find `MNavURL:1_Here` and replace the token with the filename you selected for subpage 1.

    2. Find `FNavURL:1_Here` and replace the token with the filename you selected for subpage 1.

    3. Repeat Steps 1 and 2 for `MNavURL` and `FNavURL` 2, 3, and 4.

---

3. Place site title

Use Heading 1 to present the title of the site on the home page and subpages.

    1. Find `Heading:1_Here` and replace the token with your site title.

    2. Find `Heading:2_Here` and replace the token with your site subheading or wedding message.

---

4. Place special features

Place the text of the Web site copyright in your pages.

    1. Find `WebsiteCopyright:1_Here` and replace the token with your Web site copyright text.

    2. Save and close `index.html` in your text editor.

5. Set up the subpage template

Perform the same set of edits that you completed for the `index.html` file on the subpage master template file, `subpage.html`.

1. Open `subpage.html` in your text editor.

2. Return to the beginning of this section ("Building the Site Skeleton"), and start with main Step 1, "Place navigation labels."

3. Complete main Steps 1, 2, 3, and 4 using the `subpage.html` file instead of the `index.html` file.

4. Save `subpage.html` in your text editor. Do not rename the file.

Creating Subpage Files

6. Create subpage files

Use the Save As feature in your text editor to save the `subpage.html` template with the first of the subpage filenames you selected in your content plan. Repeat this to create all subpages listed in your content plan.

Save all files to the `\1240` folder on your desktop.

1. Verify that `subpage.html` is open in your text editor.

2. Choose File ➪ Save As or similar from your text editor. Enter the filename you selected for subpage 1, and click OK.

3. Repeat Step 2 for all subpages in your content plan.

4. Repeat Step 2 for any linked articles or catalog detail pages you identified in your content plan.

7. Display your site

Open your site to check that your labels and pages display correctly.

1. Launch `index.html` from your computer by double-clicking the filename, or choose File ➪ Open (from most browsers) to open it in your browser. An empty home page should appear.

2. Click the navigation links at the top and bottom of the home page and you should see empty subpage pages.

3. Close the empty site skeleton.

Placing Content in the Home Page

8. Place home article block

Place the headings and paragraph text for the articles in `index.html` (see Figure 12-15).

1. Open `index.html` in your text editor.

2. Find `Heading:3_Here` and replace the token with your heading text. Repeat this operation for `Heading` 4 and 5.

3. Find `Paragraph:1_Here` and replace the token with your paragraph text. Repeat the operation for `Paragraph` 2 and 3.

9. Place sidebar article

Position introductory information or a wedding statement that appears on all pages of the site using this sidebar article area (see Figure 12-15).

1. Find `Heading:6_Here` and replace the token with the title for the sidebar area.

2. Find `Paragraph:4_Here` and replace the token with the text of your short article.

3. Save `index.html` in your text editor.

Placing Content in Subpages

Use the following operations to place content into all of your site subpages. Use the subpage token reference (see Figure 12-16) to see the position of the content and label tokens. Repeat this operation to enter content in all of your subpages.

10. Place subpage articles

Place article headings and text in your subpages.

1. Open the selected subpage in your text editor.

2. Find `Heading:3_Here` and replace the token with your heading text.

3. Find `Paragraph:1_Here` and replace the token with your paragraph text. Repeat this operation with `Paragraph` 2 and 3.

---

11. Place sidebar article

Position introductory information or a wedding statement that appears on all pages of the site using this sidebar article area (see Figure 12-16).

1. Find `Heading:4_Here` and replace the token with the title for the sidebar area.

2. Find `Paragraph:4_Here` and replace the token with the text of your short article.

3. Save and close the file when you have finished editing.

Finalizing Your Site

12. Edit site logo and pictures

Turn to Chapter 3 for explanation and procedures to replace the default template logo and images with your own logo and images.

13. Display your Web site

Launch `index.html` from your computer by double-clicking the filename, or choose File ➪ Open. Check your work in your browser window.

14. Edit and adjust

Make edits by opening up your home page or subpage page files in your text editor and making edits to the content. Be sure to edit only your content and not to disturb any of the surrounding code.

15. Publish

The basic parameters of what you should provide to your Web hosting company are outlined in Chapter 3. For the specifics on actually posting your live site to the Web, contact your service provider for details.

Variations

Variation 1241 Overview

This version presents the site design with headline fonts in yellow and paragraph text in gray. Otherwise the design is the same.

See the images in the CD-ROM's Gallery section.

Variation 1242 Overview	This version presents the site design with headline fonts in black and link labels in yellow. Otherwise the design is the same.
	See the images in the CD-ROM's Gallery section.

Template 1250 Blog

A personal opinion site to present Web logs and personal information, articles, op-ed pieces, and links to external sites of interest.

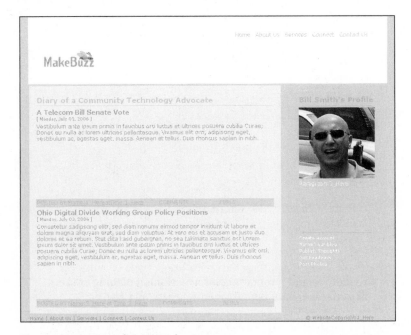

Figure 12-17: Template 1250 home page

Figure 12-18: Template 1250 subpage

Template Developer	Yana Beylinson
Filename and Location	CD-ROM: `\Templates\Chapter 12\125\1250`
Variations on this Design	1251 1252
Site Development Detail	Procedures and supporting information on placing content, links, and Web site images are presented in Chapter 3.

Design Summary

Recommended Use	Easy-to-read design is composed of article areas and link sidebars on the home page and subpages. This design allows you to create extensive links to internal subpages as well as to external sites. You can adapt the design to any information or community purpose where extensive linking to multiple topic areas or external sites is required.

Look and Feel	Quiet, simple design serves to push out the content and focus reader attention with few visual distractions. The accent photograph in the sidebar establishes the purpose of dialogue.
	The point of blogging is linking, and this design supports eight main navigation subpages plus six sidebar links on both the home page and subpages. The home page offers two lead articles and the subpage contains a single feature article or blog presentation.

Content Plan

Content Plan Overview	Before entering content in your site, make a list of the Web page labels and filenames you will use to build your Web site skeleton. Detailed coverage on building your content plan is presented in Chapter 3.
Subpages	Design supports a home page and eight principal subpages.
Sidebar	Sidebar at the right of the home page and subpages contains a headline, accent photograph, and paragraph token for a mini article or presentation of a key question or issue for comment. Each sidebar supports six links to either pages in the site or to external Web sites.
Articles	Home page includes two article areas. Subpages offer a single feature article.

Copy the Template	Follow these steps to copy the template to your hard drive:

1. Access the \Templates\Chapter 12\125\1250 folder on your CD-ROM.

2. Drag the \1250 folder to your desktop or copy and paste the \1250 folder to your desktop.

Template Headings and Tags

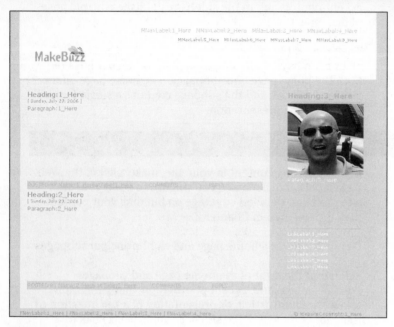

Figure 12-19: Template 1250 home page token reference

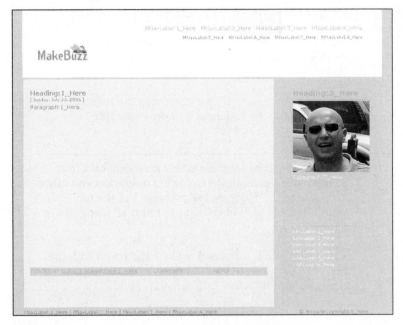

Figure 12-20: Template 1250 subpage token reference

Building Your Site Step-by-Step: 1250 Blog

Building the Site Skeleton

Use the following set of operations to enter the central navigation. Perform the exact same operations within index.html and subpage.html. Web site navigation and building the site skeleton are presented in Chapter 3.

Note that when opening index.html or subpage.html in Internet Explorer from your hard drive, a security message may appear. Click for more options, and choose to display the full content so the template displays correctly.

1. Place navigation labels	Review the list of subpage labels and filenames from your content plan. You place the labels for subpage 1 at the top (MNav) and bottom (FNav) of your page. See Figures 12-19 for home and 12-20 for subpages.

1. Open `index.html` in your text editor.

2. Find `MNavLabel:1_Here` and replace the token with the label for subpage 1. Repeat this operation for `MNavLabel` 2, 3, 4, 5, 6, 7, and 8.

3. Find `FNavLabel:1_Here` and replace the token with the label for subpage 1. Repeat this operation for `FNavLabel` 2, 3, and 4.

---

2. Place navigation links

Review the list of subpage labels and filenames from your content plan. In the following operation you place the links to the filename for subpage 1 at the top (`MNav`) and bottom (`FNav`) of your page. Enter all filenames in lowercase.

1. Find `MNavURL:1_Here` and replace the token with the filename you selected for subpage 1. Repeat this operation for `MNavURL` 2, 3, 4, 5, 6, 7, and 8.

2. Find `FNavURL:1_Here` and replace the token with the filename you selected for subpage 1. Repeat this operation for `FNavURL` 2, 3, and 4.

---

3. Place special features

Place the text of the Web site copyright in your pages.

1. Find `WebsiteCopyright:1_Here` and replace the token with your Web site copyright text.

2. Save and close `index.html` in your text editor.

---

4. Set up the subpage template

Perform the same set of edits that you completed for the `index.html` file on the subpage master template file, `subpage.html`.

1. Open `subpage.html` in your text editor.

2. Return to the beginning of this section ("Building the Site Skeleton"), and start with main Step 1, "Place navigation labels."

3. Complete main Steps 1, 2, and 3 using the `subpage.html` file instead of the `index.html` file.

4. Save `subpage.html` in your text editor. Do not rename the file.

Creating Subpage Files

5. Create subpage files

Use the Save As feature in your text editor to save the `subpage.html` template with the first of the subpage filenames you selected in your content plan. Repeat this to create all subpages listed in your content plan.

Save all files to the `\1250` folder on your desktop.

1. Verify that `subpage.html` is open in your text editor.

2. Choose File ➪ Save As or similar from your text editor. Enter the filename you selected for subpage 1, and click OK.

3. Repeat Step 2 for all subpages in your content plan.

4. Repeat Step 2 for any linked articles or catalog detail pages you identified in your content plan.

6. Display your site

Open your site to check that your labels and pages display correctly.

1. Launch `index.html` from your computer by double-clicking the filename, or choose File ➪ Open (from most browsers) to open it in your browser. An empty home page should appear.

2. Click the navigation links at the top and bottom of the home page and you should see empty subpage pages.

3. Close the empty site skeleton.

Placing Content in the Home Page

7. Place sidebar

Sidebar presents a heading above the accent photograph and an article paragraph below. You can use this to summarize or state the main issue of the blog, and link to related pages using the links below (see Figure 12-19).

1. Verify that `index.html` is open in your text editor.

2. Find `Heading:3_Here` and replace the token with the title for the sidebar area.

3. Find `Paragraph:3_Here` and replace the token with the text of your short article.

4. Find `LinkLabel:1_Here` and replace the token with the label text for this link. Repeat this operation with `LinkLabel` 2, 3, 4, 5, and 6.

5. Find `LinkURL:1_Here` and replace the token with the page filename or URL you have selected. Repeat this operation with `LinkURL` 2, 3, 4, 5, and 6.

---

8. Place articles

Place articles and postings. Note that each article takes a name token and a time token (see Figure 12-19).

1. Find `Heading:1_Here` and replace the token with your blog heading text. Repeat for `Heading` 2.

2. Find `Paragraph:1_Here` and replace the token with your paragraph text. Repeat for `Paragraph` 2.

3. Find `Name:1_Here` and replace the token with the name of the blog post author. Repeat for `Name` 2.

4. Find `Time:1_Here` and replace the token with the time of posting. Repeat for `Time` 2.

5. Save `index.html` in your text editor.

Placing Content in Subpages

Use the following operations to place content into all of your site subpages. Use the subpage token reference (see Figure 12-20) to see the position of the content and label tokens. Repeat this operation to enter content in all of your subpages.

---

9. Place sidebar

Place the headings and paragraph text for the articles in the selected subpage sidebar.

1. Open the selected subpage in your text editor.

2. Find `Heading:3_Here` and replace the token with the title for the sidebar area.

3. Find `Paragraph:3_Here` and replace the token with the text of your short article.

4. Find `LinkLabel:1_Here`. Replace the token with the label text for this link. Repeat this operation with `LinkLabel` 2, 3, 4, 5, and 6.

5. Find `LinkURL:1_Here`. Replace the token with the page filename or URL you have selected. Repeat this operation with `LinkURL` 2, 3, 4, 5, and 6.

10. Place feature article	Place articles and postings. Note that each article takes both a name token and a time token (see Figure 12-20).

1. Find `Heading:1_Here` and replace the token with your blog heading text.

2. Find `Paragraph:1_Here` and replace the token with your paragraph text.

3. Find `Name:1_Here` and replace the token with the name of the blog post author.

4. Find `Time:1_Here` and replace the token with the time of posting.

5. Save and close the file when you have finished editing.

Finalizing Your Site

10. Edit site logo and pictures	Turn to Chapter 3 for explanation and procedures to replace the default template logo and images with your own logo and images.
11. Display your Web site	Launch `index.html` from your computer by double-clicking the filename, or choose File ➪ Open. Check your work in your browser window.
12. Edit and adjust	Make edits by opening up your home page or subpage page files in your text editor and making edits to the content. Be sure to edit only your content and not to disturb any of the surrounding code.

13. Publish   The basic parameters of what you should provide to your Web hosting company are outlined in Chapter 3. For the specifics on actually posting your live site to the Web, contact your service provider for details.

Variations

Variation 1251 Overview   This version presents the site design with a white background for blog posting areas and a shade of yellow for the sidebar background. The full-page background is a pale green.

See the images in the CD-ROM's Gallery section.

Variation 1252 Overview   This version presents the site design with a soft pastel yellow background for blog posting areas, with blue heading and text fonts, and a light gray background for the sidebar. The full-page background is blue.

See the images in the CD-ROM's Gallery section.

✦   ✦   ✦

What's on the CD-ROM?

This appendix provides you with information on the contents of the CD that accompanies this book. For the latest and greatest information, please refer to the ReadMe file located at the root of the CD. Here is what you will find:

✦ System Requirements

✦ Using the CD with Windows and Macintosh

✦ What's on the CD

✦ Troubleshooting

System Requirements

Make sure that your computer meets the minimum system requirements listed in this section. If your computer doesn't match up to most of these requirements, you may have a problem using the contents of the CD.

For Windows 9x, Windows 2000, Windows NT4 (with SP 4 or later), Windows Me, or Windows XP:

✦ Intel(r) Pentium(r) III or 4 or Intel Centrino(tm) (or compatible) 800MHz processor

✦ Microsoft(r) Windows(r) XP Professional, Home Edition, or Media Center Edition 2005 with Service Pack 2

✦ 256MB of RAM (512MB recommended)

✦ 1.4GB of available hard drive space

✦ Color monitor with 16-bit color video card

✦ 1024×768 monitor resolution

✦ Microsoft DirectX 9 compatible display driver CD-ROM drive

✦ An internet connection is required to upload files to a Web server or to browse Web sites, but the templates work without it.

For Macintosh:

✦ PowerPC G3, G4, or G5 processor

✦ Mac OS X v.10.3 or 10.4

✦ 256MB of RAM

✦ 1.1GB of available hard-drive space

✦ 1024×768 16-bit (XGA) display

✦ CD-ROM drive

✦ An Internet connection is required to upload files to a Web server or to browse Web sites, but the templates work without it.

Using the CD with Windows

To install the items from the CD to your hard drive, follow these steps:

1. Insert the CD into your computer's CD-ROM drive.

2. A window appears with the following options:

   Gallery: Provides huge table of color thumbnails for each available template, including variations. Clicking any thumbnail opens a larger version of the image. Clicking the handy View Files link, takes you to a directory with all of the code for that chapter.

   Templates: Clicking this takes you to a list where you can select the templates by chapter. Click a chapter number and the list of folders each template appear in that chapter. Click the template of your choice to get to the files needed to create your Web site.

   Software: Gives you the option to install the supplied software on the CD-ROM.

   Exit: Closes the autorun window.

If you do not have autorun enabled or if the autorun window does not appear, follow the steps below to access the CD.

1. Click Start ⇨ Run.

2. In the dialog box that appears, type *d*:**start.exe**, where *d* is the letter of your CD-ROM drive. This brings up the autorun window described previously.

3. Choose the desired option from the menu. (See Step 2 in the preceding list for a description of these options.)

Using the CD with the Mac OS

To install the items from the CD to your hard drive, follow these steps:

1. Insert the CD into your CD-ROM drive.

2. Double-click the icon for the CD after it appears on the desktop.

3. Double-click the Start icon.

4. The CD-ROM interface appears. The interface provides a simple point-and-click way to explore the contents of the CD.

What's on the CD

The following sections provide a summary of the software and other materials you'll find on the CD.

Author-created materials

The CD-ROM contains complete code for all templates featured in *1 Hour Web Sites*. Readers can find the template code on the CD-ROM by clicking the Gallery or Templates buttons from the autorun interface.

Templates are numbered based on the chapter in which they appear. To locate code for a specific template, use the Gallery option and then either click the corresponding View Files link, click the Templates option and click the chapter number, or access the \Templates subdirectory and locate the number of the desired template.

The Gallery option opens a Web page containing a table of every variation and thumbnails arranged by chapter enabling the reader to shop through the designs in full color and select a template for development. The Gallery contains images for home and subpage default designs and two variations for each.

Artwork and logos on the CD-ROM are provided for your reference only. Logos are not to be reused, manipulated, or altered in any way. You must replace the logo and artwork with your own material. See Chapter 3 for more information.

Software

Adobe Photoshop Elements

Photoshop Elements, from Adobe Corporation — 30-day trial version for Windows and Macintosh.

Adobe Photoshop Elements software allows you to edit and enhance your photos, resize them for various uses, create slide shows, create Web galleries, and more.

`www.adobe.com/products/photoshopelwin/`

Note

Trial, demo, or evaluation versions are usually limited either by time or functionality (such as being unable to save projects). Some trial versions are very sensitive to system date changes. If you alter your computer's date, the programs will "time out" and will no longer be functional.

Troubleshooting

If you have difficulty installing or using any of the materials on the companion CD, try the following solutions:

- ✦ **Turn off any anti-virus software that you may have running.** Installers sometimes mimic virus activity and can make your computer incorrectly believe that it is being infected by a virus. (Be sure to turn the anti-virus software back on later.)

- ✦ **Close all running programs.** The more programs you're running, the less memory is available to other programs. Installers also typically update files and programs; if you keep other programs running, installation may not work properly.

- ✦ **Reference the ReadMe:** Please refer to the ReadMe file located at the root of the CD-ROM for the latest product information at the time of publication.

Customer Care

If you have trouble with the CD-ROM, please call the Wiley Product Technical Support phone number at (800) 762-2974. Outside the United States, call 1(317) 572-3994. You can also contact Wiley Product Technical Support at **http://support.wiley.com**. John Wiley & Sons will provide technical support only for installation and other general quality control items. For technical support on the applications themselves, consult the program's vendor or author.

To place additional orders or to request information about other Wiley products, please call (877) 762-2974.

✦   ✦   ✦

Index

Continued

Continued

Liquid Pixel
studio

Web Design & Development
Custom Programming
Logo Creation & Branding
Graphic Design
Internet Marketing

Eye catching and dynamic - Liquid Pixel Studio is a fresh company that thrives on big ideas and carefully studied methods. Specializing in web and graphic design, and web development, we create websites that are extremely attractive and remarkably solid.

We are savvy in brand identity, logo creation and all types of business identification: we can create an enduring, representative image unique to you and your business.

And because internet marketing is what makes your site profitable, we take time to analyze the competition and optimize your site for search engines. We also specialize in creating attractive email campaigns that drive traffic to your site.

We make certain that every client is with us every step of the way - through steady feedback and suggestions, we ensure your website and your business is miles ahead of its competition.

SPECIAL OFFER

Only for the readers of this book we offer 10% off the web development fee.
Contact us and learn how we can help you build a great site and market it to your advantage.
Visit liquidpixelstudio.net/1hour for more information. Initial consultation is absolutely free.

LiquidPixelStudio.net
917.319.0413

GRAPHIC ODYSSEY™
BEAUTY MEETS LOGIC™

IS IT TIME TO HIRE A PROFESSIONAL?

Many businesses rely on internal staff, bargain talent, and inexperienced freelancers to accomplish some of their most important website and graphic design needs. Instead they should be entrusting their projects to a professional design and development group that can be relied upon for experience, professionalism, expertise, and perfection.

Give us a call today to experience what you've been missing. If you prefer email, write to **success@graphicodyssey.com**.

WEBSITE DEVELOPMENT
- Websites of All Sizes
- E-commerce Solutions
- Online Database-driven Applications

GRAPHIC DESIGN
- Corporate Identities
- Brochures and Product Sell Sheets
- Direct Mail Campaigns

MULTIMEDIA AUTHORING
- Interactive CD-ROMS
- Video-based Sales Tools
- Flash-powered Online Product Demos

623.792.7940
graphicodyssey.com

Wiley Publishing, Inc. End-User License Agreement

4. Restrictions on Use of Individual Programs. You must follow the individual requirements and restrictions detailed for each individual program in the About the CD-ROM appendix of this Book. These limitations are also contained in the individual license agreements recorded on the Software Media. These limitations may include a requirement that after using the program for a specified period of time, the user must pay a registration fee or discontinue use. By opening the Software packet(s), you will be agreeing to abide by the licenses and restrictions for these individual programs that are detailed in the About the CD-ROM appendix and on the Software Media. None of the material on this Software Media or listed in this Book may ever be redistributed, in original or modified form, for commercial purposes.

5. Limited Warranty.

(a) WPI warrants that the Software and Software Media are free from defects in materials and workmanship under normal use for a period of sixty (60) days from the date of purchase of this Book. If WPI receives notification within the warranty period of defects in materials or workmanship, WPI will replace the defective Software Media.

(b) WPI AND THE AUTHOR(S) OF THE BOOK DISCLAIM ALL OTHER WARRANTIES, EXPRESS OR IMPLIED, INCLUDING WITHOUT LIMITATION IMPLIED WARRANTIES OF MERCHANTABILITY AND FITNESS FOR A PARTICULAR PURPOSE, WITH RESPECT TO THE SOFTWARE, THE PROGRAMS, THE SOURCE CODE CONTAINED THEREIN, AND/OR THE TECHNIQUES DESCRIBED IN THIS BOOK. WPI DOES NOT WARRANT THAT THE FUNCTIONS CONTAINED IN THE SOFTWARE WILL MEET YOUR REQUIREMENTS OR THAT THE OPERATION OF THE SOFTWARE WILL BE ERROR FREE.

(c) This limited warranty gives you specific legal rights, and you may have other rights that vary from jurisdiction to jurisdiction.

6. Remedies.

(a) WPI's entire liability and your exclusive remedy for defects in materials and workmanship shall be limited to replacement of the Software Media, which may be returned to WPI with a copy of your receipt at the following address: Software Media Fulfillment Department, Attn.: 1 Hour Web Site: 120 Professional Web Templates and Skins, Wiley Publishing, Inc., 10475 Crosspoint Blvd., Indianapolis, IN 46256, or call 1-800-762-2974. Please allow four to six weeks for delivery. This Limited Warranty is void if failure of the Software Media has resulted from accident, abuse, or misapplication. Any replacement Software Media will be warranted for the remainder of the original warranty period or thirty (30) days, whichever is longer.

(b) In no event shall WPI or the author be liable for any damages whatsoever (including without limitation damages for loss of business profits, business interruption, loss of business information, or any other pecuniary loss) arising from the use of or inability to use the Book or the Software, even if WPI has been advised of the possibility of such damages.

(c) Because some jurisdictions do not allow the exclusion or limitation of liability for consequential or incidental damages, the above limitation or exclusion may not apply to you.

7. **U.S. Government Restricted Rights.** Use, duplication, or disclosure of the Software for or on behalf of the United States of America, its agencies and/or instrumentalities "U.S. Government" is subject to restrictions as stated in paragraph (c)(1)(ii) of the Rights in Technical Data and Computer Software clause of DFARS 252.227-7013, or subparagraphs (c) (1) and (2) of the Commercial Computer Software - Restricted Rights clause at FAR 52.227-19, and in similar clauses in the NASA FAR supplement, as applicable.

8. **General.** This Agreement constitutes the entire understanding of the parties and revokes and supersedes all prior agreements, oral or written, between them and may not be modified or amended except in a writing signed by both parties hereto that specifically refers to this Agreement. This Agreement shall take precedence over any other documents that may be in conflict herewith. If any one or more provisions contained in this Agreement are held by any court or tribunal to be invalid, illegal, or otherwise unenforceable, each and every other provision shall remain in full force and effect.